Indigenous Peoples
In the Wake of Mabo

Indigenous Peoples
In the Wake of Mabo

Edited by Dr Kamal Puri

Contributors
Vafa Payman
Thomas Jones
Farin Sanaei
Graham Hassall
Graham Nicholson
Elizabeth Hindson
Dr Kamal Puri
Commissioner Irene Moss
The Honourable Justice Marcus Einfeld
Margaret Stephenson
June Perkins
Father Rod Cameron
Farvardin Daliri
Camilla Chance
Margaret Elias
William Ferea

Published by
Bahá'í Publications Australia
for
The Association for Bahá'í Studies - Australia

© Bahá'í Publications Australia
173 Mona Vale Road
Ingleside N.S.W. 2103
Australia

ISBN 0 909991 89 8

First Printing 1997

Text Design and artwork: Barry Anderson
Cover design: Wisdom Graphic Design & Advertising

Table of Contents

PART 3: INDIGENOUS CULTURE AND SOCIETY

EDITORIAL

Throughout 1993, the designated year of Indigenous Peoples of the World, there was a great deal of debate in Australia on issues affecting Aboriginal and Torres Strait Islander people. Yet much of the discussion focused narrowly on the High Court's revolutionary judgement in Mabo and the questions of land rights, ownership and control which surround it.

This collection of papers is intended to give a broader picture. The papers are a collection drawn from presentations to the 12th National Bahá'í Studies Conference held at The University of Queensland, Brisbane in July 1993. Although the theme of the conference - Indigenous Peoples - was specified, presenters were at liberty to select their own topics. The result was a diverse mix of papers covering both Bahá'í and secular issues. By dividing the published papers into three categories, it is hoped the readers will be able to isolate material of particular interest to them. However the structure of the book is only a guide, and many of the papers, especially those written from a Bahá'í perspective, touch upon other areas as well.

The collection presents information specifically related to the Mabo case, along with discussions of human rights in relation to indigenous people, commentaries on current social and political conditions and their impact, and essays on Aboriginal culture. It would be impossible in a single book to give a comprehensive account of issues relating to indigenous peoples and their culture. Instead, the aim of this compilation is to serve as a reminder of the rich diversity of indigenous culture and the complex range of problems faced by indigenous people.

ABOUT THE CONTRIBUTORS

Father Rod Cameron has, for over thirty years, been carrying out a study of the Aboriginal Dreamtime. He has travelled widely in Australia talking to Aborigines and listening to their sacred stories. His central aim is to bring to white Australians a deeper appreciation of the values of the Dreamtime. He has written and lectured extensively. Father Rod has a Master of Science degree and has spent years teaching science in High Schools. He now works in the Cairns Catholic Diocese as Chaplain to Aborigines in the Far North of Queensland.

Mr. Farvardin Daliri holds a BFA from Lucknow University and a postgraduate Diploma in ceramic design also from Lucknow University. He completed a Bachelor of Education at La Trobe University in 1988 and a Masters of Education at Monash University in 1991. He is currently writing a PhD thesis at James Cook University on the topic of his paper. Mr Daliri was born in Abadeh, Iran, and has been a professional artist, sculptor and model maker as well as being an art teacher. He was the coordinator of seven Bahá'í tutorial schools in the Lucknow District from 1980 - 1983 and Coordinator and Field Officer at the Migrant Resource Centre for North Tasmania, Davenport, 1985 - 1986.

Justice Marcus Einfeld has been a Justice of the Federal Court of Australia since 1986. He was the founding President of the Australian Human Rights and Equal Opportunity Commission (1986 - 1990) and has served many times on the Australian delegation to the United Nations Commission on Human Rights (Geneva). He has been actively involved in a range of international organisations, particularly in the promotion of human rights in Australia. He led the Toomelah and

Goondiwindi inquiry which exposed systematic denial of human rights to the Aboriginal people of those areas. Justice Einfeld has a distinguished legal career, having practised as a barrister for 25 years, 10 years as Queens' Counsel. Justice Einfeld holds a Bachelor of Law and a PhD.

Margaret Elias is the Chairperson of the National Spiritual Assembly of the Bahá'ís of Papua New Guinea. Ms Elias is a lawyer, specialising in industrial relations and the law. She is Permanent Chairperson of the Minimum Wages Board, and Chairperson of the Public Services Conciliation and Arbitration Tribunal, the Teaching Service Conciliation and Arbitration Tribunal and the Industrial Arbitration Tribunal in Private Sector. She was appointed to these positions two years ago and previously held the position of Deputy Chairperson of these tribunals. She is a mother of four and has been working in the Public Service of Papua New Guinea for the last 16 years.

William Ferea is the Head of Department and a Lecturer in the Department of Psychology and Philosophy of the University of Papua New Guinea. He currently lectures in logic, Marxist philosophy, comparative philosophy, philosophy and literature, and philosophy and journalism. He has previously been the Associate Dean of the Arts Faculty (Students) and the Philosophy course Adviser in 1985. His principal research areas include the concept of self, myth and cosmology in Melanesia, retributive and utilitarian justification of punishment, with special reference to the Melanesian Pay-Back system and recurring existential themes in contemporary Pacific writings. He has numerous publications, including poems, reviews, and philosophical and non-philosophical works. William Ferea holds a BA (Honours) Philosophy from the University of PNG and an MA in

Philosophy from the University of Hawaii.

Camilla Chance/Fligelman became a Bahá'í in England in 1962. She has served on a number of Local Spiritual Assemblies and on the Regional Teaching Committee of Victoria. She moved to Warrnambool 21 years ago and developed a friendship with the Warrnambool Aboriginal Community. She was elected to and served on the trust committee for the Warrnambool Aboriginal Community for one year. Camilla was a book reviewer for the Age and was employed by the Australian to review Aboriginal literature in a period where there was a gap in the understanding of, and access to, literature on Aboriginal people. Her work allowed her to contribute to bridging this gap. She has also had illustrations published in a children's book.

Graham Hassall is a Research Fellow at the Centre for Comparative Constitutional Studies, University of Melbourne. His major interests include the history, politics, sources of values, and systems of government of the Asia-Pacific region, and he is also interested in Bahá'í history. He is a founding member of the national Committee of the Association for Bahá'í Studies - Australia.

Elizabeth Hindson is employed by the Queensland University of Technology as an Associate Lecturer. Ms Hindson is currently studying for a Masters in Social Work. She was previously employed in the Queensland Division of the Aboriginal and Torres Strait Islander Affairs for 22 ½ years. She is a member of the Brisbane Bahá'í community, serving in a variety of capacities over many years.

Thomas (Tom) Jones is the Acting Senior Head Teacher of Management and Financial Services at the Hunter Institute of Technology. Since 1987 Tom has supervised the design and delivery of Aboriginal management and entrepreneurial training at the Hunter Institute in consultation with leaders and members of the Awabakal,

Koompahtoo and Mindaribba Local Area Land Councils. Tom holds and MBA, Dip Ed and AIMM.

Irene Moss (Race Discrimination Commissioner) graduated in Arts and Law from the University of Sydney and later took a Masters in Law from Harvard University in the USA. Ms Moss was appointed Race Discrimination Commissioner of the Australian Human Rights and Equal Opportunity Commission in 1986. She chaired the National Inquiry into Racist Violence, and recently, in co-operation with the United Nations Centre for Human Rights, hosted the United Nations Conference on Combating Racism. Prior to her appointment as Race Discrimination Commissioner, she worked with the newly established New South Wales Anti-Discrimination Board where she was involved in a number of landmark discrimination cases relating to sex and race discrimination, physical and intellectual disability and other human rights issues.

Graham Nicholson is Crown Counsel for the Northern Territory. He has also lectured part-time at the Northern Territory University where he is a visiting Fellow in the Faculty of Law, and is Legal Adviser to the Northern Territory Sessional Committee of the Legislative Assembly on Constitutional Development. In 1990 - 1991 he was visiting Lecturer in Law at the University of Malaya, in Malaysia. His particular areas of interest include constitutional, international and administrative law, federalism, human rights, and mining law. He will shortly be taking up an attachment to the Justice Department of the Government of Laos.

Vafa Payman is a lawyer from Melbourne. He holds a Bachelor of Economics (Hons) and a Bachelor of Laws from Monash University. He also holds a Graduate Diploma in International Law from the Australian National University. He is a member of the National Spiritual Assembly of the Bahá'ís of Australia.

June Perkins holds a Bachelor of Arts (Hons) from the University of Melbourne, and has recently been working as a Research Assistant for the Aboriginal and Multicultural Department of the University of New England researching interactions between Aboriginal Pre-schoolers via video. Her major Honours thesis was the Representation of Aboriginal Women in Film. Recently she interviewed prominent Aboriginal women in Armidale for the local paper to promote the theme of the indigenous year. Currently she is working on a collection of poems about indigenous Bahá'ís of the Australasian and Pacific regions. Her own background is that she was born in Port Moresby to an Australian father and a Papuan mother. She has grown up in a Bahá'í family since the age of four.

Associate Professor Kamal Puri was Acting Dean and Head of the T. C. Bierne Law School, University of Queensland in 1992. He is an expert in the area of intellectual property, having 18 years teaching and research experience. In 1978 he completed a PhD at the Australian National University and in 1980 was appointed as Senior Lecturer in Law at the Victoria University of Wellington, where he pioneered the teaching of intellectual property at various tertiary levels. In 1989 he joined the University of Queensland. He has numerous publications in the area of intellectual property and in 1991 he was awarded a prestigious grant by the Australian Research Council to carry out a project concerning the protection of the intellectual property of Aboriginal and other folklore works. He has also received another ARC grant to carry out research on the implications of the Mabo case for the intellectual property rights of Aborigines.

Viva Rodwell lived most of her life in Brisbane, before moving to Sydney some 15 years ago. After gaining a BA and Certificate of

Physical Education, she taught in the Queensland Education Department. In her spare time Viva gave recitals on ABC radio and sang with the ABC's Queensland Wireless Chorus. She is currently active in numerous organisations, including the Women's International League of Peace and Freedom, the United Nations Association of Australia, the Embroiderer's Guild and the NSW Art Gallery Society. She is also on the Australian Opera's auditions committee, and is an exhibiting member of the Society of Arts and Crafts of NSW. In 1991 she commenced a course in Peace studies at Macquarie University.

Farin Sanaei is a post graduate student in Optical Communication Engineering at the University of NSW. He holds a Bachelor of Engineering in Electrical Engineering from the same University. He is a member of the IEEE and IEAust. He is the chairperson the of the Spiritual Assembly of the Bahá'ís of Randwick and also chairperson of the Association for Bahá'í Studies Australia - Committee. He has served on the National Youth Committee of Australia and on other committees. He has been a member and president of the Bahá'í Society of the University of New South Wales. He is also a member of the Sydney Club of Research.

Mrs Margaret Stephenson is a lecturer at the T. C. Bierne School of Law at the University of Queensland. She practised as a solicitor in Brisbane before joining the University of Queensland's Law School where she has been a lecturer for several years. She is editor of the University of Queensland Law Journal and co-edited a recent book, Mabo: A Judicial Revolution.

PREFACE

Since its inception in Australia more than a decade ago the Association for Bahá'í Studies (ABS) has made a substantial contribution to the development of scholarship within the Bahá'í community. The Bahá'í Faith places a high value on learning, independent inquiry, and freedom of speech, and ABS has been an important vehicle for nurturing these qualities within the Bahá'í community in an organised and systematic way.

ABS has also been instrumental in opening a scholarly dialogue between the Bahá'í community and like-minded groups and individuals in the wider Australian community on issues of common interest. *"As the Bahá'í community strives to become more open, outward, and civic-minded in all its endeavours, aligning itself as much as possible with the good works and aspirations of the Australian people"*[1], this aspect of ABS's work will become even more important.

The National Conference is the leading event in the ABS Calendar, and attracts a wide diversity of people from both Australia and overseas. A number of distinguished visitors attended the conference in 1993, including, most notably, Justice Marcus Einfeld, a Justice of the Federal Court of Australia and former president of the Australian Human Rights and Equal Opportunities Commission.

The Conference theme for 1993 was "Indigenous People" - the theme of the United Nations year. Given the excited and at times vigorous public debate in Australia over the issue of native land title, the conference theme could hardly be more relevant.

The Conference theme is relevant however, not only in light of what is happening in Australia at this time, but also because of what is occurring in our region. Australia lies on the rim of the South Pacific, a region in which there are many small, indigenous communities in the early stages of nationhood. For these communities, the task of transforming their societies whilst at the same time preserving political stability is a formidable one. Amidst all our own trials as a nation at this juncture in our history, we Australians must also be aware of the needs of our Pacific neighbours and appreciate the magnitude of the challenges they face.

1 Australian Bahá'í Community, Three Year Plan - Ridván 1993 - Ridván 1996.

PART 1:
INDIGENOUS PEOPLES
BAHÁ'Í PERSPECTIVES

Chapter One
ABORIGINAL RECONCILIATION - SOME MORAL AND PSYCHOLOGICAL REQUISITES

by

Vafa Payman

This paper looks at Aboriginal reconciliation in Australia from a moral and psychological perspective, identifying some of the conditions that need to be satisfied by both Aboriginal and non-Aboriginal Australians for the process to be successful. Bahá'í views on race unity are considered, in particular, the discussion contained in a recent statement on the subject issued by the American Bahá'í Community; and an extract from 'The Advent of Divine Justice', a letter written by Shoghi Effendi, the Guardian of the Bahá'í Faith, to the Bahá'ís of the United States and Canada in 1938.

The public debate in Australia on the question of Aboriginal reconciliation has focused on the material requirements of the Aboriginal people, such as housing, education and health care. In this context, the High Court's decision in the Mabo case[1] was significant for Aborigines because by acknowledging Aboriginal ownership of land for the first time, the law in Australia has forced government to reconsider its position on the issue of land rights and compensation.

Whilst land rights and the material requirements of the Aboriginal people are obviously important as elements of the reconciliation process, no effort to solve the problems of Aboriginals in Australia is

3

likely to succeed unless there is also a proper appreciation of the moral and psychological commitments that both Aboriginals and non-Aboriginals must make. True reconciliation will not occur without a fundamental shift in thinking and behaviour by both sides. As a recent article dealing with the reconciliation process declared:

> Clearly, the reconciliation process will fail without huge changes in white thinking and white behaviour, and that is a big ask. But equally it is about blacks stopping beating their heads against the now unalterable facts of Australian history.[2]

Quoting Lois O'Donoghue, the Chairwoman of the Aboriginal and Torres Strait Islander Commission (ATSIC), the article went on: "Says O'Donoghue: "We have, to a large extent, been swept aside by the immensely powerful forces that have occupied our country. Given the history of European domination of the world it is, in fact, hard to imagine pre - 1788 Australia being allowed to remain as it was - though the process of colonisation might have been kinder and more just. We must reconcile ourselves to this fact... and work towards a realistic accommodation with modern Australia."

O'Donoghue's view is that despite the undoubted acts of terrible cruelty suffered by Aborigines, it is probable that the most destructive forces have always been invisible - disease, despair, the loss of social structures and beliefs. These forces are still at work in many communities, and they manifest themselves in alcoholism, child abuse, domestic violence and early death. For example, she says, the Royal Commission into Aboriginal deaths in custody investigated 20 deaths in Queensland; in the same period 23 Aboriginal women died as a result of family violence in three Queensland communities alone. "The principle of self-determination must be extended to include self-responsibility", she concludes."[3]

Behind every great accomplishment there lies a great moral

principle. In the High Court's decision in Mabo, the moral principle was the need to eliminate racism from a contentious area of our common law. As Brennan J. who wrote the leading majority judgement in the case declared, it was "imperative in today's world that the common law should neither be nor be seen to be frozen in an age of racial discrimination."[4] "A common law doctrine founded on unjust discrimination in the enjoyment of civil and political rights demands reconsideration."[5]

Accordingly, the High Court decided that the proposition put to it that, when the Crown assumed sovereignty over Australia, it became the universal and absolute beneficial owner of all the land and therefore that the common law itself, to quote Brennan J., "took from indigenous inhabitants any right to occupy their traditional land, exposed them to deprivation of the religious, cultural and economic sustenance which the land provides, vested the land effectively in the control of the Imperial authorities without any right to compensation and made the indigenous inhabitants intruders in their own homes and mendicants for a place to live", was unjust and that its claim to be part of the common law to be applied in contemporary Australia had to be rejected.[6] "Whatever the justification advanced in earlier days for refusing to recognise the rights and interest in land of the indigenous inhabitants of settled colonies, an unjust and discriminatory doctrine of that kind can no longer be accepted."[7]

The moral principle that guided the High Court in Mabo must also govern the reconciliation process. According to the Bahá'í Writings, racism can be eliminated if there is universal acceptance of the oneness of mankind. More than a century ago, Bahá'u'lláh wrote:

> Know ye not why we created you all from the same dust? That no one should exalt himself over the other. Ponder at all times in your hearts how ye were created. Since we have created you all from one

same substance it is incumbent on you to be even as one soul, to walk with the same feet, eat with the same mouth and dwell in the same land, that from your inmost being, by your deeds and actions the signs of oneness and the essence of detachment may be made manifest.[8]

Acceptance of the oneness of mankind, as discussed in a recent statement on race unity issued by the American Bahá'í Community,[9] has important implications for the reconciliation process. It means that we as Australians must abandon any thought that one group in our society is intrinsically different from other groups on account of race or ethnicity. Rather, we must recognise that we are all human beings and thus essentially the same.[10]

Acceptance of the oneness of mankind also means that we as Australians must develop a friendlier attitude towards people of a different race. It is not enough to give Aborigines material benefits; they must also be drawn into our social activities and accorded genuine love and respect. We human beings value the recognition we get from others. If we are discriminated against and denied this need, we lose hope and self-confidence.[11]

Acceptance of the oneness of mankind also means that Aboriginal and non-Aboriginal Australians must join together as equal partners in the pursuit of common national goals. Notwithstanding the difficulties that have been experienced in relations between the two groups, we must resist the temptation to advocate racial separation and follow separate agendas. Whilst some degree of separateness may be unavoidable at this stage in our national development, we must not split the country into different racial zones and isolate ourselves within them.[12]

As a nation, Australia right now faces many critical challenges. We must solve our economic problems. We must resolve the issue of our national identity. We must decide whether we wish to become more closely integrated, economically, politically, and culturally, with our Asian neighbours. At a more human level, we have to stop the breakdown of the family unit, the growing incidence of domestic violence, the upsurge in youth homelessness. In all these matters, and others, we can benefit from the insights and contribution of Australia's Aboriginal people. They must be invited and encouraged to participate in the decision-making processes of the nation. The goal must be to secure their involvement as equal partners and fellow citizens.

The reconciliation process is the responsibility of both Aboriginal and non-Aboriginal Australians. Neither group should believe that the process is a matter that exclusively concerns the other; both must make special efforts. In their dealings with each other, they would do well to heed the following advice of Shoghi Effendi (1897-1957), the Guardian of the Bahá'í Faith, which, though given to whites and Negroes in the United States in the late 1930s, is just as relevant to whites and Aborigines in Australia today:

> Let the white make a supreme effort in their resolve to contribute their share to the solution of the problem, to abandon once and for all their usually inherent and at times sub-conscious sense of superiority, to correct their tendency towards revealing a patronising attitude towards the members of the other race, to persuade them through their intimate, spontaneous and informal association with them of the genuineness of their friendship and the sincerity of their intentions, and to master their impatience of any lack of responsiveness on the part of a people who have received, for so long a period, such grievous and slow-healing wounds. Let the Negroes, through a corresponding effort on their part, show by every means in their power the warmth of their response, their readiness to forget the past, and their ability to wipe out every trace of suspicion that may still linger in their hearts and minds.[13]

Aborigines are a spiritual people. Bahá'ís, too, are a spiritual people, and like Aborigines they are assaulted by serpents from time to time. "Every trial doth attack man", says Bahá'u'lláh, "and every dire adversity doth assail him like the assault of a serpent."[14] But in the Bahá'í universe, there are no negatives, only positives and disguised positives. Accordingly, the assault of the serpent is not pain and calamity, but providence and growth; outwardly it is "fire and vengeance", but inwardly it is "light and mercy".[15]

The reconciliation process is about striking the right balance between the material and the spiritual, the legal and the moral, the practical and the psychological. Bahá'ís must contribute to the process, and we can begin by actively promoting the advancement of Aboriginal Bahá'ís.

In his judgement in Mabo, Brennan J. said that in discharging its duty to declare the common law of Australia, the High Court was not free to adopt rules that accord with contemporary notions of justice and human rights if their adoption would fracture the skeleton of principle which gives the body of our law its shape and internal consistency. The peace and order of Australian society was built on the legal system. The system could be modified to bring it into conformity with contemporary notions of justice and human rights, but it could not be destroyed.[16]

The High Court's decision in Mabo did not destroy our legal system. The decision, however, has shaken our body politic, and that may yet awaken the Australian people to glorious future possibilities. I wish to conclude with the following words of Bahá'u'lláh:

> O Well Beloved Ones! The tabernacle of unity hath been raised; regard ye not one another as strangers. Ye are the fruits of one tree, and the leaves of one branch.[17]

REFERENCES
1. *Mabo v. Queensland* [1992] 66 ALJR 408.
2. A. N. Maiden, 'Black Power - Taking Control', in the *Independent*

Monthly, May 1993.

3. ibid.
4. Mabo, above, note 1 at 422.
5. *ibid.*
6. *ibid.*, at 416.
7. *ibid.*, at 422.
8. Bahá'u'lláh, *The Hidden Words* (Arabic).
9. 'The Vision of Race Unity - America's Most Challenging Issue', a Statement by the National Spiritual Assembly of the Bahá'ís of the United States (1991).
10. See the discussion in ibid, pages 3-4.
11. *ibid.*, at 5 - 6.
12. *ibid.*, at 9 - 10.
13. Shoghi Effendi, *The Advent of Divine Justice*, (Bahá'í Publishing Trust, Wilmette, Illinios 1984) at 40.
14. *Bahá'í Prayers*, (Bahá'í Publishing Trust, Wilmette, Illinios 1981) at 66.
15. Bahá'u'lláh, above, note 8.
16. Above, note 1 at 416 - 417.
17. *Tablets of Bahá'u'lláh Revealed After the Kitáb-i-Aqdas*. (Haifa: Bahá'í World Centre 1982) at 164.

Chapter Two
THE BASIS OF ABORIGINAL ENTREPRENEURIAL AND MANAGERIAL SKILLS: CLAN, COMMUNITY OR BOTH?

by

Tom Jones

Aboriginal and Torres Strait Islander enterprises based on barter and exchange have existed in Australia as an integral part of their economic activities for at least 40,000 years according to the most recent estimates. Evidence exists that valued items were bartered and exchanged through an extensive distribution network across the entire continent. Their collection, production and distribution formed part of the economic, marital and religious activities and were therefore subject to the rules and regulations imposed by the clan, class and estate, the three composite elements of Aboriginal society. These rules and regulations existed to maintain the interdependence in Aboriginal society rather than to impose any centralised political structures over the component parts. The traditional marriage system was in effect an important aspect of the economic structure. It was through marriage that access to other territories was gained. Therefore the family/clan commercial and economic structure predominated and the more recent structures based on "City", "State" and "Nation" and abstract concepts such as "the Community" were unknown. Since the early 1970s, Government funding policies focused on "the Community" although it has been recognised that this concept is just as abstract, intangible and novel to Aboriginal society as it is to non-Aboriginals. The recent success of 180 Community Development Employment Projects covering over 20,000 Aboriginal and Torres Strait Islanders and other successful enterprises has increased interest in the re-emergence of entrepreneurship as a means of attacking Aboriginal unemployment.

The paper explores the current dichotomy as to whether the family/clan or community-based structures are conducive to the development of successful Aboriginal entrepreneurial and managerial skills. Or both situationally.

Introducion

This paper will begin by asking some interesting questions which have even more interesting answers:

1. What is reputedly the world's oldest entrepreneurial culture?
2. Where are the commercial ruins of the world's oldest "commercial" structure?
3. The trade routes that are considered to be the world's oldest are now the site of modern highways. What country are they in?
4. What group of people lead Australia and possibly the world in conducting programmes where the participants work for unemployment benefits?
5. How many of these peoples participate in these programs: 20?, 200?, 2,000?, 20,000?

The answer to all of these questions are found in this paper and all relate to little known facts about Australian Aboriginals and Torres Strait Islanders. The purpose of this paper is to increase the awareness of and to explore a dichotomy about their enterprises and community organisations.

Are family/clan structures more conducive to the development of successful Aboriginal entrepreneurial and managerial skills than community-based structures? Or can either or both be appropriate according to the situation?

First it is necessary to define the terms "Family", "Clan",

"Entrepreneurship", "Management", "Community" and "Situation" in the context that they are part of the ongoing process of civilisation. Then aspects of the world's ancient legends and modern Scriptures as they relate to the Bahá'í belief of "progressive revelation"[1] and the Bahá'í principle of "seeking a spiritual solution to the economic problem"[2] will be introduced.

These terms, legends, Scriptures and beliefs as they historically and currently apply to Australian Aboriginals and Torres Strait Islanders in general and to their community organisations and enterprises in particular will then be examined. Finally various strategies to address the current situation will be examined because (unfortunately like many European and Australian businesses) some Aboriginal enterprises are   perceived to have "failed"[3] and the management skills in community organisations continue to be challenged.[4]   This is important because the assumption is often made that Aboriginal people are not capable of or interested in becoming successful managers[5] and/or business people[6] when, in fact, much training for management and enterprise development has been inadequate and in some cases non-existent.[7]   In addition most of the planning is carried out and funding provided on a "community" basis rather than the more traditional family/clan basis. Many Aboriginal community-based organisations have had little or no experience in enterprises yet businesses were purchased for these communities with the expectation that they would "learn" how to manage them with the assistance of "management consultants" and day-to-day experience.

Two important questions arise out of these introductory comments:

1. Would Aboriginal enterprises and community organisations be more successful if the spiritual aspects and their cultural importance were given greater emphasis?

2. If so, how can this be achieved?

Definition and Discussion of Major Terms

A. Definitions

It is logical to assume that God, having created mankind, would wish to continuously and progressively guide His creation through a consistent and predictable process from our earliest beginnings to modern times.

Bahá'u'lláh described the "process" of civilisation when He declared that mankind has been created "...to carry forward an ever-advancing civilisation".[8]

History from a Bahá'í perspective is not a succession of wars and conflict, but the positive process of constructing and perfecting increasingly complex, divinely-ordained organisational structures.

Humankind began with the family and progressed through the tribe (clan), the city state and the nation. We are now trying to develop effective international organisations often without due regard to the nature and importance of the previous structures. Our lack of success simply reflects the lack of respect for and between these previous structures.

This concept of a continuous process is an important aspect of some of the major terms in the dichotomy under examination. Let us define and then examine these terms in the context of a "continuous process":

Family: the basic biosocial unity in society having as its nucleus two or more adults living together and co-operating in the care and rearing of their own or adopting children.[9]

Clan: a group persisting through the generations and having title to some tangible or intangible thing such as land or totemic song, ritual or lore.[10]

Community: a group of people marked by a common characteristic but living within a larger society that does not share that characteristic.[11]

Management: the process of planning, leading, organising and controlling the human and physical resources of an organisation in order to achieve stated goals.[12]

Entrepreneurship: the process...of creating or growing a business through innovative and risk-assuming management.[13]

Situation: a relative position or combination of circumstances at a given moment.[14]

B. Discussion

Family, Clan and Community

The origin of Australia's ever advancing civilisation process are lost in the "Dreamtime" and continued in isolation from the rest of the world until about four centuries ago.

Australian anthropologists differ in their interpretations of events and definitions.

Maddock[15] seemed to treat the clan and family as virtually the same entity when he stated that the rules and regulations imposed by clan, class and estate (the three composite elements of Aboriginal society) existed to maintain their interdependence rather than to impose any centralised political structures over the component parts.

Therefore to the above mentioned definitions of family and clan we can add:

Class: a classification of persons and their actions, which operates to prescribe human conduct (eg. marriage regulations) but it is a classification also of everything else in the Universe.[16]

Estate: a socially significant category, the members of which act or are acted upon collectively and which cuts across clan and class. The three estates are men, women and novices.[17]

Maddock maintains that the management of Aboriginal society and the collection, production and distribution of valued objects formed part of the economic, marital and religious activities and were therefore subject to the above rules and regulations.

The traditional marriage system was in effect an important aspect of the social and economic structure. It was through marriage that access to other territories was gained.

Anthropologists agree that the family/clan management and economic structure predominated and the more recent structures based on "city state" and "nation" were unknown.

The abstract concept "community" came into general use only in recent years and it became part of the Commonwealth definition of an Aboriginal person:

Aboriginal Person: "...is someone who is of Aboriginal descent and who identifies with their Aboriginality and who is accepted by the community in which they live as Aboriginal".

Management, Entrepreneurship and Situation

The author presented a paper to a Bahá'í Studies Conference in 1985 that used Stoner's diagram below to illustrate the many parallels of the history of modern management theory with the history of the Bahá'í Era up to the late 1970s.[18]

This theme has been taken a step further in this paper and George Cabot Lodge's model of the "New American Ideology"[19] of the 1970s has been updated by adding a third column to indicate the changing

Figure 1: Schools of Management Thought

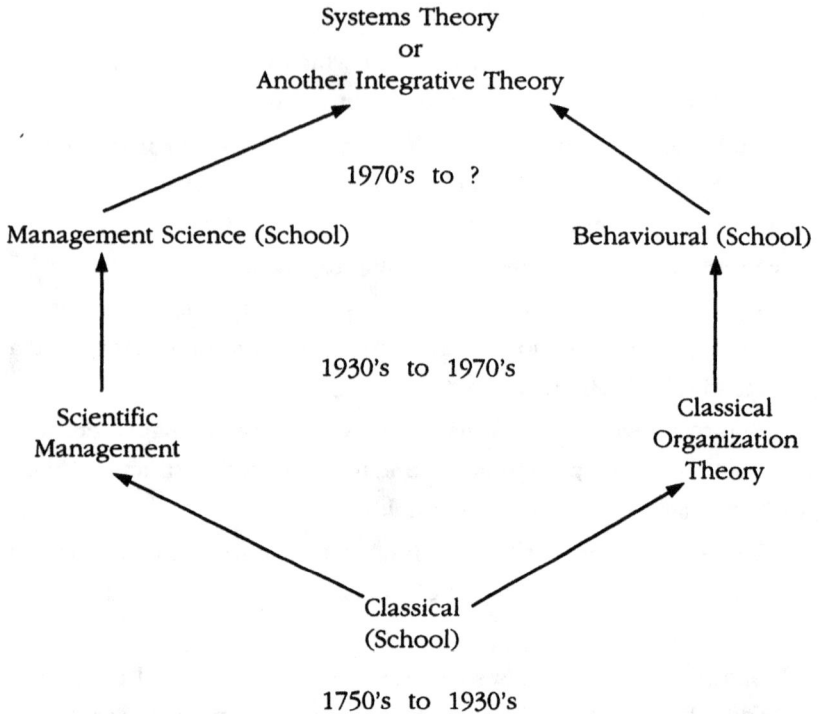

Systems Theory
or
Another Integrative Theory

1970's to ?

Management Science (School)   Behavioural (School)

1930's to 1970's

Scientific   Classical
Management   Organization
                                               Theory

Classical
(School)

1750's to 1930's

Management, 2nd edition/Stoner
© 1982 Prentice Hall Inc

political, economic and management scene of the 1990s. The attributes listed in this third column are the ancient and eternal aspirations of humankind. They are enshrined in the Bahá'í Writings and in the traditional Aboriginal lore. We have come around full circle.

After this modification, George Cabot Lodge's table more clearly reflects the continuing process of the evolution of management theory and Bahá'u'lláh's concept of humankind's purpose of carrying forward "...an ever advancing civilisation".[20]

A Modification (in hindsight) of: "THE NEW AMERICAN IDEOLOGY"		
THE OLDER RECENT 1750'S TO 1930'S IDEOLOGY	CABOT LODGE "EMERGING" 1930'S TO 1970'S IDEOLOGY	ABORIGINAL/ETERNAL BAHÁ'Í IDEOLOGY
Rugged Individualism	Communitarianism	Social Responsibility
Property Rights	Rights of Membership	Human Rights
Competion	Community Need	Co-operation
Limited Government	Activist Government	Flexible Government
Atomistic Thinking	Systems Thinking	Holistic Thinking
Imperialism	Situational Confederalism	Limited Federalism

Stoner's definition of management practice as a process is now readily accepted by theorists. Therefore, Fry's recent application of the term to entrepreneurship is novel but quite logical. Entrepreneurship is simply another form of management. However it is also an ongoing process of establishing a climate for developing organisational *creativity* (new ideas) into organisational *innovation* (new products or services) by changing the organisational culture.

Management by culture is a relatively new concept in the modern management theory but it was commonplace to traditional Aboriginals[21] and is familiar to Bahá'ís both in practice and through an article by Alan Wilcox.[22]

Management by culture is an essential ingredient in the effective management of community-based organisations. The entire world and both the Bahá'í and Aboriginal communities stand to benefit from an in-depth study of the Bahá'í experience during the last 150 years.

Two important question arise from this part of the paper:

scene of the 1990s benefit from the offer of the "Bahá'í experience" as a model for study?[23]

2. How can the Australian Aboriginals and Torres Strait Islander people apply the wisdom contained in their ancient lore to the task of improving management and encouraging innovation in their community-based organisations and small businesses?

These questions will be addressed through an examination of some aspects of the world's legends and Scriptures and the two specific Bahá'í teachings as they apply to the above definitions and discussions.

Introduction of Aspects of the World's Legends and Scriptures or

"In the Beginning was the Word"[24]

Bahá'ís understand the meaning of "the Word of God" as both the Manifestations of God on Earth and the beginning and end of all the Bounty of God. The Manifestations of God being the Lord of their "age" and the source of all religious and scientific (technological) knowledge.

Udo Schaefer[25] gives a succinct outline of the concept of the God as the Creator and the Lord of History, Who manifests Himself from time immemorial to humankind through legends and scriptures.

The Bahá'í belief in "progressive revelation" and the Bahá'í principle of "a spiritual solution to the economic problem" underpin this paper and are themes that fit easily with some accounts of the world's religious history and with many anthropological accounts of the world's economic history.

Maddock, Dalton and Herskovits were just three of the anthropologists who identified the religious basis for technological change, innovation and the regulation of economic activities in ancient and primitive cultures variously in Africa, Asia, Australia, Europe, India and the Pacific Islands.[26]

'Abdu'l-Bahá[27] explained how the confirmations of the Holy Spirit play a key role in the spiritual, technological and material education of mankind when he stated:

> ...the Holy Spirit is the very cause of the life of man; without the Holy Spirit he would have no intellect, he would be unable to acquire his scientific knowledge by which his great influence over the rest of creation is gained. The Holy Spirit gives to man the power of thought, and enables him to make discoveries by which he bends the laws of nature to his will.
>
> The Holy Spirit it is which, through the mediation of the Prophets of God, teaches spiritual values to man and enables him to attain Eternal Life.[28]

The Bahá'í Scriptures explain the meaning and purpose of the Prophets of God (who in this context are also the founders of the great religions and the countless unknown Divine Manifestations before them) and the fact that God cannot "...incarnate His Essence and reveal it unto men"[29] but that He causes "...luminous Gems of Holiness... to appear out of the realm of the spirit and... impart unto the world the... mysteries of the unchangeable Being"[30] through a succession of "...sanctified Mirrors" who are "...the Treasuries of divine knowledge and the Repositories of celestial wisdom".[31]

One Aboriginal Bahá'í, Diana Carew-Reid demonstrated this concept in the Koori context through her illustrated and annotated version of Bahá'u'lláh's prayer "Blessed is the Spot".[32]

Too many people (Aboriginal and European alike) have too little understanding of the deep spiritual nature of traditional Aboriginal culture and its worth to the modern world. Often we hear the tired old aargument that the Aboriginal culture had no possibility of survival because it was much less "powerful" than that of the Europeans who

BLESSED IS THE SPOT

'Blessed is the spot
And the house
And the place
And the city
And the heart
And the mountain
And the refuge
And the cave
And the valley
And the land
And the sea
And the island
And the meadow
Where mention of God
Hath been made...
And His praise glorified.'

Bahá'u'lláh

©Diane Carew-Reid-Koori- Jan 21st 1993.

DECIPHERING THE RAINBOW SERPENT

o O o   = Ancestors Who camped, loved, and created Physical form, Mountains, Trees, Rivers etc

= Camps or Sacred Sites, where the Ancestors camped, and these areas are maintained by Aboriginal people.

= Laws from the Alcheringa (Dreamtime) that the Ancestor Law Maker gave to Aboriginal people since the dawn of creation.

= Songlines which are Chapters of the 'Dreamtime' Aborigine people must memorize these chapters (stories) because they teach Spritual, Moroal, and Social Laws as given to them by the Ancestor Law Maker. The name 'Alcheringa' is the proper name for the Dreamtime stories.

= The 'Uncreated' Spirit Energy which manifests Physical Reality.

= The 'Star' of Divine Revelation, symbolically held in the Serpent's Mouth and symbolizes the Alpha, i.e. The Beginning which has no beginning.

= The Moon or Light or Truth of the Revelation. The Omega that is not. Omega means end. All Revelation is Progressive and aborigine people understand this concept.

Note:
At the time of writing and illustrating this prayer Diana Carew-Reid was researching her Aborigine Roots. Her Aboriginal identity was revealed by a 'Koori Elder' from New South Wales... hence the word 'koori'. Diana belongs to the Karadjari Language group of Broome. In the Karadjari language 'Dreaming' is called 'Bagarrigara'. 'Alcheringa' is from the Aranda people.

because it was much less "powerful" than that of the Europeans who settled in Australia. This narrow, secular definition of "powerful" appears to suggest that a culture could only be powerful if it was backed by the might of material and not spiritual force. It certainly cannot explain why social and spiritual traditions continue to play such a powerful role in the lives of many of Australia's Aborigines despite two centuries of efforts by European settlers to wipe their traditions out.

Critics of the *Mabo* decision often refer to the "guilt industry" which ignores the fact that *Mabo* is not about guilt but about justice and justice is loved by God:

> O SON OF SPIRIT! The best beloved of all things in My sight is Justice; turn not away therefrom if thou desirest Me, and neglect it not that I may confide in thee. By its aid thou shalt see with thine own eyes and not through the eyes of others, and thou shalt know of thine own knowledge and not through the knowledge of thy neighbour. Ponder this in thy heart; how it behooveth thee to be. Verily Justice is My gift to thee and a sign of My loving-kindness. Set it then before thine eyes.
>
> Bahá'u'lláh.[33]

The ABC television documentary, *Exile and the Kingdom* (screened on Wednesday, July 7, 1993 at 8:30 pm) provides a good basis for making an informed judgement on Aboriginal land rights of the land's spiritual importance. Perth film makers Frank Rijavic and Noeline Harrison produced the documentary from a story by Roger Solomon (John Pat's uncle). The documentary features the Injibandi/Ngaluma people who have been misunderstood, ignored and abused since the coastal town of Roebourne sprang up as a centre for white pearling and pastoral endeavours in the 1860's.

Listed below are some quotes from the documentary:

> It was the dispossession and removal of Aboriginal people from their land which has had the most profound impact on Aboriginal

society. The nexus between the inadequate or insufficient land provision for Aboriginal people and the behaviour which leads to a high rate of arrests and detention is repeatedly observed in the reports of the deaths.

Mr. Elliot Johnson, QC, Chief Commissioner,
Royal Commission into Black Deaths in Custody.

All them millionaires, like Lang Hancock, he's a millionaire today from the blackfella... and from all the minerals what they find, the black fellas get nothing... as long as they're rich, they're gone and we still poor. ...got no country.

Pilbara Aborigine.

Four important questions arise from this part of the paper:

1. Has the Holy Spirit guided humanity since time immemorial in all of our spiritual, material and technological progress?

2. Will the modern humanity continue to remain technological giants but spiritual midgets until they recognise the above fact?

3. Will Aboriginal community-based organisations, private enterprises and entrepreneurial efforts be enhanced through a renewed appreciation of the importance of the spiritual dimension?

4. Will the entire world's political, economic and social endeavours be enhanced through a renaissance of indigenous spirituality?

Aboriginal Economics and Enterprises

Aboriginal and Torres Strait Islander enterprises based on barter and exchange have existed in Australia as an integral part of their economic activities for at least 40,000 years according to the most recent estimate. Evidence exists that valued items were bartered and exchanged through extensive distribution networks across the entire continent. F. D. McCarthy[34] illustrated one such network.

The collection and/or production and distribution of these shells and other valued objects[35] formed part of economic, marital and religious activities. According to Maddock these were subject to the co-operative rules and regulations imposed by clan, class and estate,

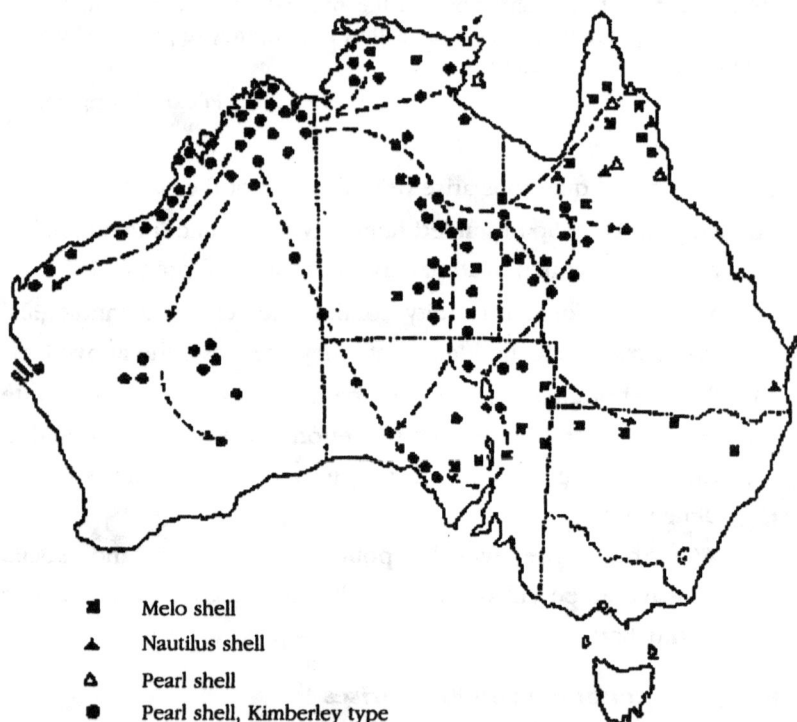

▇	Melo shell
▲	Nautilus shell
△	Pearl shell
●	Pearl shell, Kimberley type

Shell Ornaments
The distribution of the Kimberley pearlshell and Princess Charlotte Bay baler-shell ornaments, showing how highly-coveted objects used for purposes of magic and as status symbols are traded throughout the continent.
F. McCarthy

the three composite elements of Aboriginal society.

Many aspects of the traditional systems of co-operative rules and regulations have been lost or changed radically since the advent of European settlement two centuries ago. However, for several prior centuries many groups of indigenous people bartered co-operatively with sea-going Asian and European traders.

Although Aboriginal people played an important role in the economic growth of modern Australia,[36] the first two hundred years of European settlement were not conducive to the emergence of and indigenous entrepreneurial class. This often resulted from the direct intervention by the government of the day through a series of 'protective' and other Acts of Parliament.

Aboriginal academic Dr. Eve Fesl[37] when discussing the attitude under the "Protection Acts" quoted Protector Roth:

...no practically useful results can possibly accrue by teaching our mainland blacks composition, fractions, decimals or any other subjects that will in any way enable them to come into competition with Europeans.

An example of this intervention was the pastoral industry. It has long been recognised that Aboriginals were the backbone of the sheep and cattle industry, because their ability to work long hours was a major contributing factor to the wealth and success of many pastoral properties.

When Aboriginal people gained leases of land to grow crops and run cattle and thus carve out their own place in the growing economy, government policies of the day did not allow Aboriginal people to accumulate any real wealth and many of the leases were revoked when it was obvious that they were becoming successful. Until the early 1970s Aboriginal people continued to contribute their labour and environmental knowledge to the growth of the Australian economy but were never fully compensated.

However there were some remarkable success stories mostly based on family/clan structures in many parts of Australia. Some notable Hunter Region examples of these were:

- Bill and Robert Smith's railway construction firm (1969 - 1979)
- Glenn Ridgeway and family's Post Office/Mixed Business at Tamilba Bay up to the present day.
- The Manton Family at Karuah.

A period of change commenced in the 1970s with various government funded programs such as the "Family Resettlement Program"[38] This particular program was aimed at improving the living condition of Aboriginal people but sometimes at the cost of traditional family, clan, and locality loyalties. From the early 1970s government funding policies focused on "the community" although it has been recognised that his concept is just as abstract, intangible and novel to Aboriginal society as it is to non-Aboriginals.

The recent success of 180 community development employment Projects covering over 20,000 Aboriginal and Torres Strait Islanders and other successful enterprises has increased interest in the re-emergence of entrepreneurship as a means of attacking Aboriginal unemployment.

In 1976, in response to repeated requests from various Aboriginal communities for an alternative to the unemployment benefit, a pilot scheme (called Community Development Employment Projects or CDEP's) to provide additional work opportunities for Aboriginal people living in remote areas was introduced in one community.[39] By 1978 the CDEP scheme had grown to include a further 10 remote area communities and by the time the 'Miller Report' was released in 1985 there were 32 CDEP's.

In 1980, the Commonwealth Government established by legislation the Aboriginal Development Commission (ADC). Its goal was:

> To maximise the well-being, self determination and self-management of all Australian Aboriginal and Torres Strait Islanders so they can enjoy a level of economic and social opportunity equal to that of other Australians.

One of the major strategies developed by the ADC to reach this goal of economic independence was:

> To increase the opportunity for economic independence, self-sufficiency and self-management, and to improve the employment and income of Aboriginal by providing loans for the acquisition or development of commercially viable businesses.

In 1983, the NSW Aboriginal Land Rights Act was introduced which provided Local, Regional and State Land Councils the opportunity to invest in and develop enterprises. The Land Councils' successes and failures in enterprise development and studies commissioned (including the "Miller Report") clearly indicate the importance of management training for successful enterprise development.

In September 1985 the Report to the Federal Government by the Committee of Review of Aboriginal Employment and Training (the "Miller Report") was released and many new policies and initiatives were implemented as a result of the "Miller Report" including community and individual training in the area of small business and the "Aboriginal Enterprise Initiative Scheme" to encourage unemployed persons to create their own self employment. This scheme was administered through the Federal Department of Education Employment and Training (DEET) until 1992 when the program was transferred to the Business Funding section of the Aboriginal and Torres Strait Islander Commission (ATSIC). The scheme offered a small business management course, wage supplement for the first twelve months and access to a loan through the Commonwealth Department Bank.

What the scheme lacked however, was access to after care support to ensure survival during the first twelve months of operation.

Another result of the "Miller Report" was the implementation of the Federal Government's "Aboriginal Employment Development Policy" (AEDP). Under the AEDP the scope and flexibility of the CDEP's was increased. This included expansion of the CDEP's to include communities in rural areas, small rural towns, urban areas and specific interest groups (eg. language groups) and a broadening of the definition of "productive work".

In 1989 the "Aboriginal Development Commission" (ADC) was replaced by the "Aboriginal and Torres Strait Islander Commission" (ATSIC) which assumed the administration of the CDEP's and the program was transferred to ATSIC's Business Funding section.

By June 30, 1990 there were 166 CDEP projects in Australia involving approximately 15,000 people.

In 1992, the Aboriginal Enterprise Development Officers (AEDO) program was introduced into six NSW Business Enterprise Centres (BEC's) funded through the Self Employment Development Program of the NSW Department of Industrial Relations, Employment, Training and Further Education. (DIRETFE).

Briefly, the Aboriginal Enterprise Development Officers' Program is an advisory service to Aboriginal people who are interested in starting a small business. Like all pilot programs it has its shortcomings. However its major advantage is being able to mould programs that include the overall requirements of Aboriginal people wanting to establish businesses, including effective training based on established needs. Whilst it has been acknowledged that aspects of preparation, eg., training, financing, and support services, are crucial to providing a successful outcome, most programs have failed to co-ordinate or provide a total package to assist Aboriginal people to enter into the area of enterprises.

Since the introduction of government funded programs aimed at encouraging people to enter into community/individual enterprises there has been insufficient focus placed on the need for program providers to adopt an integral approach to service delivery.

A proposal is now being examined[40] which may result in the BEC's, through the AEDO programs acting as agents for ATSIC enterprise loans. This proposal will undoubtedly place greater emphasis on the AEDO programs and the need for them to deliver a total program of enterprise development.

The successes and failures of the last twenty years have been the subject of much debate, therefore, urgent research is necessary to provide the information required for planning effective service delivery. Already a consensus is emerging on two important points: first, Aboriginal people throughout Australia want the opportunity to gain and maintain their own form of economic independence and not remain entrenched in a circle of government grant funding and poverty; and second, Aboriginal people are still traditionally oriented and the structures of the family and the clan are the mechanisms through which they exist and find greatest fulfilment.

The Community Development Employment Projects and many other successful Aboriginal enterprises (both community and clan/family based); the appointment of the six Aboriginal Enterprise Officers; the renewed interest in Aboriginal art, music, medicinal secrets; and the accompanying problems of compensation, copyright, etc. are all pointers to the future.

They will ensure an increased interest in the re-emergence of Aboriginal entrepreneurship not simply as a means of attacking

Aboriginal unemployment but also as recognition of its rightful place in world history.

The questions that arise from this part of the paper are:

1. What research is required to monitor the success, failures and specific requirements of Aboriginal enterprises?

2. What specific strategies need to be adopted to develop Aboriginal enterprises to their full potential?

Research and Strategies for the Future

A. Research

This section is a brief account of a recent research project and some suggested strategies for the future. The research carried out by Jill Byrnes in 1987 on 50 Aboriginal enterprises shows that there are three broad categories:

1. Those like the Yeperenye Shopping Centre which are owned by the local Aboriginal community, employ some Aboriginal staff but are run by professional managers for at least the next 10 years;

2. Those like B. E. & L. I. Pell & Sons which are run by a family group and are building onto an already high level of management skill;

3. Those like "Goorie Mabul" that are run by talented people who are trying their hand and risking their money in an entrepreneurial business.

My research has indicated that all three groups require different levels of training and mentor support. However all of them would seem to be able to benefit from an even higher level of traditional cultural emphasis. The training being offered to date is also quite deficient in this important particular.

However in all cases there is a need for community groups to come to terms with differing and sometimes antagonistic family/clan loyalties. Training and mentor support in this important particular is often sadly lacking.

All three groups of enterprises seem to need this emphasis according to the family/clan mix and their situation in terms of business age and size. Arriving at the successful mix seems to be the most important overall problem.

B. Strategies

To accomplish this some or all of the following strategies should be considered, evaluated and, if appropriate, implemented.

1. De-secularisation and de-politisation of the current community attitudes through emphasising:

   a) That Australian Aboriginal people are part of the world's oldest and one of the wisest living religions;

   b) That they have much to offer in environmental studies, employment initiatives, and world trade and tourism.

2. Concentration on management by culture through:

   a) Liaison with community groups who have had considerable experience in this field such as Bahá'ís;

   b) Utilising such ancient go-between persons such as the "Puntimai" of the Awabakal people of the Hunter Region.

3. Management education emphasis to always reflect Aboriginal traditions, values and respect for ancient mores.

4. Improved networking, for example:

   a)   A "Black Yellow Pages";

   b) Networking amongst and between various religious groupings -Traditional, Christian, Bahá'í, etc.

This list is not exhaustive and several Aboriginal student groups, teachers/lecturers and business counsellors are working on improving and extending it at the moment.

Endnotes

1. For a succinct description of this belief see: Schaefer Udo, *The Imperishable Dominion.*, (George Ronald Publishers, Oxford, 1983.), Chapter 7.

2. National Assembly of the Bahá'ís of the United States, *Bahá'í World Faith.*, (Bahá'í Publishing Trust, Wilmette, Illinois, USA, 1943.), at 240, 247, 375 - 378 and many others.

3. Jill Byrnes, *Enterprises in Aboriginal Australia: Fifty Case Studies.*, The Rural Development Centre, University of New England, Armidale. 1988., at 2.

4. 'Fisher's Challenge on Black Spending', *The Sun Herald*, June 27, 1993, at 23.

5. Three years ago the author was privileged to play a part in the management training at Newcastle for the Awabakal Local Area Land Council when it re-structured into the following 12 autonomous and efficiently conducted divisions: Child Care Centre, Pre-School, Youth Centre, Elders Community Transport Services, Disability Services, Family Support and Welfare Service, Aboriginal Housing Association, Youth Accommodation, Medical Centre, Dental Service, Employment and Training Centre, Culture and Resource Centre.

6. As indicated earlier, over 20,000 Aboriginals and Torres Strait Islanders are working for 'unemployment benefits' and indications are that there will soon be exponential growth in Aboriginal Enterprises and Entrepreneurship.

7. The NSW LALC Model is widely considered to be a worthwhile model for study and implementation but like several other organisations and Government Departments it attracted adverse comments for its financial performance. See the *Report to NSW Parliament*, (NSW Auditor-General (Mr. Harris), June 16, 1993.).

8. *Gleanings from the Writings of Bahá'u'lláh*, 110:1.

9. *Webster's Third New International Dictionary*.

10. Kenneth Maddock, *The Australian Aborigine: A Portrait of Their Society*,

Grolier Press, 1974.

11. *Webster's Third New International Dictionary.*

12. A. F. Stoner, R. Collins & P. W. Yetton., *Management in Australia,* (Prentice-Hall, Sydney, 1985.)

13. F. L. Fry., *Entrepreneurship, A Planned Approach,* (West Publishing Company, Minneapolis, 1993.) at 29 - 30.

14. *ibid.*

15. Above, note 10.

16. *ibid.*

17. *ibid.*

18. For example, while Shaykh Ahmad (1743 - 1826) and Siyyid Kazim (1793 - 1843) sought the 'Lord of the New Age', classical management theorists were seeking a new beginning; Robert Owen (1771 - 1858) 'conceived of the manager's role as one of reform' (Stoner, above, note 12 at 38) and Charles Babbage (1792 - 1871) designed a mechanical calculator, as a forerunner to the 'information age' which began on May 23, 1844 with the invention of the telegraph. Babbage also carried out some early method studies (Stoner at 39).

19. George Cabot Lodge, *The New American Ideology,* (Knopf Press, New York, 1976.) at 16.

20. Above, note 8.

21. During the author's studies of traditional Aboriginal society he has identified this and many other management activities such as 'skills audits' of young children, etc. This is correctly the topic of another paper.

22. 'Empowering the Community'., edited from an article written by Alan Wilcox, *Australian Bahá'í Bulletin,* (May 1993) at 4.

23. A statement by the Universal House of Justice, *The Promise of World Peace: To the Peoples of the World* (Bahá'í Publications, Australia, 1986.) at 27.

24. New Testament, John 1:1.

25. Schaefer at 104 - 109.

26. 26 Maddock, above, note 10; Dalton, George (Ed.) *Tribal and Peasant Economics,* Natural History Press, Garden City, New York, 1967); Herkovits, Melville J. *Economic Anthropology: A Study in Comparative Economics,* (Knopf, New York, 1952.)

27. 'Abdu'l-Bahá (1844 - 1921) the eldest son of Bahá'u'lláh (the Founder of the Bahá'í Faith) and the Exemplar and Interpreter of the Bahá'í Writings.

28. *Some Answered Questions,* Chapter LIX

29. *Gleanings from the Writings of Bahá'u'lláh*, at 49.
30. *Kitáb-i-Íqán*, at 99 - 100.
31. *ibid*.
32. *Australian Bahá'í Bulletin*, (May 1993) at 16.
33. *The Hidden Words of Bahá'u'lláh*.
34. F. D. McCarthy, *The Australian Encyclopaedia*, (The Grolier Society of Australia, Sydney, 1981, Volume 1.) at 30.
35. Typical of the valued items involved were foodstuffs; medicinal and narcotic leaves, stems and plants; pigments and other raw materials; finished goods such as stone implements, weapons, ornaments, sound instruments and occasionally sacred objects and art, including song and dance.
36. For brief details see, Professor G. Bolton, 'A View from the Edge: an Australian Stocktaking.' (1992 Boyer Lectures, ABC Books, Sydney, 1992.) at 4 - 6.
37. Dr. Fesl, 'The Koori Contribution', in *Furious Agreement: Forty Prominent Australian Focus on the Next Fifty Years*. (Michael Dugan (Ed.), Penguin Books, Ringwood, Vic., 1991.)
38. The Family Resettlement Program was designed to relocate Aboriginal people to urban industrial areas and thus allow them greater access to education and employment opportunities. However it also had the effect of cutting many family, clan and locality loyalties and forming 'communities' that were not based on (and sometimes antagonistic to) these traditional loyalties. A new set of problems began to replace the old.
39. For further historical and practical details see *Community Development Employment Projects: User Guide*, Aboriginal and Torres Strait Islander Commission, January, 1991.
40. See Hunter Region Aboriginal Enterprises Development in the Hunter Region.

Chapter Three
THE ELIMINATION OF RACISM; AN ESSENTIAL PREREQUISITE FOR THE PROGRESS OF HUMANITY.

by

Farin Sanaei.

Racism is a major barrier to peace. Its elimination is imperative for unity and harmony between Aborigines and non Aborigines in Australia. In this paper the definition and spectrum of racism are discussed. Then the causes of the practice of racism are explored. This is followed by an analysis of the effects and consequences of racism on individuals, on society and on the progress of humanity, particularly in achieving peace and unity in the world. In conclusion effective and

Introduction

One of the fundamental causes of gross inequality and injustice between Aborigines and non-Aborigines in Australia is racism. Racism is one of the most challenging issues confronting not only Australian society today but also humanity at large. To ignore the problem is to expose the world to physical, moral and spiritual danger.

Bahá'u'lláh, the Prophet Founder of the Bahá'í Faith, wrote:

...the well being of mankind, its peace and security, are unattainable unless and until its unity is firmly established.[1]

To address the problem of racism effectively, it is appropriate to look at the definition and spectrum of racism, determine its underlying causes, analyse the effects and consequences of racism on individuals, on society, and on the progress of humanity, particularly on achieving peace and unity in the world. Only them will we be able to set an agenda to combat racism effectively.

Definition of Racism

What do we mean by racism? Who is racist?

The first thing to realise is that racism has been born out of human ignorance. As 'Abdu'l-Bahá, the successor and son of Bahá'u'lláh explains:

> The earth has one surface. God has not divided this surface by boundaries and barriers to separate races and peoples. Man has set up and established these imaginary lines, giving to each restricted area a name and a limitation of a native land or nationhood.[2]

Often when we talk about race relations, we come across two different words, racialism and racism. Racialism refers to prejudiced beliefs and behaviour. It is a process by which attributes, such as colour, country of origin or language, are transformed into identities, and people come to be treated as members of a group. When these become fully systematised into a philosophy of "race" superiority, and become a part of the way in which society as a whole is organised, then it is called racism. Racist ideology distinguishes and discriminates against those identified as racially "others". As a consequence they are labelled and treated as "others" or "inferiors". Racism is thus both an ideology and a social practice.[3] As a result, at the root of racism is the attempt to keep a particular group of people, marked out by their physical and cultural characteristics, poor and powerless.

In 1951 UNESCO convened a meeting of scientists who stated in their Statement on the Nature of Race and Racial Differences, that "available scientific knowledge provides no basis for believing that the groups of mankind differ in their innate capacity for intellectual and emotional development." In another statement UNESCO points out that, "the human problems arising from so called "race" relations are social in origin rather than biological. The basic problem is racism, namely, antisocial beliefs and acts which are based on the fallacy that discriminatory inter-group relations are justifiable on biological grounds."[4]

Prejudice means "to prejudge". However in the context of racial and ethnic relations it refers to negative prejudgment.

In terms of prejudice and discrimination we may divide people into categories:[5]

1. The "unprejudiced non-discriminator" who upholds, in belief and practice, the idea of freedom and equality.

2. The "unprejudiced discriminator" who is not personally prejudiced, but sometimes discriminates against other groups because it seems socially and financially convenient to do so.

3. The "prejudiced non-discriminator" who feels hostile to other groups, but recognises that law and social pressures are opposed to discrimination. This person does not translate prejudice into action.

4. The "prejudiced discriminator" who does not believe in the values of freedom and equality and consistently discriminates in both words and actions.

It is difficult to keep personal prejudice from eventually leading to some form of discrimination. Therefore, it is not enough just to believe in freedom from all prejudices. We must courageously and diligently put this in action. Therefore the ultimate goal for individuals and the society at large must be to achieve the first category, namely the unprejudiced non-discriminator.

Causes of Racism

Why and how racism started, and why it still exists.

Initially racism grew out of slavery and was used to justify slavery. Racialist practices and racist social and political systems were developed wherever countries were colonised. Such practices kept the local people under control in the lowest section of the society, and prevented them from taking any power themselves. Such systems ensured that they provided cheap labour.

Throughout the centuries, racism has been exported along with the settlers to different countries, such as Australia and New Zealand, and has taken on a number of different forms over the years. Today's racism uses the language of difference rather than inferiority, and so tries to deny the accusations of racism.

Racism has also taken a form of religious prejudice. For centuries, Catholicism had held that a person could only be fully human if he or she was a believer within the one true Church. This implied that those who worshipped different Gods under different religious systems were, therefore, an inferior sort of human being.[6]

'Abdu'l-Bahá explained that rivalry between:

> ...the different races of mankind was first caused by the struggle for existence by wild animals. This struggle is no longer necessary; nay rather interdependence and co-operation are seen to produce the highest welfare in nations. The struggle that now continues is caused by prejudice and bigotry.[7]
>
> The breeding ground of all these tragedies (wars and conflicts) is prejudice: prejudice of race and nation, of religion, of political opinion; and the root cause of prejudice is blind imitation of the past - imitation in religion, in racial attitudes, in national bias, in politics.[8]

Therefore there is no valid or justifiable reason for being racist, racialist or prejudice. Prejudice or race is a pure illusion, a simple superstition. And as long as this "blind imitation of the past" continues, the foundations of our social order will remain shaken.

Effects of Racism

What are the effects of racialism and racism on individual, society, and the world at large?

Racism has cost the world dearly. Systems of white domination in America, Asia, and Africa have left a trail of blood and anguish down through history that has imposed on the present generation a legacy of hatred and racial conflict. Centuries of white racial dominance have created centuries of racial distrust among non-whites; centuries of distrust that have festered into countless manifestations of racial disunity in every multiracial society in the world.[9]

Looking through the history of mankind, we can say that racism is not just a set of ideas or beliefs, it has a very important economic function. It not only degrades and humiliates, but it also impoverishes, in every way, the people who are its target. It makes the cheap labour force that the capitalist system demanded almost free.

While the culture of colonialism attempted to make colonised people feel inferior in every way, so that they would submit more easily to colonial rules, it also had the effect on the white people of making them think they really were racially superior. They swallowed their own propaganda. This made itself manifest in every aspect of white culture. An example is Hitler's theories of the racial superiority of the German people which were developed directly from early writers, scholars, and thinkers. His attempt to wipe the Jews and Gypsies off the face of the earth was their logical conclusion.

Mari Matsuda, in her book *Public Response to Racist Speech*, explains the effect of racist remarks on individuals:

As much as one may try to resist a piece of hate propaganda, the effect on one's esteem and sense of personal security is devastating. To be hated, despised, and alone is the ultimate fear of all human beings. However irrational racist speech may be, it hits right at the emotional place where we feel the most pain.[10]

Bahá'ís are particularly concerned about the devastating effects that racism can have on the lives of its victims, destroying their sense of human worth and their capacity for individual and collective development. Racism is an insult to human dignity, a cause of hatred and division, a disease that devastates societies. Prejudice and discrimination have created a disparity in the standards of living, providing some with excessive economic advantage while denying others the bare necessities for leading healthy and dignified lives. In the words of 'Abdu'l-Bahá:

In every period war has been waged on one country or another and that war was due to either religious prejudice, racial prejudice, political prejudice, or patriotic prejudice. It has therefore been ascertained and proved that all prejudices are destructive of the human edifice.[11]

Many citizens of multicultural societies fail to understand the connection between their domestic racial policies and world peace. Racism as a chronic social, psychological, and spiritual illness retards the society's healthy growth and development as well as that of racial minorities and the larger society. Prejudice prevents them from understanding the truth. Prejudice is a fruitful source of war, strife, divisions, hatred and bloodshed. Thus as long as prejudices exist among mankind, universal peace can not become a reality in the world.

In the past 200 years of Australian history, racism had destroyed the lives of many Aborigines, insulted their beliefs and customs, and has made them desperate for a decent human life. As a result, we see divisions and alienations in our society today.

The existing discriminatory and unbalanced level of social justice and gross contrast of Aboriginal living standards with non Aboriginals, are direct consequences of prejudiced race relations in this country. It was not until 1967 that Aboriginals were counted as human beings in national census. From 1980 to 1989, 99 Aboriginal and Torres Strait Islanders have committed suicide in police custody.[12] At present the unemployment rate of Aboriginals is estimated to be four times the rate for non-Aboriginals. Similarly, ill health, improper housing, and low levels of education among Aboriginals are some of the devastating effects of racism in our social structure. These imbalances in our Australian community have cost us dearly financially, psychologically, and morally. Disillusionment, hatred and alienation are some of the results of such imbalances.

How To Combat Racism

Now that we know the causes and the effects of racialism and racism, how do we go about eliminating them?

No matter what form the struggle for racial justice, unity, fellowship and love has assumed (either political, economical or cultural) its deepest roots are spiritual in nature. When individuals and communities are connected with the spiritual roots of these struggles, they are transformed. Thus we need a transformative agenda which in the process of seeking racial justice, unity, fellowship and love transforms and elevates peoples and communities. An agenda that explains the interconnection between all the above elements and social progress. An agenda which seeks a basic change in perceptions and values about human beings. An agenda which creates an appreciation of the organic oneness of the human family. An agenda that embraces and advocates love for one's fellow human beings as a prerequisite for building and healing communities.

As a part of this spiritual struggle, unity must be understood as the key precondition for all forms of social progress. The emergence of a global society and a united world demands wider unity. All social groups have to be educated to understand that at this stage of human evolution on this planet, where interdependence is a structural reality, *everyone*, no matter who they are or where they are on the social scale, has a vital role to play in solving the problems associated with racism. This calls for nothing less that a unity of vision and purpose. This universal vision together with co-operation and collaboration will guide us along the path to permanent racial unity. The result of this co-operation and collaboration will be a friendship bond, which in turn would enhance the unity of our vision and purpose, and transform other countless social relationships in the society.

Social and economic progress in every multiracial society today is dependent on the degree to which racial groups learn to live, work and play together in love and harmony. Where racial unity, based on social justice and nurtured by love and fellowship, is lacking or absent, multicultural societies are forced to waste precious time, energy and resources managing crises.[13] A true example of this is the American society.

Racism is not limited to few countries such as America and South Africa. Racism started as an international social virus and it remains so today in every multicultural society in the world. If this disease is not treated effectively we will suffer long term retardation in our social progress.

The main strategies to combat racism are transformation and education. Educating the present generation about the urgency of establishing racial justice and unity in their respective societies will save us from many more decades of racial turmoil.

They must be exposed to the great historical cost in human misery and social conflict that racism has exacted from the entire society. They must be made to understand that there can not be any lasting peace in any multicultural society without genuine love and fellowship among racial groups. Then, it must be demonstrated to them that such love and fellowship among the various races of their societies will not only reduce and ultimately eliminate racism and racial conflicts but also elevate the entire society to new levels of material and spiritual development. The spectrum of the educational programs must include all kinds of audiences: schools, universities, community groups and the mass media.

In 1936, Shoghi Effendi (1897 - 1957), the appointed Guardian of the Bahá'í Faith, described how a universal love among Bahá'ís has "burned away their prejudice" and "made them lovers of mankind". He said:

> While preserving their patriotism and safeguarding their lesser loyalties, it has made them lovers of mankind,... This universal, this transcending love which the followers of the Bahá'í Faith feel for their fellow men of whatever race, creed, class or nation, is neither mysterious nor can it be said to have been artificially stimulated. It is both spontaneous and genuine.[14]

Bahá'ís throughout the world are involved in building an international community of diverse people, many from previously mutually antagonistic backgrounds. They are encouraged to accept all people regardless of their differences.

'Abdu'l-Bahá said:

> Let them look no upon a man's colour but upon his heart. If the heart be filled with light, that man is nigh unto the threshold of His Lord; but if not, that man is careless of His Lord, be he white or be he

black.[15]

Moreover, the Bahá'í community goes out of its way to arrange its affairs to encourage minorities to participate in all areas of its community life. It encourages its followers to have true interaction with others and goes as far as encouraging interracial marriages.

If any discrimination at all is to be tolerated, it should be a discrimination not against, but rather in favour of the minority, be it racial or otherwise. It is important to note that this is for no other reason except to stimulate and encourage unity of the human race and to further the interests of the community. Outside of such a context of spiritual unity, the policy would be interpreted as a form of "reverse discrimination".

Shoghi Effendi, the Guardian of the Bahá'í Faith, addressing the people of America, on how to solve their long term racial problems, says:

> Let the white make a supreme effort to abandon once and for all their usually inherent and at time subconscious sense of superiority, to correct their tendency towards revealing a patronising attitude towards the members of the other race, to persuade them through their intimate, spontaneous and informal association with them of the genuineness of their friendship and the sincerity of their intentions, and to master their impatience of any lack of responsiveness on the part of a people who have received, for so long a period, such grievous and slow healing wounds.[16]

> On the other hand", he says, "let the members of the other race show by every means in their power the warmth of their response, their readiness to forget the past, and their ability to wipe out every trace of suspicion that may still remain in their hearts and minds.[17]

It must be realised that the solution of so vast a problem is not a matter that exclusively concerns one group or race. It must also be realised that such a problem can not either easily or immediately be resolved. Nothing short of genuine love, extreme patience, true humility, mature wisdom and tact, sound initiative, and deliberate, persistent, and prayerful effort can succeed in removing such a social disease.

We must make continuous effort to expose ourselves to the other ethnic cultures, and to associate and collaborate with them on community issues, and to break down barriers of suspicion and misunderstanding.

We must also reconsider all our own prejudices and inherited customs in the light of our contemporary situation, and where change is called for, we must have the courage to work towards that change.

A recent development in rectifying the imbalances and injustices caused by racism is the High Court's decision in *Mabo's* case. The important moral principle behind this judgement was to eliminate racism from the area of our common law. It was a judgement to reconsider our way of thinking towards race relations in Australia.

Diversity of colour, nationality and culture enhances the human experience and should never be made a barrier to harmonious relationships, to friendships or to marriages.

Conclusion

In conclusion let us not forget that racism is a "blind imitation of the past". It has been and still is the most fundamental cause of human sufferings. And most importantly, let us not forget that:

> ...the oneness of humanity, a spiritual truth abundantly confirmed by science, implies an organic change in the structure of present-day society. The fundamental solution to racial and ethnic conflict rests ultimately on the common recognition of the oneness of humankind. And education in the principle of the oneness of humanity is the shortest route out of poverty and prejudice.[18]

In the final analysis there can be only one race and that is the human race. The world today has reached that stage of technological

45

development where people must decide to be one world or none.

Dr. Martin Luther King, Jr. put it succinctly:

As I stand here and look upon thousands of Negro faces, and the thousands of white faces, intermingled like the waters of a river, I see only one face - the face of the future.

Endnotes

1. Bahá'u'lláh, *Gleanings* at 286.
2. 'Abdu'l-Bahá, *The Promulgation of Universal Peace.* at 300.
3. J. Pettman, *The Politics of Race*, (Peace Research Centre, ANU, 1988) at 5.
4. Herman Santa Cruz, *Racial Discrimination*, (New York, United Nations, 1971) at 13 and 22.
5. G. Allport, *Social Dilemma.*
6. Institute of Race Relations, *Roots of Racism*, (1982) at 24.
7. 'Abdu'l-Bahá, *Selections from the Writings of 'Abdu'l-Bahá*, at 300.
8. *ibid* at 247.
9. R. W. Thompson, *Racial Unity; An Imperative for Social Progress*, Bahá'í Studies Publication, Canada, (1990) at 1.
10. Mari Matsuda, *Public Response to Racist Speech: Considering the Victim's Story*, (1989) 97 Michigan Law Review at 2332 - 2333.
11. 'Abdu'l-Bahá, above, note 6 at 299.
12. Final Report of the Royal Commission into Aboriginal Death in Custody (1991).
13. *ibid.*, at 5.
14. Shoghi Effendi, *The World Order of Bahá'u'lláh*, (2nd ed., Bahá'í Publishing Trust, Wilmette Illinois, 1974) at 197 - 198.
15. 'Abdu'l-Bahá, above, note 6 at 113.
16. Shoghi Effendi, *The Advent of Divine Justice*, (4th ed., Bahá'í Publishing Trust, Wilmette, Illinois, 1984) at 40.
17. *ibid.*
18. Bahá'í International Community Statement on Elimination of Racism and Racial Discrimination, Feb. 1993.

Chapter Four
THE AUSTRALIAN BAHÁ'Í COMMUNITY AND THE ABORIGINAL PEOPLE: EARLY INTERACTIONS.

by

Graham Hassall

This paper examines the origins of the interactions between the Bahá'í community and Aborigines. It looks into early approaches made by the Bahá'í community to Aboriginal people, and the nature of the interaction that followed these approaches in its first decades. The interaction is placed on the context of the guidance provided by the writings of Shoghi Effendi in relation to Aboriginal people as well as in the context of the relationship between Aboriginal and white people of the time.

Background

Little is known about the first Aboriginal Bahá'ís, or about the approaches made by the Bahá'ís toward the Aboriginal community. This paper thus marks an initial inquiry into early interactions between the Bahá'í community and Aboriginal Australians. Its scope is limited, both in terms of sources consulted, and time-frame. It relies on archival records[1], on such publications as the Australian *Bahá'í Bulletin*, and on a limited number of interviews. It concentrates on the period prior to 1963. In that year the Bahá'í community completed a world-wide, and decade-long plan of expansion, known as the "Ten Year Crusade". For the Australian Bahá'ís, the Crusade had been a period of intensive activity that had called on all the spiritual, mental and physical resources at their command. At its completion, however, the Bahá'ís remained relatively unknown to the wider community. They were in one hundred and eleven centres (including thirty Local Assemblies and thirty-eight groups); and comprised several hundred members, including approximately twenty Aboriginal people.

A study such as this is important for several reasons. Firstly, it allows us to appreciate the efforts and achievements of the Bahá'ís of an earlier period - efforts which provide the foundations for our own activities, and without which our present accomplishments and aspirations would not be possible. Secondly, through such an inquiry into the experience of others we can moderate our own attitudes and actions. We are able to contemplate their accomplishments and limitations as part of our inheritance as Bahá'ís in this country. Furthermore, this consideration of the past builds in us a sense of compassion for the experience of the Aboriginal people, and the sensitivity that is required for building a relationship between all the peoples that the forces of history have brought together in Australia.

Policy And Approaches To 1955

There was minimal contact between the Bahá'í community and Aboriginals before the 1950s. Since the introduction of the Bahá'í Faith to Australia by Clara and Hyde Dunn in 1920, the small group of members they were able to raise were predominantly city-dwellers, whose efforts to spread their new faith were made in the mainstream of Australian society - which was predominantly European.[2] That the Bahá'ís adhered to the principle of racial equality did not move them to seek out Aboriginal members; neither did they speak or act against the racially discriminatory laws and attitudes that existed in Australian society. This silence, however, must be placed in the context of a reluctance by the Bahá'ís to raise their voice on any specific issue of concern in Australian society. They saw their task as being the laying of foundations for the activities of future Bahá'í institutions.

The first contact between the Bahá'í community and Aboriginal issues was not with Aboriginals themselves, but with guardians of Aboriginal welfare. Thus a member of the Aborigines Welfare Board spoke on "Aboriginal Youth Welfare" at a meeting in Sydney in March 1945.[3] Michael Sawtell, a member of the Aborigines Welfare Board, spoke at a 'World Religion Day' meeting at the National Hazíratu'l-Quds (head quarters) in Sydney in February 1953,[4] and at the Yerrinbool school in 1955. He also facilitated contact with Aboriginals in La Perouse.(at 7.)

Perhaps the goals Shoghi Effendi set for the Bahá'ís of Australia and New Zealand to accomplish during the World Crusade had expanded their horizons, and pushed them beyond the expression of principles into the realm of action. Pioneers ventured among the Melanesians of Papua New Guinea, the Solomon Islands, New Caledonia, the New Hebrides (now Vanuatu) and Fiji; they also settled among the Polynesians of Tahiti, Tonga, and Samoa; and the Malays of Portuguese Timor.[5] Several Pacific Island Bahá'ís subsequently visited Australia, stayed with Bahá'í families, and participated in the community's activities.[6]

These initiatives in the Indian and Pacific Oceans, however, cannot disguise the conservative approach of the Australian and New Zealand Bahá'ís to teaching indigenous peoples at home. Although delegates to the 1953 National Convention recommended that a "committee be established for the promotion of the Faith among the Maoris of New Zealand and the Aborigines of Australia", the National Spiritual

Assembly decided to "defer action" until more information was collected.[7] From this time until a series of recommendations on the matter were received from Shoghi Effendi, Aboriginals heard of the Faith from a small group of dedicated individuals.

Advice Of The Guardian

Shoghi Effendi made reference in letters to individuals to the approach Bahá'ís might adopt when teaching Aboriginals. In April 1952, he wrote (via his secretary) to Viva Rodwell in Brisbane concerning a young Aboriginal woman who had become a Bahá'í:

> He was delighted to hear that Betty Anderson is not only such a devoted and active Bahá'í youth, but that she has Aboriginal blood. He hopes that she will be instrumental, with your help, and that of the other believers, in carrying the Message to her relatives. It is only right that the people who were the original inhabitants of Australia should receive the Teachings of Bahá'u'lláh, and we cannot doubt that when they embrace them, it will have a great effect not only on their characters, but on their position in relation to the life of their country.[8]

In 1955 Margaret Forrest, another Brisbane Bahá'í, received a reply from Shoghi Effendi to questions she had asked regarding the teaching of "foreign students" and Aboriginals, and regarding participation in welfare activities:

> The Guardian thinks perhaps a different approach to the Aborigines might attract them; one of being interested in their lives and their folklore, and of trying to become their friend, rather than trying to change them or improve them.
>
> If you could form a friendship with an Aborigine who had more spiritual and mental capacity than the average, you might find out that out of this friendship would spring an interest in the Faith; but no doubt great patience is required to enter into the thought of these people, so different from ourselves in background and in training.
>
> He feels you should concentrate on teaching people who will be able to grasp the Faith; and, although work with spastic children is no doubt highly meritorious as a philanthropic activity, in view of the fact

that only we Bahá'ís can give the Message to the people in these dark days, he thinks it is a pity for a Bahá'í to waste too much time on that kind of work. Direct teaching is more important, especially teaching the Aborigines.[9]

The advice contained in these letters provided the foundation of the subsequent approach to Aboriginal teaching: take an interest in Aborigines as people, particularly those of exceptional capacity - because it is they who would be best able to interpret the Bahá'í teachings to their people; learn their folklore - for the purpose of establishing friendships rather than to "change them or improve them"; and approach the teaching of Aborigines with a patient attitude.

Guidance From The Guardian To The National Assembly

Apart from these few words of advice to individuals, on three occasions the Guardian emphasised the National Assembly the importance of teaching indigenous peoples:

[1954] He attaches great importance to teaching the Aboriginal Australians, and also in converting more Maoris to the Faith, and hopes that the Bahá'ís will devote some attention to contacting both of these minority groups.[10]

[1955] Your Assembly should bear in mind the necessity, in the future at any rate, of having firmly grounded Local Assemblies in all of the states of Australia and New Zealand; and also the importance of increasing the representation of the minority races, such as Aborigines and the Maoris, within the Bahá'í community. Special efforts should be made to contact these people and to teach them; and the Bahá'ís in Australia and New Zealand should consider that every one of them that can be won to the Faith is a precious acquisition.[11]

[1956] The beloved Guardian is very anxious that constructive steps be taken at this time looking to the teaching of the Aborigines in both Australia and New Zealand.

The beloved Master has often referred to the importance of the original inhabitants of a country being brought into the Faith, as the Cause of God will be the means of stimulating and activating these peoples and the cause of their progress in society.[12]

He feels that it would be well for your Assembly to appoint two committees, one in charge of teaching the Aborigines, and one, a committee of New Zealand people, who will be in charge of teaching the Maoris in New Zealand.[13]

Formation Of National Aborigine Committees

In June 1956 the National Assembly responded to the Guardian's repeated suggestions by appointing a five-member National Aboriginal Committee. Jeff and Viva Rodwell, Jean Millway, and Betty Anderson were appointed in Brisbane, and Greta Lake was appointed in Sydney. The committee first met in Brisbane on 27 July 1956.[14] Jeff Rodwell was appointed chair, Viva Rodwell secretary, and Betty Anderson treasurer. The Committee reviewed reports sent in by Bahá'ís already involved in contacting Aborigines (Greta Lake in Sydney, Katherine Harcus in Adelaide, Frank Saunders in the Northern Territory, and Rolph Schiller in Duchess, Queensland), and consulted on possible elements of a national plan. It also requested clarification of its terms of reference, which, by August, the national body confirmed as being "to plan contact work with Aboriginal people".[15]

Australia's federal structure meant that laws relating to Aboriginals differed in each state. The NAC made efforts to collect the relevant state laws, ordinances and regulations, and also obtained a copy of the *Aboriginal Act*, which controlled the life of Aboriginal Australians. It sought in addition information on the numbers of Aborigines in different parts of the country, and sought information on the circumstances in which they were living from the Departments of Aboriginal Welfare in each state.

Articles were placed in the Bahá'í Bulletin encouraging Bahá'ís to pioneer to areas close to Aboriginal communities.[16] The committee appealed for a Bahá'í to move to the more distant parts of Australia:

...if such pioneers chose the Northern Territory or the vast areas of

West Queensland, North West Australia, or Central South Australia they would also serve in the double capacity of both pioneering virgin territory or Australia, and of assisting in implementing the Guardian's desire to bring the Aboriginal people into the Faith.[17]

Appeals for pioneers to move to Aboriginal areas obtained no immediate response. Members of the committee, on the other hand, made progress through developing friendships with individual Aborigines, and reports based largely on their own efforts were contributed to the *Bahá'í Bulletin*:

> Both in Sydney and Brisbane, Bahá'ís are endeavouring to implement the Guardian's desire by actions, rather than words. Befriending Aboriginals, taking them into your home, visiting them when hospitalised and showing an active interest in their welfare, are all ways in which some Bahá'ís are, and you too can help in this work. You may be able to contact these dark brothers through visiting the Native Affairs exhibit at the Royal Show as was done in Brisbane, although whenever contact is made in a State of Mission organisation, great discretion should be observed. Even if numbers of Bahá'ís could show by actions alone, without any verbal teaching at present, the spirit of the Faith, what a wonderful help it would be.[18]

Queensland and New South Wales were not, however, the only states in which Bahá'ís commenced a commitment to teaching Aborigines. In 1955, Adelaide Bahá'í Ann Pearce had moved to Goolwa, at the mouth of South Australia's Murray River, to be nearer to Aboriginal communities. She established children's classes, and through contact with Marjorie Tripp met Ephraim Tripp, who in January 1960 became a Bahá'í.[19] The NAC reported:

> Mrs Pearce has made them real friends, and they enjoy her hospitality and her friendship. Since she first showed them the Bahá'í way of life, she is now able to tell them of the Faith so dear to us. It is by deeds, not words, that these souls will be brought to Bahá'u'lláh.[20]

Another Adelaide Bahá'í, Clarice Stanton, was in contact with tribal people from Yalata, at Fowlers Bay on the southern edge of the Nullabor Plains, who were from Kooniba near Ceduna and from

Oldea.

In April 1957, the National Assembly characterised the work of drawing Aboriginals to the Bahá'í cause as "a task of great difficulty".[21] Following the reading of the NAC's report to National Convention in 1957, the delegates felt the best place to contact Aboriginals was Darwin, since "the natives in other States are mostly under mission control and therefore out of reach of the Bahá'ís". The report of this discussion concluded:

> Aborigine people want to be taught how to do things. It is necessary to make friends with them in order to teach them - this is obviously a basic point in teaching anyone anywhere.
>
> The native people must be treated as human beings - they must be made to feel equality as individuals. They must be helped to think for themselves.[22]
>
> The Aborigine people are very shy and diffident and are very much in need of love and understanding. They do not want pity - they want to be treated as ordinary Australian citizens.[23]

The need to state such sentiments is indicative of the relations existing between black and white Australians at the time. Aborigines were not even Australian citizens. Their forbears had been dispossessed of land and property, and had been decimated by disease and murder. They did not possess the right to vote, were not counted in the census, were denied permission to drink alcohol (a good rule, but applied discriminately, and for the wrong reasons!), and required permits to enter certain areas, including movie theatres; they were forced to live on the fringes of modern society. It was in this social context that the Bahá'ís went to speak to them of racial equality, and universal brotherhood. Who were these Europeans to speak of such things? It was little wonder, therefore, that communicating the Bahá'í message across this vast divide took time, and no doubt required much soul-searching by the Bahá'ís themselves.

The NAC reported progress in the "slow process of being accepted and trusted."[24] The National Teaching Committee reported increased activity in teaching Aborigines during the year 1958 - 1959, in Brisbane, Goolwa, Unley, Sydney, Tamworth and Lismore.[25] Mrs Pearce continued her work in Goolwa, and the Hewsons in Adelaide had entertained and given accommodation to Aborigines. At Christmas in 1959, Mrs Rose Hawthorne gave a party for the Aboriginal youth, for which she received a letter of thanks from the Board of Aborigine Advancement League.[26] South Australian Aborigines spread work of the Bahá'í teachings to relatives in Western Australia. In Brisbane the Rodwells sponsored youth meetings, and recorded Aboriginal elders speaking and singing. They became close friends with Mr George McKenzie,[27] Margaret Valadian, Margaret Williams, the first Aboriginal woman to attend university,[28] and with renowned singer Harold Blair.

While all such initiatives were welcomed, diverse views emerged concerning the extent to which the Bahá'ís should combine their efforts with those of other organisations. In Tamworth, NSW, Colin and Allaine Duncan were active from the late 1950s in the Association for the Assimilation of the Aborigines, which among other activities taught trades and arts skills at the local Technical College. But not all Bahá'ís felt that it was necessary to become involved in existing movements. The issue was discussed following presentation of the NAC's report at National Convention in 1958:

> Several speakers stressed the Guardians instruction that Bahá'ís were to be leaders of the field, pointing out that our task was not one of welfare in competition with the missions, but was to befriend the Aborigine and to teach him the Faith. Bahá'ís as individuals could and should take any opportunity offered to them of making contact with Aboriginal people.[29]

Hand of the Cause[30] Collis Featherstone made a recommendation, which the delegates approved, "that the NSA consider the establishment of legally incorporated Bahá'í Aboriginal Societies".[31] Whereas little seems to have come of this idea, the "dangers of affiliating with existing secular "welfare" and similar societies for the Aboriginal people" were stressed in the NAC's report to National Convention in 1959. The Committee emphasised, however, "the need for the Aboriginal people to be treated as a friend in the same manner as contacts among the white population."[32]

It might be thought that the National Teaching Committee gave less emphasis to the issue of Aboriginal teaching at this time than to other issues. Its report for 1957 - 1958, for instance, simply stated "Aborigine contacts - the teaching work has been blessed by increasing contact with Aborigine people in all states."[33] But is must be remembered that at this time there were a mere ten Local Assemblies in Australia, and the community's resources were now also required for construction of the Mashriqu'l-Adhkar (House of Worship) in Sydney.

The issue was brought into sharper focus in September 1963, when the Federal Council for Aboriginal Advancement's secretary, Faith Bandler, sought the support of the Bahá'ís in "helping Aborigines to reclaim their hunting ground and home" at Yirrkala in the Northern Territory's Gove Peninsula, where the mining of Bauxite had been proposed. The National Assembly replied that, deeply as the Bahá'ís sympathised with the Aboriginal people, the Assembly had:

> ...no power as an incorporated body administering the affairs of a national religious community, to take part in this legal action. (at 54)

Developments 1959 - 1961

Between 1959 and 1961, efforts to reach the Aboriginal community received impetus from visits by several international Bahá'í travellers, and were rewarded by an increased number of Aboriginal enrolments.

In 1959 Enoch Olinga, a Hand of the Cause from Uganda, Africa, toured Australia and the Pacific Islands. Together with Collis Featherstone Mr Olinga visited many Aboriginal communities in South Australia, and he visited others in New South Wales.[34]

Ephraim Tripp

The most effective teaching activities during the period 1961 - 1963 took place in South Australia, principally in Murray Bridge and Renmark. Through the efforts of Ann Pearce, Ephraim Tripp became a Bahá'í in January 1960. Members of this family joined the following year. On 10 - 11 of June 1961, the Bahá'ís of Renmark, Murray Bridge and Victor Harbour, supported a "part study, part social" weekend attended also by Aboriginals from the Point McLeay Mission. Sixteen of the forty people present were Aboriginal. It was after this meeting that a close friend of Ephraim Tripp, Fred Murray of Renmark, became a Bahá'í.

Fred Murray

Fred Murray was not the first Australian Aboriginal to become a Bahá'í nor the most educated. He was, however, the first "full-blooded" Aboriginal to join, and he entered the community with a clear understanding of its mission to bring the races together. Murray had been born on the Esperance Peninsular in 1844. He had travelled the country areas of South Australia, working on a camel train, dam-sinking, and horse-breaking. Although illiterate, he recognised in the life and teachings of Bahá'u'lláh the fulfilment of tribal belief that Mumina (the creator) would send the spiritual teacher and law to his people. Murray's years as a Bahá'í were brief, but filled with purpose. When Ruhiyyih Khanum visited South Australia in September 1961 (on her way to the dedication of the Mashriqu'l-Adhkar in Sydney) she met

Fred Murray at a meeting at Narring. In February 1962, Murray accompanied Dr Muhajir and the Howards on an extensive visit to Aboriginal communities. In 1963, Fred travelled to London to attend the first World Congress. When the Congress Committee sought the attendance of an Aborigine (it planned to have Bahá'ís of all races represented), Ruhiyyih Khanum had suggested Murray, and had sent 1000 pounds to cover expenses. He travelled to the Congress with Margaret and Noel Bluett.

Harry Penrith

In Sydney, Greta Lake had by 1960 established a firm friendship with Harry Penrith, who many years later became better known as Burnum Burnum. The committee reported:

> The Aboriginal young man, Harry Penrith, continues to visit the Lake home and shows an increasing interest in the Faith. He attended the Summer School and has been to the Temple and a number of Public Meetings.[35]

Other Developments 1959 - 1961

Canberra Bahá'ís were visiting Aborigines in Leeton. The Duncans continued their work in Tamworth. Others meeting Aboriginals included Thelma Hewson in Adelaide, the Rodwells in Brisbane.[36] In Sydney Greta Lake was attending lectures on Aboriginal education at Sydney University. In response to the Committee's report to National Convention, the delegates felt that "teaching work with the native people should be conducted on an individual basis, with the genuine Bahá'í love for all mankind clearly demonstrated."[37] The Committee said it was through "white and Aboriginal people freely intermingling, that the truth of the claims of the Faith are proven through demonstration of its power to establish the oneness of mankind in the hearts of men. In this way, the world is to be rescued from the tragedies of prejudice, intolerance and division."[38]

The NAC Moves to South Australia

In June 1961, the National Assembly moved the National Aborigines Committee to South Australia. Members of the committee now included Howard and Myrtle Harwood, resident at Cooltong, Ephraim and Beryl Tripp and Madge and Maurice Williams. The committee's objective was to "advise and guide the National Assembly and believers on methods of taking the Faith to the Aborigines throughout Australia". Its terms of reference were "to teach the Faith to the Aborigines with power to admit Aborigine believers where necessary".[39] In South Australia, activities continued in Gawler, Murray Bridge, Loxton, and Tailem Bend. In October 1961, Howard Harwood reported to the South Australian Regional Teaching Committee that the Tipps had heard of receptivity to the Bahá'í Teachings in the lower Murray area. (at 23.) A gathering in Murray Bridge 22 - 23 July 1961, attracted an audience of 78, including 58 from the Point McLeay Mission. Hand of the Cause Collis Featherstone screened films of the Intercontinental Conference in New Delhi.[40] There were also a group of three Aboriginal Bahá'ís at Victor Harbour in 1961. Frank Khan visited the state in 1961. (at 35)

From this time the approach taken toward Aboriginal teaching was much influenced by the ideas and enthusiasm of Howard Harwood, an orchardist from Cooltong who later served on the Continental Board of Counsellors. The Annual Report of the NAC in 1961 included the secretary's assessment of the situation:

> The Australian Aborigines present one of the most complex present day social problems because of the enormous number of types and their related social environments, not to mention the differing climates of policy layed down and pursued by state and federal authorities.
>
> There are however, certain points that can be established as

general. The Aborigine is quickly attracted to the Spirit of the Faith; they do not show their feelings very much, they do not ask questions or cause argument for or against, they are very shy, sensitive, peace-loving people who generally feel extremely inferior; they are divided and scattered and are in need of an unabating demonstration of love that only comes through knowledge of the Teachings and a very deep desire to be of service.[41]

During 1961 - 1962, Howard and Myrtle Harwood had made two special trips of over 2,000 miles to visit Aboriginals in South Australia and Victoria. *Bahá'í News* for October 1961 reported that the committee was formulating plans "to further teaching work among Aboriginal people all over Australia - a project which was very dear to the heart of the beloved Guardian."[42]

The Visit Of Ruhiyyih Khanum

In the second half of 1961 Ruhiyyih Khanum visited Australia, primarily to represent the Hands of the Cause in the Holy Land at the dedication of the Sydney Mashriqu'l-Adhkar. She expressed a wish to visit the Aborigines, and to spend the night with an Aboriginal family. When the committee was refused permission for her to visit Point McClay Government Settlement by the South Australian State Protector of Aborigines,[43] she stayed with John and Irene Bingapore at Tailem Bend. Aboriginals from the Point McClay settlement visited Ruhiyyih Khanum at Narrung, a small town close to the settlement. Others travelled further to attend the meeting of abut 40 people. Geoff and Edie Carter and their seven children travelled more than 200 kilometres from Loxton to be present. They became Bahá'ís several months later. Mrs Bingapore became a Bahá'í 18 months later. Others present who later joined included Silvie and John Rankin.

Ruhiyyih Khanum stayed in Darwin for five days following the dedication of the Sydney Mashriqu'l-Adhkar, and the Darwin Bahá'ís, including Aaron Blomely and Tony Scott, who had made friends with Aboriginals from Bathurst and Groote islands, were able to arrange meetings.44 None of these contacts, however, resulted in Aboriginals becoming Bahá'ís, mostly, a situation the Bahá'ís attributed to the control over the Aboriginal lives by the missions.

NAC Policy 1962 - 1963

In the year 1961 - 1962, the number of Aboriginal Bahá'ís increased from five to ten. In February 1962, Dr. Muhajir visited several Australian states. In Victoria, he spoke at meetings in Condah and Pernim Mission station.[45] Although he made a successful visit to Renmark[46] he, like Ruhiyyih Khanum, was refused permission to visit Point McClay Government Aborigine Settlement - in this case he and Howard Harwood reportedly being ordered off the settlement by a drunken superintendent (at 34). Following his visit to Allawah Grove, outside Perth, regular visits were made to Aborigines living there.[47]

Dr. Muhajir's approach to teaching in general, and teaching Aborigines in particular, provided a jolt to attitudes toward planning and action held by the Australian Bahá'ís. He felt there should be Aboriginal Committees in each state rather than a single national committee,[48] and he related success in teaching Aborigines to success in other endeavours.[49] No doubt the NAC was buoyed by Dr. Muhajir's encouraging visit. It published guidelines, advocating personal visits to Aborigines by Bahá'ís, through which the principle of equality could be demonstrated. The committee further suggested that families be visited frequently, that only small pamphlets be given out (unless bigger books were requested); that it was best to work with Bahá'í institutions rather than through other organisations; and that it was best not to wait for permission to visit, or to bother with advertising, or extending invitations, but to "just go".[50]

Literature

Providing literature that introduced the Bahá'í teachings to an Aboriginal audience in an appropriate manner was not addressed until the 1960s. In July 1962, the NAC explored the prospect of printing a booklet in an Aboriginal language (at 28) and sought examples of booklets from Regional Assemblies in Africa and the South Pacific (at 29).[51] The committee viewed materials printed for an American Indian audience but decided they were unsuited to use with Aboriginals (at 45). It also explored the idea of presenting Bahá'í principles through picture books,[52] but was at the time unable to find a person who could provide the illustrations.[53]

In the 1960s the National Teaching Committee commenced encouraging involvement in Aboriginal teaching, urging RTC's to organise events for Aboriginal communities during Easter:

> During the past few years, conditions of inequality and lack of opportunity which had existed for centuries are being changed, all over the world, as the spirit of justice moves in the hearts of men everywhere. As in other countries it seems that it is the destiny of the Faith in Australia to bring justice and equality to the Aboriginal people, that mankind may be enriched through the particular talents with which they have been endowed.[54]

In June 1962, the NAC wrote to all Local Assemblies and Regional Teaching Committees to find out where Aborigines were being taught the Faith (at 28, the letter reproduced at 30). Reports to this request provided the first national summary of teaching activities (at 31).

By mid-1962, Aboriginal teaching activities had increased throughout Australia. Hobart reported that there were no Aborigines in Tasmania, but part-Aborigines lived on Cape Barren and Flinders Islands. Early in 1962, Rod Alberts, of Condah, a nephew of Harry Carter, became a Bahá'í during a visit to Victoria by the Harwoods and Harry Carter.[55] Douglas Rankin, who became a Bahá'í in South

Australia, moved to Melbourne and became the ninth Bahá'í in the Victorian capital, allowing a Local Assembly to be formed at Riḍván 1962.

In Darwin, Bahá'í Naw-Rúz (new year) was celebrated with a barbecue, and at Easter a group of 15 Bahá'ís and their friends camped on the Douglas River, spending their evening talking "around the campfire".[56] Darwin Assembly was formed at Riḍván 1962. The first Torres Strait Islander to become a Bahá'í (Nola/Pam Blomely) was reported in the annual report for 1963.[57] Soon after its formation Darwin Assembly established an adult education course for Aborigines. It commenced one night per week, attended initially by some 20 youth.[58] When the class was extended to two nights per week it attracted the attention of the Church Missionary Society, which asked the participants not to attend, and commenced holding hymn sessions at the same time.[59]

At Easter 1962, Madge and Maurice Williams and Harry Carter travelled north, meeting Aboriginals in Carrieton, Peterborough, Hawker, and Port Augusta.[60] In May 1962, Beryl Tripp reported to a teaching conference in Adelaide that 'practically all the Aborigines in South Australia' had now heard of the Faith, and urged the Bahá'ís to now establish closer contact with them.[61] In September the Williams made another tour through South Australia, reaching the southern terminus of the Birdsville Track, and visiting Georgetown, Quorn, Hawker, Copley, Leigh Creek and Beltana.[62] In November 1962, the National Assembly asked the NAC to arrange for Harry Carter to visit Blacktown in Sydney (at 33): an interstate teaching tour what was later described as a "significant step forward".[63]

In January 1963, the NAC met with Hands of the Cause Collis Featherstone and William Sears (at 37). In March 1963 the United

Aborigines Committee Mission intercepted mail being sent to the Jackson children at Nepabunna, Port Augusta, South Australia, and refused to allow them to receive the Bahá'í children's newsletters (at 47). The mission wrote to the South Australia RTC and requested the newsletter of the Child Education Committee not be sent to families there. Howard Harwood, secretary of the NAC, felt this opposition would do "more good than harm".[64] The Committee noted also that all Aboriginal mission settlements were coming under the control of the government, and church influence over the lives of Aborigines was declining.[65]

There were now approximately 20 Aboriginal Bahá'ís, and these Bahá'ís were on six Local Assemblies: Melbourne, Newcastle, Payneham, Gawler, Murray Bridge and Renmark (at 48). Those who became Bahá'ís during 1962 - 1963 included Mrs Elaine Murray and her husband Freddy Murray (whose father was Fred Murray); Mrs Poland in Blacktown; Mr and Mrs L. A. Rigney and Mrs W. Williams in Gawler; Mr D. Carter and Mr. Clive and Mrs Rigney in Murray Bridge; and Joseph Egan and his mother Mrs J. Egan of Coll Col in New South Wales. About half the Aboriginal Bahá'ís came from the Minen, Bunanditj, Narrogin, and Pointbarli tribes; the tribal origins of the other half were unknown.[66] At Ridván 1963, the National Assembly reported:

> The Aborigine community has shown marked increase in numbers and several new centres have been established by Aborigine believers.[67]

In the same report the National Teaching Committee reported "warm co-operation" with the NAC.[68]

Developments 1963 - 1965

At least 16 Aborigines became Bahá'ís between February 1963 and

February 1965.[69] The first All Aborigines Teaching Conferences was held in Murray Bridge on 9 June 1963.[70] In July 1963, the NAC reported to the National Assembly that officers of the South Australian Aborigines Affairs Department were impressed with the behaviour of those who had become Bahá'ís (at 51).

In January 1964, the NAC noted a difference in conditions in the north and south of Australia. The NAC felt that the work it was doing was best done at a local level, through LSA's and RTC's, and resolved that the committee be discontinued:[71]

> The NAC has the view that no one in Australia really has the experience enough to advise the NSA of taking the Faith to the Aborigines and feel that teaching should start with believers going to the north and centre of Australia such as Alice Springs, Broome, etc. and live, learning to go from the ground level and work from there.

The NAC felt, furthermore, that Bahá'ís "generally were not active enough amongst coloured people and that action must be taken to change this." (at 54).

Aboriginal Society And Bahá'í Law

Identification with the principles of Bahá'u'lláh was not in itself a sufficient buttress against the pressures that faced those individuals of whatever race who joined his Cause. For Aborigines, however, the pressures were greater, as the sources of law and morality that exist in all cultures had disappeared from most Aboriginal communities. Consequently, the ability to construct a meaningful existence was harder; and the opportunities for development more limited. Bahá'ís were no less prone to such pressures, and some Aboriginal Bahá'í families were weakened by alcoholism and by the break-down of relationships. The use of alcohol was not only against Bahá'í law, but its use by Aborigines was not permitted under Australian law, and led to their imprisonment. A candid assessment of the situation, and attempt at interpretation was offered by Howard Harwood at a NAC consultation in January 1965:

> Even when they become Bahá'ís they have good intentions but with the flick of an eyelash it happens. Then in jail. For some unknown reason, when they have become Bahá'ís, it is often hard to get them to come to study the Faith and so deepen themselves. Prayer seems to be the main way to reach them, perhaps we who claim to be Bahá'ís do not pray enough. (at 62)

Bahá'í marriage laws were also difficult to implement within the Aboriginal community: many did not know their natural parents, but required the consent of their parents for marriage. In February 1965, the NAC put a number of questions to the National Assembly. It wished to know what to do:

1. when one of the Bahá'í marriage parties has been born out of wedlock and raised in an institution and does no know who the parents are;

2. when one of the Bahá'í marriage parties has a known mother but unknown father;

3. when one of the Bahá'í marriage parties does no know his or her father or mother and has been fostered but not legally adopted;

4. when one of the Bahá'í marriage parties knows his or her mother but has been legally adopted by another couple; and

5. in many cases, fostering is done at an early age. The child has never been told that he or she is fostered or of his or her circumstances. In view of this would it be correct to accept the written consent of these foster parents? (at 64, Heggie answers at 65).

Dissolving The National Aboriginal Committee

In June 1965 the National Spiritual Assembly accepted the National

Aboriginal Committee's decision that it be disbanded "having in mind (its) recommendation that Aborigine believers should be treated as any other believer". After almost a decade of experience, the committee felt considerable differences existed in the Aboriginal communities of the north and south of Australia, and that the work it had been doing was best attempted at the local level, by Local Spiritual Assemblies and Regional Teaching Committees. Thereafter, responsibility for taking the message of Bahá'u'lláh to Aboriginals was taken up by the National Teaching Committee.

The experience of the National Aborigine Committee raises interesting questions concerning propagation of the Bahá'í Teachings amongst a specific cultural group within Australian Society. The first concerns the relationship between mode of organisation and effective action. There was a desire, on the one hand, to recognise the "special nature" of the task by appointing for it an administrative committee. There was a gradual realisation, however, that the existence of such an administrative committee had generated the impression within the Bahá'í community that "Aboriginal Teachings" was being undertaken by a small group of devoted "experts". The Committee's concern was that the Bahá'í Community in general had relinquished too much responsibility for the task, which it felt belonged to the community as a whole. In later year an "Aboriginal and Torres Strait Islander" Committee was once more established then dissolved. Finding the balance between "unity" - in which all tasks belonged to all members of the community - and "diversity" - in which members of the community engaged in a range of diverse but complementary and mutually-supportive activities - was still being sought.

A second question concerns the effectiveness with which the Bahá'í Teachings were communicated to Aboriginal Australians. The progress made by 1965, although limited, was none the less significant, and made through the considerable efforts of a small number of individuals. By 1968 the Bahá'í community included members of the Andilyaugwa (Groote Island), Bunanditj, Jirkia Minning, Junjan, Minen, and Narrogin tribes. This progress laid the basis for the achievements of the 1980s, when there were conversions by Aboriginals at Onslow in the far north-west of Western Australia. Acceptance of the Bahá'í Faith by Herbert Parker, an important tribal elder, in 1985, and Jack Malardy leader of the Karradjarrie people at La Grange in 1987 heralded acceptance of the Bahá'í Faith by more than one hundred Aboriginals. By the 1990s the Australian Bahá'í community included approximately 400 indigenous members.

Endnotes

1. Australian National Bahá'í Archives, Mona Vale, New South Wales.
2. See Graham Hassall, 'Outpost of a World Religion: the Bahá'í Faith in Australia 1920 - 1947', Journal of Religious History, 16:3, June 1991 at 315 - 338.
3. *Bahá'í Quarterly* 36, July 1945, at 9.
4. *Bahá'í Bulletin* 60, April 1953, at 4.
5. See Graham Hassall, 'Pacific Bahá'í Communities 1953 - 1964', in Donald H. Rubenstein (ed. *Pacific History: Papers from the 8th Pacific History Conference*, University of Guam Press and Micronesian Area Research Centre, 1992).
6. Fijian Bahá'í Isireli Racule, for instance, visited numerous Australian centres during 1956 - 1957, and spent time with Aborigines in Tamworth: Regional Teaching Committee for New South Wales. Annual Report, in National Spiritual Assembly of the Bahá'ís of Australia and New Zealand, Annual Report 1957 at 16.
7. *Bahá'í Bulletin* 62, June 1953, at 5.
8. Shoghi Effendi to Viva Rodwell, 30 April 1952.
9. Shoghi Effendi to Margaret Forrest, 9 April 1955.
10. Shoghi Effendi to National Spiritual Assembly, 16 June 1954.

11. Shoghi Effendi to National Spiritual Assembly, 24 July 1955.
12. This paragraph was published in *Bahá'í Bulletin* 24, June 1956, at 5.
13. Shoghi Effendi to National Spiritual Assembly, 10 March 1956.
14. Frank Wyss was invited to the first three meetings, to assist in 'formulating a program of work': NAC to NSA, 18 April 1957. 15 NSA (James Heggie) to National Aborigine Committee, 13 August 1956.
15. NSA (James Heggie) to National Aboriginal Committee, 13 August 1956.
16. Bahá'í Bulletin 35, May 1957, at 2.
17. National Aborigine Committee, Annual Report, in National Spiritual Assembly of the Bahá'ís of Australia and New Zealand. Annual Reports 1957 - 1958 at 26.
18. Viva Rodwell, 'Appeal for help among Aborigines', *Bahá'í Bulletin* 29, November 1956 at 4. In 1956 a Brisbane Bahá'í was invited to speak on the Aboriginal situation at a Congregational Church: Convention Report BE (Bahá'í Year) 113 (1956), in *Bahá'í Bulletin* 25, July 1956 at 5. The Rev. Rees Thomas invited Viva Rodwell and Betty Anderson to address the congregation of the City Congregational Church once more in 1957.
19. Ephraim Tripp was from an unknown tribe and was also of part-Maori descent.
20. *Bahá'í Bulletin* 68, March 1960 at 10.
21. National Spiritual Assembly of the Bahá'ís of Australia and New Zealand, Annual Report 1957 at 4.
22. Annual Bahá'í Convention - Australia, 1957 at 7.
23. *Bahá'í Bulletin* 68, March 1960 at 10.
24. Aborigine Committee. Annual Report, BE 115 at 20.
25. National Teaching Committee, Annual Report, in National Spiritual Assembly of the Bahá'ís of Australia, Annual Report BE 115 (1958 - 1959) at 12. The Teaching Committee for South Australia reported, 'Aborigine contact work has been carried out by Unley, Marion Group and at Goolwa,' *ibid.*, at 14.
26. *Bahá'í Bulletin* 68, March 1960 at 11.
27. Aborigine Committee, National Spiritual Assembly of the Bahá'ís of Australia Annual Report BE 117 (1961), at 18.
28. At the beginning of 1958 Margaret Willams transferred from Brisbane to Melbourne University.
29. Convention Report, Annual Bahá'í Convention Australia, BE 115 (1958) at 8.

30. Shoghi Effendi (Head of the Bahá'í Faith 1921 - 1957) designated a number of outstanding Bahá'ís as "Hands of the Cause", and charged them with special responsibilities relating to the protection and development of the Bahá'í community worldwide. The Hands of the Cause referred to in this paper are H. Collis Featherstone, Ruhiyyih Khanum (widow of Shoghi Effendi), Enoch Olinga, Rahmat Muhajir, and William Sears.

31. Convention Report, Annual Bahá'í Convention Australia, BE 115 (1958) at 8.

32. Convention Report, Annual Bahá'í Convention Australia, BE 116 (1959) at 5.

33. National Teaching Committee Report 1957 - 1958 at 4.

34. Places visited by Mr. Olinga included La Perouse and Tamworth.

35. National Aborigine Committee, National Spiritual Assembly of the Bahá'ís of Australia, Annual Report BE 116 (1960) at 26.

36. National Aborigine Committee, National Spiritual Assembly of the Bahá'ís of Australia, Annual Report BE 116 (1960) at 26 - 27.

37. Report of Annual Bahá'í Convention - Australia BE 118 (1961) at 5.

38. *Bahá'í Bulletin* 85, August 1961 at 8.

39. Bahá'í Directory Australia 1962 - 1963 at 3.

40. *Bahá'í Bulletin* 86, September 1961 at 12.

41. National Aborigines Committee. National Spiritual Assembly of the Bahá'ís of Australia Annual Report BE 118 at 31.

42. *Bahá'í News* 367:13, October 1961.

43. Ruhiyyih Khanum was refused permission to visit Point McClay Government Aborigine Settlement.

44. *Bahá'í Bulletin* 88, November 1961 at 12.

45. *Bahá'í Bulletin* 93, April 1962 at 6.

46. National Teaching Committee Report in National Spiritual Assembly of the Bahá'ís of Australia, Annual Report, BE 118 (1962) at 12.

47. National Teaching Committee Report in National Spiritual Assembly of the Bahá'ís of Australia, Annual Report BE 118 (1962) AT 19. Madge Featherstone visited when in Perth in May - June 1962.

48. To Pam Ringwood, 5 March 1962, NTC Correspondence 1962. (0888/0258 National Bahá'í Archives.)

49. NTC to RTC's 12 March 1962, NTC Correspondence 1962. (0888/0258 National Bahá'í Archives.)

50. *Bahá'í Bulletin* 100, November 1962 at 15.

51. In July 1962, the National Assembly ordered 1000 copies of *Convincing Answers*, and 100 copies of *Trustees of the Merciful* at 32.
52. The NSA replied to the committee that it felt Aborigines could 'accept the simple truths of the Bahá'í Faith as well as Australians generally' but did not rule out the idea of 'teaching the Faith in pictures'. NSA (James Heggie) to NAC, 1 August 1962, at 34.
53. NAC Annual Report BE 122, April 1965, at 67.
54. *Bahá'í Bulletin* 93, April 1962, at 4.
55. *Bahá'í Bulletin* 92, March 1962 at 11.
56. *Bahá'í Bulletin* 95, June 1962 at 8.
57. National Teaching Committee Report in National Spiritual Assembly of the Bahá'ís of Australia, Annual Report BE 118 (1962) at 20.
58. *Bahá'í Bulletin* 96, July 1962 at 8.
59. *Bahá'í Bulletin* 100, November 1962 at 11.
60. *Bahá'í Bulletin* 95, June 1962 at 8. Travel by the Williams' in South Australia was reported in Bahá'í News 382:18, January 1963 folder at 35.
61. *Bahá'í Bulletin* 96, July 1962, at 10.
62. *Bahá'í Bulletin* 99, October 1962 at 14. 'During this visit, contact was renewed with many Aboriginals who had been met during a previous visit in May. Many discussions of the Faith were held, and slides of Bahá'í Holy Places and Bahá'í gatherings shown. In all areas, they were warmly received and they found the native people receptive to the Teachings. A measure of their reception was that the Aboriginal people in several places showed them rock carvings, which are sacred to them. In addition to the Aboriginal people, there are many descendants of Afghan parents in this part of Australia, quite a number of whom are Muslims.'
63. National Spiritual Assembly of the Bahá'ís of Australia. Annual Report BE 119 (1963) at 9.
64. National Aboriginal Committee Report in National Spiritual Assembly of the Bahá'ís of Australia, Annual Report BE 119 (1963) at 12 - 13.
65. at 41.
66. NAC to National Spiritual Assembly, 24 December 1962.
67. National Spiritual Assembly of the Bahá'ís of Australia. Annual Report BE 119 (1963) at 2.
68. National Spiritual Assembly of the Bahá'ís of Australia. Annual Report BE 119 (1963) at 9.
69. Report on 'Teaching Among the Aborigines' by Madge Williams at 63 - 64.

70. *ibid.*, at 49.
71. at 55.

Chapter Five
ABORIGINAL CUSTOMARY RITES - THE CHALLENGE TO BAHÁ'Í AUSTRALIA

by

Graham Nicholson

This paper briefly addresses the current legal developments in Australia and elsewhere in the recognition of Aboriginal customary rights, both as to land and in other respects and both domestically and internationally. The paper will relate to the Bahá'í writings on the position of indigenous peoples in Bahá'u'lláh's model of a New World Order. The paper poses the question whether Bahá'í Australia is at present adequately addressing the position of indigenous rights, both from a point of view of those secular developments and in terms of the Bahá'í writings. How far can Bahá'í Australia go before becoming enmeshed in the politics of indigenous rights? What more needs to be done to articulate the Bahá'í position? To what degree can indigenous rights be better secured under the Bahá'í model?

It is now well accepted that Australia as an island continent was settled by a race of dark-skinned peoples many thousands of years prior to European settlement. Some say this occupation goes back more than 40,000 years. The origin of these peoples is not certain, although a commonly advanced theory is that they migrated from South-East Asia during the ice-ages and the consequent lowering of sea levels. They gradually spread out over the whole of the continent, including Tasmania. They adapted to a harsh land and survived. They were isolated from the rest of the world for a very long time. As a result, they developed unique forms of culture and religion not paralleled anywhere else in the world. The complexity and subtlety of their arrangements have only been recognised by non-Aboriginals in comparatively recent times. It is now widely accepted that they had and to some extent still have unique social, legal and religious systems and beliefs and that these enabled them to survive in harmony with their somewhat harsh environment. It is an achievement that dwarfs that of the European people in this continent.

This state of relative equilibrium was dramatically affected by European settlement of Australia. With limited exceptions, this new wave of settlement was carried out with little or no regard to the Aboriginal people and to their systems and beliefs. The absence of co-ordinated or sophisticated Aboriginal institutions or policies to deal with this invasion and the lack of advanced technologies, meant that these people could easily be pushed back and marginalised. Occasional isolated acts of resistance on their part could usually be dealt with quickly and effectively. The legal theory was developed that the land was virtually uninhabited, available for European settlement by grant from the Crown. Rights under Aboriginal law were not recognised. Missionary zeal was often combined with a colonial mentality to subjugate, to convert and then to isolate the survivors. To many, Aboriginals were heathens and barbarians. It reflected a 19th century attitude which, despite rising humanitarian concerns, fitted in conveniently with Darwinian-Spenserian concepts, and with inherited concepts of superiority derived from European 'civilisation'. To some extent we still live with that inheritance today. It is at its roots a racist concept.

The effect on Aboriginal peoples in Australia was not very

dissimilar to that of other colonised indigenous peoples in other parts of the world, which had resulted in marginalisation, disintegration and loss of culture, language and identity, impoverishment, etc.

Aboriginal people in Australia have perhaps suffered more than most. In part, this stems from the lack of any recognition by European settlers of Aboriginal customs and beliefs. For many years, concerns about the plight of the Aboriginal people were a "non-issue" to white Australia. To some, they were thought of as a dying race. To others they could safely be ignored. Others saw a need to exterminate Aboriginal culture and to mainstream the survivors at the lower levels of the dominant race.

It is mainly in the north and the centre of Australia, where European settlement has been more spasmodic and more recent, that traditional Aboriginal culture and society has been able to survive as a living system.

The lack of recognition of Aboriginal customs and beliefs was reflected in the law introduced by the European settlers. There was virtually a total failure to accept and apply Aboriginal rights arising from their pre-European settlement circumstances. This was later reflected in the *Australian Constitution* in 1901, which expressly excluded Aboriginal people. It was not until 1967 that this position was modified by national referendum to remove the exclusions as to Aborigines. In a sense, this has left the Constitution neutral on the matter. There is still no constitutional recognition of the Aboriginal people or their special place as the indigenous people of Australia.

In much the same way, the Australian courts have interpreted and applied the common law inherited from England in a way that has largely excluded any reference to Aboriginal customs and beliefs. To a very limited extent, this has been modified by legislation, but generally speaking Aboriginal customary law is not regarded as being part of the law of the land. The most significant breakthrough in this regard is the recent High Court decision in *Mabo*, a landmark in giving formal legal recognition to customary rights to land. Whether this will lead in time to some wider acceptance of customary rights remains to be seen. It seems likely that the decision will continue to be a catalyst for a wider debate, perhaps leading in time to national legislative or even constitutional change.

The developments in Australia have to some degree paralleled the debate in the international arena on the matter of indigenous rights. Article 27 of the *International Covenant on Civil and Political Rights* confirms certain rights of "minorities", although indigenous spokespersons reject this as an appropriate title for indigenous peoples. More explicitly, the recent adoption of *ILO Convention 169 on Indigenous Rights* has placed the matter firmly on the international human rights agenda. Work is proceeding under the auspices of the UN Economic and Social Council (to which the Bahá'í International Community has consultative status as an NGO), through the working group on Indigenous Rights, to settle the terms of a draft UN Declaration on Indigenous Rights. This may in time lead to a UN Convention on the subject. Much of the debate centres on calls for the legal recognition of indigenous peoples as distinct peoples in their own right, with certain pre-existing rights, including the right to self-determination.

From a Bahá'í point of view, the debate should be accepted as part of the struggle by indigenous people for recognition and acceptance as equals. The call of Bahá'u'lláh for the adoption of the concept of the "oneness of humanity" obviously extends to and includes all indigenous peoples. They are part of the one great human family. To the extent that the present social and legal system is based on racist values and attitudes which do not accept indigenous people as equals, then that system is not entitled to respect from a Bahá'í. On the other hand, a Bahá'í is required by the teachings of his or her faith to respond to any deficiencies in a way that does not create disunity or disharmony, and he or she must be obedient to the government and to the law. It is here that the dilemma exists for a Bahá'í.

A good starting point in dealing with this dilemma is the call of the Bahá'í Faith for the total elimination of race prejudice. This principle is quite clear in the teachings, although its practical implementation presents no simple task. The roots of prejudice are deep-seated and are regularly fed by a fresh diet by contemporary society. There is a need to identify those aspects of society which have a discriminatory effect, particularly as they impact upon the individual concerned. A decision has them to be made as to how to respond to those aspects of society but within the framework of the Bahá'í teachings. Sometimes a pro-active role may be required. Sometimes forbearance is required. The matter requires careful judgement, patience and much effort. The fact that a particular group in society may be viewed as being socially backward or reticent, politically immature or even with members whose hygienic standards are below those of the observer, cannot be allowed to colour the response. If the test is one of total non-discrimination, it cannot be made conditional upon the achievement of standards expected in the dominant society. It must be an unreserved acceptance of fellow human beings, of whatever race or background, for what they are, as equal members of the one human race.

The high standard required by the Bahá'í Faith does not end there. The principle of positive discrimination, as found, for example, in the "special measures" provision of the *Racial Discrimination Convention*, is expressly endorsed in the Bahá'í writings. This requires that indigenous peoples and minorities should receive a special measure of love, nurturing, encouragement and safeguarding. This includes giving them priority in matters of Bahá'í administration. The disadvantages that these people have endured in the past must be countered by making them feel that they are truly partners and equals.

The principle of positive discrimination, or affirmative action, is now a part of the law of Australia as a result of the *Racial Discrimination Act 1975*. Its implementation often gives rise to strong feelings of resentment. We have probably all heard the view expressed that Aboriginal people should not be given special advantages when so many other Australians are struggling. There are several responses to such views.

For example, it is possible to view any such positive measures as not being discriminatory at all, a view endorsed by the Supreme Court of the USA. They may be designed to correct a pre-existing imbalance or inequity. Of course, views will differ as to where that balance should be redrawn, and it may be necessary to take a broad view across the spectrum of Aboriginal affairs.

Special measures may also be seen as a form of redress to compensate for the loss of indigenous rights which are no longer capable of being reinstated.

A Bahá'í response is that in so far as special measures are incorporated into the law, they must be accepted and obeyed as such. It should not be a cause for complaint that individual Aborigines may seek to take excessive advantage of that law or even to abuse it. After all, abuse of the law is common to all sectors of society. But beyond the obligation to obey the secular law is the spiritual obligation to work towards a Bahá'í community based on racial unity, love and fellowship.

Where the general law does give effect to the rights of indigenous people, such as in the *Mabo* case, it is clear that Bahá'ís must be obedient to and respect that law, not only to the letter of the law but in its spirit as well.

This has wide repercussions, yet to be fully thought through by the Australian Bahá'í community. If it is accepted that Aboriginal people once inhabited the whole of the continent, then presumably at one time all land in Australia must have been the subject of customary ownership. Much of it may still be the subject of such ownership. The fact that it is a form of ownership that is not easily equated with individual proprietary interests with which European settlers were accustomed is irrelevant.

The decision in *Mabo* makes it clear that in some cases a customary title can coexist with existing land uses. In other cases, such as where there had been an inconsistent Crown grant, customary title may be extinguished. Among leading indigenous thinkers, there is considerable opposition to the concept of extinguishment, and the High Court has required a clear intention to extinguish title. The possible survival at law of a customary title, particularly in the north and centre of Australia, cannot be discounted.

Bahá'ís need to consider what obligations this may impose under Bahá'í law. For example, when we hold our next convention or conference, should we not first ascertain if the locality of the function is acceptable to any traditional owners. We would do the same for any other landowner. If we are contemplating the acquisition of a Bahá'í centre or other facility, we need to consider the same question. At the very least the Bahá'í principle of consultation should be employed to ensure that any Aboriginal inhabitants are identified (if possible), recognised and their rights respected. Courtesy may demand a similar approach even if the customary rights have been legally extinguished but where traditional relations with the land in question are still maintained.

Another example of a situation where the rights of indigenous people should be taken into account relates to matters of religion. At international law there is a broad but qualified right to religious freedom, but this has not yet been incorporated into Australian domestic law except for the limited provision in section 116 of the *Australian Constitution*. At common law, there is no guarantee of religious freedom in this country. Commonly, since European settlement, Aboriginal religion has been largely relegated to the status of myth or superstition, largely unprotected by the law.

From a Bahá'í point of view, Aboriginal traditional beliefs should be accepted as a valid and genuine form of religious belief. Contrary to the popular view, they are not just legends and fictional stories, but can represent a deeply held spiritual belief system. It may well be that they are based on a spiritual premise that incorporates the concept of a transcendental, all-powerful creator, even if that deity is too sacred to be mentioned in other than symbolic terms.

Religion is central to Aboriginal society and customs. It is the connecting factor between the traditional living Aborigine, his fellow Aborigines and with the land. It has been one of the main factors in Aboriginal survival.

The Bahá'í writings stress that all religions (apart from a few which are the result of human perversity) are derived from the same divine source and have the same spiritual principles as their base. All should be respected and treasured as part of humanity's heritage. Bahá'ís are commanded to consort with the followers of all religions in a spirit of fellowship and understanding. The fact that a particular religion may seem rather alien to western concepts, provides no excuse for making any exceptions to these teachings. There is therefore an obligation on Bahá'ís to treat Aboriginal religion, where it is genuinely believed in and practised, with the same respect one would extend to any of the great religions of the world. Any reference to Aboriginal religion as mere primitive mythology or storytelling is by this standard offensive and contrary to Bahá'í law. The trivialisation of Aboriginal religion for commercial or other reasons is particularly objectionable. The relative lack of any restrictions in domestic law on this form of conduct does not exonerate it from blame.

The obligations to show respect for Aboriginal religion extends to such matters as having proper regard for Aboriginal burial grounds, which are common throughout Australia, and sacred sites, which are also common, in order to avoid any act amounting to sacrilege or desecration. In some jurisdictions, such as the Northern Territory, this is already part of domestic law.

Perhaps more difficult from a Bahá'í perspective is the matter of indigenous claims to self-determination. This is a matter now accepted as a right of all distinct peoples in International law (see Article 1 of both the *International Covenant on Economic, Social and Cultural Rights* and the *International Covenant on Civil and Political Rights.* Australia is party to both covenants and has legislated with respect to the latter covenant). However within Australia, as in other countries, it is not a right enforceable in domestic law in the sense of giving a right to indigenous "peoples" to secede and become independent.

Increasingly however, there is acceptance of a more limited right of internal self-determination of indigenous people and minorities within the nation-state, although the content of that right and its implications have not been fully spelled out. It appears to be a right that goes beyond Article 27 of the *International Covenant on Civil and Political Rights*, whereby minorities can enjoy their own culture, profess and practice their own religion and use their own language, but how much further it goes is uncertain.

Many Aboriginal spokespersons in Australia are now advocating a grant of substantial Aboriginal self-determination within Australia. Suggestions have been made that such a grant could conveniently be made to areas such as the Torres Strait, perhaps far north Queensland, parts of the Northern Territory and the Kimberleys of Western Australia. Such a grant could, under one option, be outside the framework of the existing federal system, although still under the umbrella of the national government and parliament. Other proposals would see greater Aboriginal autonomy at a local or regional level by adjustment of the federal system. Commonly, the claims for increased control are combined with claims to traditional land. There is much talk of an Aboriginal treaty and a right of self-determination entrenched in constitutional law. No clear consensus has yet emerged as to methodology or content, although proposals have recently been made to the federal Government.

It is becoming increasingly recognised by the wider community that the many difficulties facing the Aboriginal people and communities cannot be effectively tackled without a greater measure of control (and responsibility) by those people and their communities. Paternalistic solution imposed from outside, no matter how well-intentioned, are not effective. The Aboriginal people should exercise greater control over their own affairs.

The issue has the capacity to become politically divisive. Extremes of views on either side, pro-Aboriginal and anti-Aboriginal, are now not uncommon. Many non-Aboriginal people resent the special measures already available to assist Aboriginal people and are not favourably disposed to further such measures or claims. This divisiveness is a problem for Bahá'ís, given the injunction in the Bahá'í writings against any political involvement. The very purpose of the Bahá'í Faith is to achieve the unity of the human race, and all divisiveness, including political divisiveness, is to be avoided. For Bahá'ís, it is particularly critical that racial unity be achieved and maintained in their own community. Bahá'í administrative structures should fairly reflect the diversity of humanity and not a particular racial orientation. These principles will necessarily limit the extent to which Bahá'ís can become involved in movements for greater separateness, autonomy and rights for Aboriginal people.

But it is submitted that this does not totally prevent support by Bahá'ís for more fair and equitable arrangements for indigenous people in the wider community and the upholding of their rights. They have generally not been treated as equals in the past. Inferior conditions still exist and their rights are often still denied. This is still a lack of respect for their customs and beliefs. How far Bahá'ís can go in supporting non-Bahá'í moves for the advancement of indigenous peoples will often be a matter of fine judgement. When in doubt, the Bahá'í institutions should be consulted. For the Bahá'í, the real solution is a spiritual one which involves the acceptance of indigenous peoples as fully equals in the one human family under one God. Within that one family, there is of course room for great diversity, but it must be diversity that compliments the unity of the whole rather than fragments it. It is ultimately a matter of imbalance. Shoghi Effendi has written:

> We should meet them as equals, well-wishers, people who admire and respect their ancient descent, and who feel that they will be interested, as we are, in a living religion.

Indigenous Peoples

(letter dated 21 September 1951 to the Comite de Ensenanza
Bahá'í para los Indigenas).

Genuine equality is in this view an absolute pre-requisite. This is consistent with the emphasis in the Bahá'í writings on the need for every adult to take full responsibility for his or her progress and development in all the aspects of life - social, material, moral and spiritual. The Bahá'í International Community, in a submission on indigenous rights, has asserted that those rights should emphasise four main principles:

1. Respect for indigenous communities and their cultures and the elimination of prejudice;

2. An appreciation of the value of cultural diversity in the wider community;

3. The full participation of indigenous people both in the wider national society and in decisions that directly affect them, to enable them to provide a higher level of social, economic and spiritual well-being and to preserve their unique cultures and identities;

4. Co-operation between indigenous peoples and their governments, based on mutual respect rather than separation or antagonism.

Thus the Bahá'í view stresses indigenous peoples acting in co-operation with the wider community and the government rather than in confrontation with it. This must be premised on an acceptance of the principle of diversity. Within such an attitudinal framework, indigenous rights and self-determination can be actively protected and developed.

The quest for Aboriginal advancement separate from the rest of the community cannot, in the Bahá'í view, be seen as a final goal in itself.

It should be seen as a step towards a wider unity, otherwise the results will be limited and will create barriers and tensions between the various races. The unity which is productive of unlimited results is the unity of humankind, which recognises that all are the servants of one God and are equal in the sight of God. This is the only unity that is capable of reconciling the many races and peoples of the world. It is quite compatible with the recognition and acceptance of these lesser unities, providing that these are seen as part of an equal partnership in the greater global enterprise.

A society which is established on the framework of the assumed superiority of one particular group over others will be an impediment to the achievement of this wider unity. It has to be admitted that since European settlement on this county, Australia has been established on such a basis. The late and somewhat grudging admission that indigenous peoples do have a legitimate place in this society with legal rights may be thought of as too little too late. But what is important now is to work towards a future society which fairly reflects the legitimate interests of all, no one being superior to others. It is a vision of a social and spiritual partnership. The vision of the Council for Aboriginal Reconciliation is compelling in this regard:

> A united Australia which respects this land of ours; values the Aboriginal and Torres Strait Islander heritage'; and provides justice and equity for all.

Transposed into the context of Bahá'u'lláh's vision of the New World Order, this becomes a global partnership, one in which the many indigenous peoples of various lands are admitted as full and equal partners for the first time in human history, with their cultures being accepted and valued as part of the heritage of all humankind. Only within such a New World Order can the rights of indigenous people be fully and fairly implemented. It will be a society in which distinctions of colour, race and background will cease to be of any special importance in themselves except as a treasury containing the diversity of humanity and the great beauty of its various members.

The Bahá'ís of Australia need to develop a greater understanding of Bahá'u'lláh's global vision and how it can operate within Australia. They need to be able to respond to any situations of confrontation and division between Aboriginal and non-Aboriginal people in a way that better reflects that vision and offers an alternative. This is the challenge to Bahá'í Australia. A challenge which is becoming increasingly pressing.

Selected Bibliography

1. *Aboriginal Law Bulletin* (Vol. 3 No. 61, April 1993)
2. Association for Bahá'í Studies, Australia, *Integration and Cultural Diversity* (1988, Bahá'í Publications Australia)
3. Bahá'í International Community, *A Pattern for Justice* (1973 - 1974, unpublished)
4. Bailey, Peter, *Human Rights: Australia in an International Context* (1990, Butterworths)
5. Brennan, Frank, *Sharing the Country* (1991, Penguin)
6. Brennan, Frank, *Reconciling our Differences* (1992, Aurora Books)
7. Buddon, Chris, *Reconciliation, Celebration and Aboriginal People* (1988, Assembly Social Responsibility and Justice Committee)
8. Cassidy, Frank, (Ed.) *Aboriginal Self-Determination* (1991, Oolichan Books)
9. Commonwealth of Australia, *Mabo: the High Court Decision on Native Title* (June 1993)
10. Coombes, H C, *Kulinma* (1978, ANU Press)
11. Council for Aboriginal Reconciliation, *Walking Together* (1993 various issues)
12. Council for Aboriginal Reconciliation, *Making Things Right* (1993)
13. Crawford, James (Ed.) *The Rights of Peoples* (1988 Clarendon)
14. Hazlehurst, Rayleen M. (Ed.) *Ivory Scales: Black Australia and the Law*

(1987, NSW University Press)

15. Hocking, Barbara, *International Law and Aboriginal Human Rights* (1988 Law Book Co.)

16. Human Rights and Equal Opportunity Commission, *Racist Violence* (1991 AGPS)

17. Jull, Peter, *Australian Nationhood and Outback Indigenous Peoples* (November 1991, NARU)

18. Law Reform Commission, *The Recognition of Aboriginal Customary Laws* Vols 1 & 2 (1986, AGPS)

19. Maddock, Kenneth, *Our Land is Our Land* (1983, Penguin)

20. McRae, H., Nettheim, G. and Beacroft L., *Aboriginal Legal Issues* (1991 Law Book Co.)

Chapter Six

ABORIGINAL FAMILIES

by

Elizabeth Hindson

Australian Aborigines are in a state of transition. Due to historical events they occupy a disadvantaged position in Australian society. They are however, endeavouring to rectify this by improving their social, economic, political and cultural status. They are striving to carve a position in this society which will elevate their status to one that is at least equal in all respects to other Australians. The achievement of this goal, however, might mean the creation of tensions brought about by competing values. In this paper the writer evaluates how might the teachings of the Bahá'í Faith serve to light a pathway for the resolution of such dilemmas.

Australian Aborigines are not homogenous; they can have very diverse characteristics, for example:

- They live in all parts of the country, mostly in urban areas.
- Their social and economic situations vary.
- Most are of mixed racial origins.
- There is great variation with respect to the level of Western education received.
- Some are group oriented, others individualistic.
- For some English is a second language while others know only a few words of an Aboriginal language.
- Attitudes, beliefs and values vary.

It is thus often difficult to make sweeping generalisations about Aborigines, however, statements will be qualified as necessary.

The objectives of this paper are twofold:

(i) To endeavour to acquaint non-Aboriginal people with the circumstances of Aboriginal families of today through the provision of social statistics with explanations and reference to some specific issues that are of concern and threat to Aboriginal family life. There are many negative articles on Aborigines in the press and though there is much truth in these, many achievements are being made. However, the better informed we are about one another, the better understanding there will be.

(ii) To illustrate that many Aboriginal people have become enthusiastic scholars of Aboriginal traditional culture and that there has been a resurgence in pride and a belief that traditional culture has worth in our contemporary world. The interest in urban dwellers arose firstly in the art forms (music, visual arts, languages). Some groups have shown interest in such things as gender roles and customary law. They have experimented in the reintroduction of these practices and values. The education of children in traditional ways has been trialed by some groups.

Pre-colonial Aboriginal Australia is described by anthropologists as being a very stable society. Aborigines were fairly isolated from other human populations but with respect to those with whom there was contact, it seems that such contact had little influence on the way of life. Stability and a high degree of order was maintained by social structures: tribal boundaries were apparently known and not infringed upon, intertribal relationships were clear and observed and the kinship system determined people's relationships towards one another, that is, who could marry whom; who was responsible for whom; who one was required to avoid.

Colonisation in 1788 however had a marked and irreversible effect on Aboriginal society. The breakdown and destitution of the tribe and family was set entrain.

Mankind of course has always had to deal with or adapt to social change. Social change, however occurs from a variety of causes some of which are sudden, violent and destructive. In other instances it can occur slowly and painlessly. It is sometimes even welcomed.

Recent historians[1] write of the violent and disruptive nature of the contact between early settlers and the indigenous people of this continent. The reality of contact was previously ignored or hidden hence the actual truth comes as a great surprise to many Australians.

While previous government policies relating to Aborigines may have been considered the wisest during their time, in retrospect they are now considered repressive. In Queensland, for example, it is only in the last 20 to 25 years (barely one generation) that restrictions governing many aspects of the lives of Aborigines were lifted. The dependency and powerlessness that past legislation and policies created for many Aboriginal families will simply take time to overcome. It is for these reasons, however, that we see many of the present social and economic conditions.

As mentioned previously, Aboriginal groups are very diverse. Despite these differences within the Aboriginal community they continue to see themselves as Aborigines. They feel a oneness and there are efforts being made by Aboriginal to strengthen that oneness. The colour of the skin, where one lives and the language spoken is often irrelevant though this may not be so in the more traditional groups.

It is often said by various people... "But they are not real Aborigines"... (speaking about urban dwellers, especially with a light coloured skin). Many Aboriginal people take offence at such remarks.

Many people have this stereotyped view of Aborigines, probably as being dark skinned and of behaving in "quaint" ways. One does not have to be living a traditional lifestyle to be an Aborigine. Aborigines have adapted and taken on new lifestyles and values but this does not make such people any less "Aboriginal". Most of these people are closely identified in the Aboriginal community and they associate in the Aboriginal community.

There is an official definition of "Aborigine" - one who is of Aboriginal descent, who identifies as an Aborigine and who is accepted in the community in which he or she lives as an Aborigine.

The importance of the study of Aboriginal families stems from two reasons:

(i) The family is the smallest unity of society. It is the bedrock of society. It is the group which gives support and love to its members; it is the first socialising agent of the child; it is the first nurturer and carer of its members.[2] Families are thus the building blocks of society. Societies are only as strong as the units which make it up.

(ii) From professional experience where present research reveals that families are undergoing all kinds of distress and pressures stemming from insecure financial supports, homelessness, broken homes, child neglect, domestic violence and substance abuse. Many of the problems were chronic and it was evident that any help welfare systems could give was simply a band aid response. It became obvious that Aboriginal people need to look elsewhere for the solution to social problems and answers for the meaning of life, for something that would offer hope.

Many people express great frustration when the discussion of Aborigines arises. There is also anger and resentment expressed about the amount of funds expended on Aborigines. Aborigines working with their own people are also known to express such attitudes. There is certainly agreement that continuing appraisals as to how we are approaching the issues need to be conducted. However, as mentioned above, it is only in the last 20 to 25 years that any real effort has been made to rectify two centuries of neglect.

Aboriginal family disintegration was brought about by destruction of their society, that is:

- The removal of groups from their lands (at least groups who did not 'disappear' by other means).
- The institutionalisation of groups/families.
- The control of their movement.
- Control over employment (resulting in separation of families).
- Introduction of a food ration system.
- Placement of some mothers and children into dormitories and removal of the responsibility of mothers for their children.
- Arranged marriages by Government authorities or prohibition of certain marriages by Government authorities.
- Control over individuals' finances.
- Provision of inferior health and education services.
- Prohibition of the use of Aboriginal languages and customs.

These measures stripped people of all independence resulting in complete dependency on Government officialdom. It also resulted in low self-esteem and negative attitudes towards their culture. While policy was meant to be "protective" and in instances it no doubt was, it also had detrimental effects and was in fact destructive.

In addition, Aboriginal people suffered due to poor health, inadequate education facilities and substandard housing. However, racial discrimination and prejudice expressed towards the people was probably the most soul destroying of experiences. Most members can report such experiences.

Aborigines are now expected to assume all responsibility for themselves despite the fact that they have been recognised as equals for a relatively short time. Unfortunately it is not simple for many, especially those who were most effected by past policies. Aborigines do however, want the benefits of a modern society, to be treated at equals, and to feel proud of their heritage.

Some of the following statistics however, will illustrate the effort needed to bridge the gap.

Health

While the birth rate in the Aboriginal population is higher, they die younger.[3]

Aboriginal and Torres Strait Islanders,[4] Qld:

	Whole of Queensland	Aboriginal and T.S.I.
Percentage under 20 yrs	32.5%	53%
Percentage over 65 yrs	10.8%	2.8%

The decline starts at about the age of 30 to 34 for males and females though it is higher for males. The main causes of death are circulatory diseases, injury/poisoning (including death due to violence) and respiratory diseases. The declining population from age 30 years would no doubt influence the quality of life in young families with the diminishing numbers of members of what would normally be the main income earners and carers. Families are more burdened with a high rate of illness in the group that would usually be the more robust. Where poor health is chronic, the income coming into the home would no doubt be affected. There is also the additional strain in caring for incapacitated family members.

Household Size And Family Characteristics

On average, Aboriginal households are larger than those of other Queenslanders: 4.1 members versus 3.2 members. Very few Aborigines live alone: 7.4% versus 17.8%. Aboriginal households are thus more crowded. While few live alone, this is not necessarily out of choice. Aborigines have difficulty in obtaining housing because of racial prejudice. It is also more economical to "share". Overcrowding however, does cause tensions and the additional guests are not necessarily welcome. Relatives find it difficult to refuse one another on the other hand.

Child-rearing begins earlier for Aboriginal women: of women 20 to 24 years of age, 65% had 1 or more children as opposed to 28.5% of other non-Aboriginal women. Aboriginal women also have more children: 3 women in 10 have 5 or more as opposed to 1 in 10 of other women. Also, ¾ of Aboriginal families had dependant children as opposed to ½ of other families. While birth rates of Aborigines are higher, they are however, falling.

Far fewer Aborigines have a formal marriage, though cohabitation has become quite common in the non-Aboriginal community. Cohabitation amongst Aborigines can occur at an early age especially in Aboriginal towns. Some of the reasons could be related to the fact that Aboriginal youth are thought to mature earlier, that is they are expected to become more independent at an earlier age. Secondly, as few do well in the education system they have less opportunity to obtain employment especially skilled employment. In fact, employment of any kind in Aboriginal towns is limited. The youth are thus not career oriented. Parenthood at an early age becomes the career for many young people. Also, as poor health is common in families, the caring role for families is often assumed by alternative members.

Despite the profile that has just been described, conditions have improved from the perspective of education, financial resources and health. Infant mortality in particular, though still three times the rate as that for other Australians has been reduced significantly.

Studies have also shown that Aboriginal parents' aspirations for their children's education are high though they do not expect their children to actually achieve these aspirations. Similar attitudes are held about employment. It could be said that Aboriginal life aspirations are not so very different to that of other Australians.

Among the major issues facing Aboriginal people are:

- Substance abuse, primarily alcohol.
- Domestic violence, especially in Aboriginal towns.
- Child abuse and neglect.
- Unemployment.
- Poor health
- Racial discrimination and prejudice.
- Instability in marital relationships.

Most of the above are related to alcohol abuse.

Underpinning such problems as substance abuse, domestic violence, child abuse and marital instability is the breakdown of Aboriginal social control systems. In considering this it is useful to reflect on some of the features of traditional life especially as some Aboriginal groups are looking to this as a model for today. Some of the traditional rules were referred to earlier in this paper.

While there is a growing interest in the revival of traditional dance, music and languages, it is suggested that a review of co-operation within the group would also be worthwhile. These attitudes and practices were important in the past for survival and it would seem that they are still viable. Aborigines themselves speak of the lack of responsibility of family members towards one another, support of members tends to be "one way".[5]

In traditional Aboriginal life consultation was also practised by the members who had responsibility for the group. Usually the decision makers were the elders or those considered to have "wisdom". The Aboriginal traditional group or family are thus "group" oriented. While the individual has certain rights the group is also considered important.

Certainly some traditional practices may be distasteful and unacceptable to contemporary Aboriginal groups and families. In addition they may no longer serve any useful purpose. Being "traditional" does not automatically imply superiority. At the same time there are certain practices, attitudes and values that have meaning and worth at any time.[6]

Indigenous Australians have cause to be proud of their heritage. The adoption of some of the traditional values and practices would do much to help reshape their contemporary situations and bring stability again to their lives.

APPENDIX

TABLE 1. FAMILY COMPOSITION BY MAJOR SECTION OF STATE, QLD

Families in Aboriginal and T.S.I.[1] Dwellings								
Family Composition	Urban		Non-urban		Total		Total Families	
	No.	Percentage	No.	Percentage	No.	Percentage	No.	Percentage
Single parent family with dependant children	1,524	16	722	15.6	2,246	15.9	42,214	6.1
Single parent family with dependant children and adult family members	873	9.1	481	10.4	1,354	9.6	13,526	2
TOTAL SINGLE PARENT FAMILIES	2,397	25.1	1,203	26.1	3,600	25.4	55,740	8.1
Couple Only	1,157	12.1	502	10.9	1,659	11.7	218,986	31.8
Couple with dependant children	3,393	35.5	1,452	31.4	4,845	34.2	242,953	35.3
Couple with adult family members	456	4.8	244	5.3	700	4.9	68,361	9.9
Couple with dependant children and adult family members	1,524	16	902	19.5	2,426	17.1	61,367	8.9
TOTAL COUPLE FAMILIES	6,530	68.4	3,100	67.10	9,630	68	591,667	85.9
Related adult families	623	6.5	315	6.8	938	6.6	41,673	6
TOTAL FAMILIES	9,550	100	4,617	100	14,167	100	689,076	100

Source: Tables CA0045, CX0072 (Census 1986)

[1] T.S.I. - Torres Strait Islanders

The proportion of Aboriginal and TSI families with an annual income of $15,000 or less was 34.6%, compared with 26.6% for the total population. Only 11.5% of Aboriginal and TSI families earned over $32,000 annually, whereas 24.6% of all families had incomes in this range.

In some relatively large Aboriginal and TSI families, there would have been a larger number of family members in the employed labour force, but this factor was not strong enough to offset higher levels of unemployment amongst Aboriginal and TSI people and the higher proportion of Aboriginal and TSI people in lower paid occupations. The median income of Aboriginal and TSI families ($16,789) was lower than that of all families ($21,932).

TABLE 2 ANNUAL FAMILY INCOME, QUEENSLAND

Income	Aboriginal and T.S.I. Population		Total Population	
	Number	Percent	Number	Percent
$0-$9,000	1,934	13.7	46,868	6.8
$9,001-$15,000	2,960	20.9	136,219	19.8
$15,001-$22,000	2,611	18.4	117,356	17
$22,001-$32,000	1,992	14.1	128,534	18.7
$32,001-$40,000	847	6	73,801	10.7
$40,001 & over	778	5.5	95,797	13.9
Not Stated	2,674	18.9	71,388	10.4
Spouse Temporarily Absent	370	2.6	19,114	2.8
TOTAL	**14,167**	**100**	**689,076**	**100**
Source: Tables CA0066, CSD035 (Census 1986)				

Single parent families in the Aboriginal and TSI community represented one-quarter (25.4%) of all Aboriginal and TSI families.

Additionally, single parent families with a dependent child or children constituted 69.2% of Aboriginal and TSI families with annual income of $9,000 or less.

TABLE 3 ABORIGINAL AND TSI FAMILIES: ANNUAL FAMILY INCOME BY FAMILY COMPOSITION, QUEENSLAND

Income	Family Composition							Total
	Single Parent Families		Couple Families					
	Parent and dependant child(ren) only	Parent, dependant child(ren) and adult(s)	Couple Only	Couple and dependant child(ren) only	Couple and adult family members	Couple, dependant child(ren) and adult(s)	Related Adults	
$0-9,000	1,244	95	156	250	20	55	113	1,934
$9,001-15,000	531	287	451	1,230	78	154	224	2,959
$15,001-22,000	149	287	298	1,182	116	372	204	2,610
$22,001-32,000	20	200	283	723	136	481	149	1,992
$32,001-40,000	5	58	164	256	61	261	42	847
$40,001 & over	1	62	70	175	110	321	38	779
Not Stated	296	365	193	830	151	676	165	2,673
Spouse Temp. Absent	-	-	44	193	28	103	-	370
TOTAL	2,246	1,354	1,659	4,845	700	2,426	938	14,167

Source: CA0045 (Census 1986)

In the Aboriginal and TSI community, most couple families received higher incomes than single parent families. Almost one-third (31.6%)

of couple families received incomes of $22,000 or more annually, compared with 9.6% of single parent families. However, there were more family members present in couple families which contained an average of 4.4 persons compared with an average of 3.8 persons in single parent families.

Endnotes

1. Refer to commentaries of Henry Reynolds and Ray Evans.
2. Bahá'u'lláh, founder of the Bahá'í Faith, says that if the family unit is weak, so will be the community.
3. Census 1986. see Appendix.
4. The 1986 census did not separate Aborigines from Torres Strait Islanders. However as Torres Strait Islanders are few, but with very similar conditions, for the purposes of this study, their inclusion in these statistics is justified.
5. The Bahá'í writings state: "If love and agreement are manifest in a single family, that family will advance, become illumined and spiritual; but if enmity and hatred exist within it destruction and dispersion are inevitable." An important feature of a healthy family in Bahá'í terms is that of the use of consultation, recognising the equality of the husband and wife.
6. Of indigenous people Bahá'u'lláh wrote: "To gather jewels have I come to this world. If one speck of a jewel be hid in a stone and that stone be beyond the seven seas, until I have found and secured that jewel my hand shall not stay from its search."

Chapter Seven
RECOLLECTIONS OF EARLY BAHÁ'Í INVOLVEMENT WITH INDIGENOUS PEOPLE

by

Viva Rodwell

This paper gives the author's personal recollections of the early stages of the relationship between the Bahá'í Faith in Australia and Australia's indigenous people. It begins with recollections of Elizabeth Hindson, Viva's foster daughter, who was one of the first persons of Aboriginal descent to enter the Faith. The paper continues to examine the involvement of Bahá'ís in the establishment of a society for Aboriginal development in the 1950s in Brisbane and recounts the work of a number of Bahá'ís in bringing the Faith to Aboriginal people. Also recounted is the story of Willie Mackenzie, an Aboriginal man who contributed greatly to the recording of his tribes' history, language and grammar. The early development of the faith among Aboriginal people in the Brisbane area is particularly examined.

It was being asked to recall early Bahá'í involvement with indigenous people that led to these recollections of over forty years ago.

There were two triggering factors that propelled me to involvement with our indigenous people. Strangely enough, it was not the fact that our dear Elizabeth Hindson, then a young Betty Anderson, was our foster daughter. We knew Elizabeth was part Aboriginal but somehow, it was almost subconscious knowledge, for to us, she was just our Betty.

Our Betty accepted the Faith in 1952 and on advice from a more experienced Bahá'í, probably Jim Heggie, I advised the Guardian that Betty was part Aboriginal. The following is the Guardian's reply, written by his wife, Hand of the Cause, Ruhiyyih Rabbani.

Haifa Israel

April 30th, 1952

Viva Rodwell

Dear Bahá'í Sister,

Your letter of April 8th has been received, and the beloved Guardian has instructed me to answer you on his behalf.

He was delighted to hear that Betty Anderson is not only such a devoted and active Bahá'í youth but that she has Aboriginal blood. He hopes she will be instrumental, with your help, and that of the other believers, in carrying the Message to her relatives. It is only right that the people who were the original inhabitants of Australia should receive the Teachings of Bahá'u'lláh, and we cannot doubt that when they embrace them, it will have a great effect, not only on their characters, but on their position in relation to the life of their country.

He was very happy to hear you are all so active in serving the Faith there, and assure you one and all of his loving prayers.

With Bahá'í Greetings

R. Rabbani

There is also a note in the Guardian's own hand:

May the Almighty bless, guide and sustain you and enable you to further the best interests of His Faith.

Your True Brother, Shoghi.

In 1953 the young Bahá'í, Elizabeth pioneered to Ballarat for six months, returning to our home, her home, until 1960 when she again pioneered to Newcastle where she stayed until she attended the 1963 Congress in London.

On returning from England, Elizabeth decided to work among Aboriginal people and decided on doing Social Studies at Queensland

University in 1964. There she was involved in A.B.S.C.O.L., which promoted scholarships for people of Aboriginal descent. When she obtained her degree, she commenced work in the State's Aboriginal and Island Affairs Department, and has never ceased to be involved in Aboriginal welfare.

I have a letter written by Mother Dunn in 1955 where she says, "I am so glad they have asked dear Betty to write about her people." She goes on, "Give her my dear love. She is a lovely girl. I have put her photograph in a nice gold frame and have it in my bedroom where I can see her all the time. She is so good to look at."

Mr. Faizi in 1954, in a letter asked about Betty's pioneering effort. He said, "I hope and pray she will soon attain her heart's desire in pioneering", and in an earlier letter refers to her as "our little golden key". With all her Aboriginal involvement over the years, I hope someone will document the life of "our little golden key".

We entertained many Asian students in those early days as the Colombo Plan meant, that we in Brisbane, received increasing numbers of mature students from India, Pakistan, Malaysia, Indonesia, Singapore, Fiji and other countries. They were very lonely, missing their spouses and families and, the early ones especially, found our college food very unattractive. Being Bahá'ís, we tried to show our overseas' visitors love and hospitality.

One day, one asked, "Why don't you ever have Aboriginals at you functions?" That made me think. Why didn't we? That was the first factor of influence.

The second evolved from the first. I was attending current affairs lectures and we were encouraged to suggest suitable topics. I asked the lecturer that we study "Aboriginals in today's world". Believing in having each topic presented in part by a member of that race or country, the lecturer asked if anyone knew of an Aboriginal who could give a talk. for some time, excellent letters to the Editor had been published in the Brisbane Courier Mail under the name of Cyril Richards, Salisbury. In those days Salisbury and Ipswich had quite a number of Aboriginals living there. I traced this gentleman and found him to be very shy but he was really happy to speak at this forum of interested people.

Just before the lecture night, maybe a day, the University lecturer, Tom Truman, phoned my to say that the Education Department had contacted him and Cyril Richards was not allowed to speak. I immediately thought of "discrimination" and so dressed and went to town to investigate. I had been a teacher in the State Service and felt it may be a problem in my own profession. At the time I was very pregnant with my fourth child.

On asking to speak to the Director of Education I was told he was busy and couldn't see me. I said I would wait on the seat outside the office. After some time, a person approached me asking if I were the person interested in the Aboriginal speaker. Somebody, certainly not me, had contacted the press. Anyway, eventually, I did see the Director and he presented an incontrovertible argument. Only approved speakers could speak under the auspices of the State Department. I couldn't say that we had already had speakers of other nationalities, for I did not want to involve the university lecturer, so that was the end of that specific talk.

However, Tom Truman suggested we arrange another meeting at a different venue and invite people to hear Cyril Richards speak. He asked me to convene the meeting as he felt, as a university lecturer, he should not do so. I can't remember the exact meeting but it was a success with tremendous assistance from the Brisbane Bahá'ís. That was the beginning of an organisation for Aboriginal development. I can't remember the name but it became a registered charity. That must have been about 1954. Tom was the first president and an Church of Christ minister the second. I was secretary throughout. The early Bahá'ís such as Mr. and Mrs. Squelch, Ann Stark's grandparents, Margery Moore, Ann's mother, Jean Milway, Margaret Forrest and Muriel Shelland were staunch supporters.

We were really active. Our Elizabeth (Hindson now) trained to be a girl guide leader for Aboriginal girls and Margaret Forrest (later Headland) did the training as a Brown Owl for a Brownie pack. These two ladies did a great job but activities ceased in that area when the Housing Commission resumed the land being used. I remember we ran a Sports Day for Aboriginals and we also visited people in Salisbury and Ipswich.

I spoke on Aboriginal needs at Rotary and a couple of Rotarians offered assistance. I remember one man offered an apprentice to an Aboriginal boy in engineering. To publicise this offer, I spoke on ABC to Queensland audiences and asked Aboriginals to apply and to write to me as secretary to express their educational and work needs. I waited for floods of letters but none came. I guess it was too early. Broadcasting stations 4BC and 4BH were also helpful in giving me time on radio.

The society continued, but eventually the bulk of support was from Bahá'ís. Frank Wyss came back from the Holy Land and we asked Frank what the Guardian had to say about Aboriginal teaching. Frank was reluctant to make a statement but we gathered that the Guardian had intimated that Bahá'ís should work under their own auspices. So the society was disbanded.

During those early years we met with wonderful people who were devoted to furthering the advancement of Aboriginal people, people such as the poet Judith Wright and Kath Walker who still today teaches her people the culture of the first inhabitants of this country. .

One such devoted lady was Mrs. Joyce Wilding. She opened her home at West End, Brisbane to Aboriginal people. Joyce lived by prayer. I have been in her home when she literally had no food but a large number of Aboriginal people to feed. She had complete faith that God would provide, and of course, God always did. Sometimes, it would be food and sometimes money.

She was a mother to all Aboriginals who needed any kind of assistance. She would even go into a park at night to rescue a woman or child who needed help. She was a truly great woman, an Australian "Mother Teresa". Joyce was a woman whom I was proud to call friend and she was always so accepting of the Bahá'í Faith. She was given an award by the Government in the Birthday Honours list and it was one award which she mightily deserved. Joyce regarded herself as a Bahá'í and I think she formally accepted the Faith before her death.

It was about this time I think, that there was a plea for a pamphlet for outback Aboriginals and I wrote one called the *"Family of Man"*. I never used it but Madge Williams told me that she and Maurice had found it and gave it much use in South Australia.

Another person who enriched my life was a full blood Aborigine 'Uncle' William Mackenzie. Uncle Willie could not read or write but I believe he could speak fourteen dialects and was sought after by anthropologists. Uncle Willie was a true gentleman. He lived at the Salvation Army Hostel and was respected by everyone. He always called Joyce Wilding and me "daughter" and I felt it was an honour. Always unexpectedly, he would knock on the front door, having come to see me by tram plus a short walk. We always had refreshments and sometimes, he would ask me to read some paper he had brought. At times, it was just a social call and once in a while, when I asked him diplomatically if he needed any money, he would say, "Yes daughter, could I have 5 pounds", this was only rare. A week or so later, another knock on the door and Uncle Willie would be there. After tea, he would diplomatically return the 5 pounds.

Uncle Willie was respected by the Government too, and was asked by dignitaries to illustrate the throwing of the boomerang. At his very large funeral parliamentarians were present. Towards the end of his life, Uncle Willie gave me a book by Tom Petrie on whose property I think he worked. He gave it to me to keep safely and ensure its survival. I gave it to the Queensland University years ago. The other thing he gave to my safekeeping was a tattered grammar and vocabulary belonging to the Wangerriburra Tribe. That, I thought, I had lost. We were flooded in Brisbane in 1974 and, through peoples honesty and goodness, we lost very little, but things got mixed up. However recently, in sorting out our personal papers, as you do when you get old, I found an envelope with the grammar and vocabulary of the Wangerriburra Tribe, commonly known as the Albert Tribe. I do not know who compiled it or when it was published, though it bears the authority of Anthony James Cumming, Government Printer, Brisbane.

The historical foreword is fascinating and the information came from John Allen, whose Aboriginal name was Bullumm. It says:

> Bullumm is a highly intelligent half blood, and is almost the last of a once numerous tribe. He is perhaps the best educated and most intelligent of his class in Australia. He speaks excellent English and reads fluently, writes well and is conversant with all the common topics of the day. He is a thorough bushman and a pioneer of Western Queensland. As showing his reliability and capacity, it may be mentioned that he was at one time in receipt of 1000 pounds a year

for mail-carrying contracts with the Queensland Government.

It goes on to say that Bullumm left his tribe at about twelve years of age and speaks of the integrity of this man of sixty who laboriously recalls the grammar and vocabulary of his tribe.

One section of his recalled history I found fascinating because I lived at Yeronga, next to Yerongpilly. The passage read:

> The tribe had long outgrown cannibalism. They loathed the practice, and, in union with their immediate neighbours on east, west and south who also abstained from human flesh, they kept up a simmering warfare with the cannibalistic tribes of the Brisbane River, and the country to the north thereof. The simmer, at times became a boil-over and Bullumm has vivid recollections of graphic descriptions by the tribal storytellers to the assembled tribes of the great battle at Yerongpilly, where the allied forces of the 'progressive' tribes from the Tweed to Logan routed with great slaughter, the Brisbane River blacks.

It goes on to say:

> Bullumm has read carefully and with great interest the writings of the late Mr. Tom Petrie on the customs and habits of the blacks, and considers the descriptions true and realistic. They may be taken to apply equally to Albert blacks, excepting the parts relating to the cannibal and burial customs.

This last of my trusts from Uncle Willie Mackenzie I will now give to the Queensland University Aboriginal Department.

On a trip to summer school we were staying with Aub and Greta Lake who took us to La Perouse to meet with Aboriginal people, especially a young man, Harry Penrith. Harry later accepted the Faith and we have met with him on and off over the passing years, though now he is known as Burnum Burnum.

It was about that time in the fifties we acquired a tape recorder, a seven-inch-reel Phillips and it was fairly large and heavy. I decided to record interviews with outstanding Aboriginals. Uncle Willie was recorded of course. The Aboriginal pastor, Reverend Doug Nicholls was recorded when I met him with his wife. Later, he was appointed Governor of South Australia.

I remember how excited I was to learn, I think from Mariette Bolton, that Georgia Lee was a Bahá'í. At that time Georgia, who was I think a Torres Strait Islander, was performing at Chequers, a large and prestigious night-club in Sydney. I met with and recorded an interview with that charming lady. It was exciting to a fairly new Bahá'í to hear that she accepted the Faith in Iceland I think, and had been performing with Louis Armstrong.

My contact with the quite famous Aboriginal singer, Harold Blair was most interesting. I saw him first at the Melbourne music emporium where he worked part-time, and went to Ringwood to his home where I met his wife and baby daughter.

Later I wanted to do a further interview and he invited me to a house near where I was staying. It was at Toorak, the Melbourne centre for Moral Rearmament. I was met at the door of this impressive house by a tall, charming man who introduced himself and commented on the sadness of the passing of the Guardian. It must have been in 1957. It transpired that he had been at Balliol College, Oxford University, with Shoghi Effendi and he showed me the press cutting he had cut out of the newspaper.

It struck me how interesting it was that at the time of Shoghi Effendi's period at Balliol College, there also, was Dr. Frank Buckman who initiated that world-wide organisation for peace and progress, Moral Rearmament. Moral Rearmament apparently sponsored certain people of worth and moral consciousness. Later, at a function of theirs, I met Princess Helena, who was said to be Queen Marie of Romania's granddaughter. Queen Marie was a Bahá'í.

To return to Harold Blair, who tragically died so young; I recorded this second interview at Toorak. Moral Rearmament was a world wide organisation seeking freedom from prejudice and had wonderful principles but it has been a long time since I have heard of that body.

There were other Aboriginals recorded too, but, sad to relate, I don't know the whereabouts of those special reels. We gave some Bahá'í at some time, old reels just for the tape but I cannot imagine giving away such tapes of interest. But, unfortunately, I have not found them.

Among other Aboriginals whom I knew quite will was Margaret Valadian who was a constant visitor to our Yeronga home, and who went on holidays with us. Margaret knew quite a lot of the Faith but she never became a Bahá'í. However, she did become highly educated with a B.A. and an M.A. from Queensland and Hawaii Universities.

We bought a home, "Rhossilli" in Ipswich to introduce the Faith in that locality and to firesides at that home came some interesting people such as the present Governor General, Bill Hayden and Senator Neville Bonner, the Aboriginal senator. Neville Bonner came to Rhossilli long before he entered politics.

Wonderful friendships were made with Aboriginals by those early Ipswich Bahá'ís such as Rob Munckton, Bob Patterson (who pioneered to Samoa), Jean, Val and Nancy Milway, Madge Bourke and Wendy Hall's family. Wendy is now Wendy England.

I taught at Ipswich High School during this period and have fond memories of an Aboriginal family, the Kings. I taught Wayne and knew Chris and Felicity as well as their mother. They were a talented family and I would be interested to hear of their development over the years.

Lots of seeds were sewn in Brisbane and Ipswich. I was recently rereading a letter from the dear late Hand of the Cause, Mr. Faizi whom I took with Mr. Furutan to Ipswich. It gave me great joy, so I will share an extract with you.

I remember in one of my trips to the northern provinces of Iran, the friends had a series of celebrations for the coming to the Cause of two very outstanding youths, who were both very learned and extremely enthusiastic. They both belonged to the families of priests and judges and, as such, their Faith made a great upheaval in the district. In one of the gatherings there came a very old teacher of the Cause who had just been released from prison. When he saw the two new believers and came to know the names of their fathers too, he joyfully brought out a sack out of his bag; then drew out a diary of more than fifty years teaching. He thumbed the pages and asked the Chairman if he could read some pages from that book. We were all brimful of joy and happiness, and, more than all, was the Chairman who knew what precious gems of stories that book contained. He read the following: 'One night, the friends told me that there were two learned men who desire information about the Cause. Both of them were very outstanding in their religious erudition and worldly position. With great alarm, precaution and wisdom, a meeting was arranged to which both came. After hours of discussion they left. The only thing which made all the friends happy was that the meeting had not ended in a riot or confusion against the Cause, as the meetings with the priests most often did in those days.'

Then the old teacher closed his book and said, "This is the story of forty years ago. Some seeds were sown in those days and now we reap the crops. Do you know that those two men were the fathers of these two believers who have just embraced the Cause?"

Mr. Faizi goes on:

Well, dear friends, this little story and hundreds like that show how much we should be patient for the results. The seeds you so lovingly sew these days, perhaps will reach the stage of fruition in the next generation. We must do our best and leave the rest to the Almighty, who will, in due time, crown our efforts with success.

I will end with those inspiring and encouraging words of Mr. Faizi. If I have omitted mentioning certain people, I can but plead advanced years, and apologise.

PART 2:
IN THE WAKE OF THE MABO DECISION.

Chapter Eight
HUMAN RIGHTS OF INDIGENOUS PEOPLES[1]

by

Dr. Kamal Puri

Indigenous people are entitled to community respect for their human rights. In this paper, the author refers to several international declarations that set universal human rights standards. Although legally not enforceable unless incorporated into domestic law, these declarations do have a strong moral force. Australia's accession to the relevant international conventions on human rights and the recent judicial pronouncements in Mabo and Dietrich indicate the importance the Australian government has begun to attach to human rights of its indigenous peoples.

What Are Human Rights?

The topic of human rights involves relationships among individuals, and between individuals and the State. Human rights can be best protected through adequate legislation, an independent judiciary and the establishment of autonomous institutions. In addition, effective educational campaigns, taking due account of the cultural and traditional aspects, can be carried out at national and local levels to raise public awareness regarding protection and promotion of human rights. Ratification by Australia of human rights instruments is simply not enough if the laws do not also provide for all of the legal powers and institutions necessary to ensure their effective realisation.

In 1986, the Australian Law Reform Commission concluded that in a number of respects present Australian law or its administration fail to respect fully the rights of Aboriginal people. Thus the non-recognition of Aboriginal marriages, and the excessive intervention by child welfare agencies in Aboriginal families that has been a feature of welfare practice in Australia, constitutes a failure to respect Aboriginal family life. Furthermore, aspects of police interrogation and court procedure have sometimes led in effect to Aboriginal defendants being compelled to confess guilt. The need to respect the human rights and cultural identity of Aboriginal people supports the case for appropriate forms of recognition of Aboriginal customary laws.[2]

World's Oldest Living Culture

Out of the estimated 15,000 cultures remaining on earth, Australian Aborigines represent the world's oldest living culture. Scientific data has established that Aborigines have occupied Australia for more than 40,000 years. In 1981, the Commonwealth Department of Aboriginal Affairs estimated that out of Australia's population of 16 million, there were about 168,000 Aborigines, representing 1.1 percent of the total population living in Australia. Contrast this figure, with the estimated population of Aborigines in Australia at the time of European settlement in 1788 of between a half and one million. While the population of the world has increased at an exponential rate because of medical and scientific advances, the Aboriginal population has suffered a reverse. It is horrendous to realise that in the first hundred years of British settlement in Australia, only 60,000 of an estimated 500,000 to one million Aborigines, survived the devastation caused by racial conflicts, introduced disease and alcohol.

Who Is An Aborigine?

The term "Aborigine"[3] is normally taken to mean a person of Aboriginal descent identifying as an Aborigine and recognized as such.

Physical similarities, a common history, a common religion or spiritual beliefs, and a common culture are factors that create a sense of identity amongst members of a race. As the people of a group identify themselves and are identified by others as a race by reference to their common history, religion, spiritual beliefs or culture, as well as by reference to their biological origins and physical similarities, an indication is given of their Aboriginality.[4] The criteria which is commonly being used is the one adopted by the Department of Aboriginal Affairs, viz descent, self-identification, and community acceptance.[5]

Although Aborigines have a long history, it was not until 1770 that the first European observations of Aboriginal civilisation and its rich cultural store were made. In that year, the legendary sailor, Captain Cook, laid claim on behalf of the British sovereign to the land that was later to be called Australia. Cook recorded in his diary his impressions of the native people in the following words:

> Being wholly unacquainted not only with the superfluous but the necessary conveniences so much sought after in Europe, they are happy in not knowing the use of them. They live in a tranquillity not disturbed by the inequality of condition: the Earth and Sea of their own accord furnishes them with all things necessary for life, they covet not magnificent houses, household stuff and similar; they live in a warm and fine climate and enjoy a very wholesome air.[6]

A telling illustration of the change of attitudes in the first hundred years of European settlement is provided by the contrast between what Cook observed in 1770 and what Captain Wharton F.R.S. wrote as editor of a transcription of the Log Book in 1893, describing Aborigines as "wild beasts to be extirpated."[7]

From the commencement of British settlement in 1788 until very recently, little respect has been shown by the laws of the Commonwealth, six States and two Territories of Australia for the rich

117

Aboriginal culture and their proprietary rights in land as well as intellectual property, and their human rights.[8] In spite of their very long occupation of Australia and their rich cultural heritage, Aborigines have long been treated as unequals and aliens[9] in their own country.[10] The economic and political realities have remained masked for a long time by a view of Aborigines as primitive, if not subhuman, a view which revealed underlying disregard for the Aboriginal race and their basic human rights. However, legal developments in the past 20 to 25 years display changing attitudes, accompanied by the growth of political awareness, cultural pride, and political organisation on the part of Aboriginal people. It is only in recent years that attempts have been made to acknowledge and rectify past injustices. Aborigines did not become entitled to vote at federal elections until 1962.[11]

The Settled/Conquered Colony[12]

The British colonists treated Australia as terra nullius - a land without owners, without a system of government and with no recognizable commerce. With the colonisation of Australia after 1788, a new legal regime was imposed, based on the common law. Australia was treated, for the purposes of its acquisition and the application of English law, as a settled colony, that is, one uninhabited by a recognised sovereign or by a people with recognisable institutions and laws. No treaties were concluded with Aboriginal groups, and no arrangements were made with them to acquire their land, or to regulate dealings between them and the colonists. They were treated as individuals, not as groups or communities.

Aboriginal people were therefore fully subjected to English law.[13] The law did not recognise Aboriginal customary laws and consequently did not recognise the Aboriginal peoples' right of self-determination. This stance was reaffirmed in the *Milirrupum v.*

Nabalco Pty Ltd.[14] In this case a group of Aborigines sued a mining company and the Commonwealth claiming relief in relation to the possession and enjoyment of areas of land owned by them under customary laws. Blackburn J of the Northern Territory Supreme Court decided that Aborigines had no legal claim to the land since all applicable English law came into operation in the colony from the date of settlement.[15]

Mabo v. The State Of Queensland[16]

This view that Aboriginal rights were completely terminated by the act of annexation was unequivocally rejected in the recent decision of the High Court in Mabo. In this path-breaking judgment, the highest court of the land has recognised the native title of Aborigines, which the Court ruled had not been automatically extinguished by white colonisation.

The High Court by a majority of 6 to 1 (Dawson J dissenting) incontrovertibly recognised the prior legal occupation by Aborigines of the Murray Islands in the Torres Strait. As a result, the Meriam people, who were in occupation of the Islands for generations before the first European contact, were granted occupation, use and enjoyment of their native lands in accordance with their indigenous laws or customs. This landmark ruling has established a major precedent for future land rights and arguably intellectual property and human rights cases.[17]

The decision in Mabo is significant for all Aboriginal people because the High Court has for the first time examined, and rejected, the validity of the following two fundamental propositions which had been endorsed by long-established authority and used as a basis of the real property law in Australia for more than one hundred and fifty years:

(i) that the territory of Australia was, in 1788, terra nullius in the sense of being "unoccupied or uninhabited" for legal purposes; and

(ii) that full legal and beneficial ownership of all the lands of this continent are vested in the Crown, unaffected by any claims of the Aboriginal inhabitants.[18]

According to the High Court these propositions which have provided a legal basis for and justification of the dispossession of Aborigines are no longer valid.[19] The Court further observed:

> The acts and events by which that dispossession in legal theory was carried into practical effect constitute the darkest aspect of the history of this nation. The nation as a whole must remain diminished unless and until there is an acknowledgment of, and retreat from, those past injustices.[20]

Sources Of Australia's Human Rights Obligations

The three general sources of what may loosely be termed Australia's "human rights" obligations are:

(i) International Instruments;

(ii) Domestic legislation; and

(iii) The common law and more specifically, the extent to which it recognises international jurisprudence on the subject.

(i) International Instruments

With respect to this source, the following four instruments are the most significant:

A. *International Covenant on Economic, Social and Cultural Rights 1966.*

B. *International Covenant on Civil and Political Rights 1966.* This came into force on 23 March 1976. Australia ratified this Covenant on 13 August 1980.[21] Under this Covenant, the First Optional Protocol was issued in December 1966. Australia ratified this Protocol on 25 September 1991 and it became effective from 25 December 1991. Australia's accession to the *First Optional Protocol* makes it possible for individuals within Australia who consider that any of their human rights, as set out in the International Covenant on Civil and Political Rights, have been violated or infringed, to take their case to the United Nations Human Rights Committee. It should be stated that the rules of the Human Rights Committee require that individuals seeking to have their complaints considered under the Protocol would need to establish to the satisfaction of the Committee that all available domestic remedies were exhausted or that the relevant legal processes had been unreasonably prolonged.[22] It should be acknowledged that Australia's accession to the *First Optional Protocol* underlies the importance accorded by the government to the protection of human rights and its conviction that the human rights performance of Australian governments at all levels should be fully open to international scrutiny.

C. *International Convention on the Elimination of all Forms of Racial Discrimination 1969.* Australia ratified this Convention on 30 September 1975.[23]

D. *International Convention Against Torture and Other Cruel Inhumane and Degrading Treatment 1984.* It may be noted here that the *Royal Commission into Aboriginal Deaths in Custody* recently recommended that Australia should make a declaration under Article 22 of the Convention enabling individual petition to the United Nations Committee Against Torture in a similar fashion to the right of individual petition under the *First Optional Protocol* to the *International Covenant on Civil and Political Rights.*[24]

(ii) Domestic Legislation

When States ratify a human rights instrument, they either

incorporate its provisions directly into their domestic legislation or undertake to comply in other ways with the obligations contained therein. It follows that universal human rights standards and norms today find their expression in the municipal laws of most countries. In Australia, four Commonwealth statutes stand out which are specifically designed to protect and promote human rights. They are:

Racial Discrimination Act 1975. This was enacted pursuant to the *International Convention on the Elimination of All Forms of Racial Discrimination*. The major objectives of this Act are first, to promote the equality before the law of all persons regardless of their race, colour or national or ethnic origin; and second to make discrimination against people on the basis of their race, colour or national or ethnic origin unlawful.

Human Rights and Equal Opportunity Commission Act 1986. This was enacted pursuant to five international instruments to which Australia is a party.[25] The Act establishes and empowers the Human Rights and Equal Opportunity Commission to deal with specific instances of abuse as well as having a broad policy formulating function. The Commission also has the function of examining international instruments and federal laws to ensure that they contain nothing inconsistent with Australia's human rights obligations.

Sex Discrimination Act 1984. The Act gives force to Australia's obligations under the *Convention on the Elimination of All Forms of Discrimination Against Women*. Its major objectives are first, to promote equality between men and women; second, to eliminate discrimination on the basis of sex, marital status or pregnancy; and third, to eliminate sexual harassment at work and in educational institutions.

Privacy Act 1988. The Act gives effect to the *Organisation for*

Economic Development (OECD) Guidelines on the Protection of Privacy and Transborder Flows of Personal Data and the International Covenant on Civil and Political Rights (Article 17).

Although Australia's legislative reforms in protecting and promoting human rights have a good track record (for example, political rights for women were recognised soon after independence in 1902), at the same time, its "white Australia" immigration policy was condemned in most parts of the world. This policy was publicly discarded in 1973.

The Australian government as well as the general public was largely unaware of the abuses of Aboriginal human rights until 1974 when, at the time of opening of Parliament in Canberra there was strong demonstration by Aboriginal people protesting against their deplorable situation. The resulting increased awareness led to the enactment of several pieces of legislation both at federal and state levels, including the *Race Discrimination Act 1975* and the *Human Rights and Equal Opportunity Commission Act 1986* and the development of an attitude of "multiculturalism" in the country.

However, Australia's poor record regarding the protection of Aboriginal human rights was again drawn to the world's attention in January 1988 when thousands gathered in Sydney to protest against Australia's bicentennial celebration of the arrival of its first white settlers. Boycotting the festivities, the Aborigines pointed out that for them the two hundred years had been one of annihilation, dispossession, and increasing poverty. They had become outcasts in their own home, living on reservations or in urban slums, suffering infant mortality three times the national average and earning half the national average wage. These protestations have had a positive result in the sense that government policies now increasingly recognise the special needs of Aborigines to retain their own culture, customs, traditions and life-styles. The Commonwealth government has taken a number of significant measures which seek to provide protection for Aboriginal cultural heritage, eg. the *Australian Heritage Commission Act 1975* which protects places associated with the Aboriginal history, culture and beliefs; the *Aboriginal and Torres Strait Islander Heritage Protection Act 1984* to protect significant Aboriginal sacred sites and objects; the *Museum of Australia Act 1980*, and the *Protection of Movable Cultural Heritage Act 1986*. Several States have followed suit and enacted legislation to safeguard and preserve Aboriginal culture.

(iii) Common Law Recognition

One particularly relevant facet of the Mabo decision is the Court's reference to human rights as enshrined in the international treaties and the likely effect these will have on the future of Australia's indigenous peoples. Brennan J made several references to the way the common law should adapt itself to human rights principles. Thus, his Honour stated:[26]

> The opening up of international remedies to individuals pursuant to Australia's accession to the Optional Protocol to the International Covenant on Civil and Political Rights... brings to bear on the common law the powerful influence of the Covenant and the international standards it imports... International law is a legitimate and important influence on the development of the common law, especially when international law declares the existence of universal human rights.

In several post-*Mabo* decisions, Kirby P. of the New South Wales Court of Appeal emphasized that regard should be had to human rights principles in deciding cases in domestic courts.[27]

Relationship Of Australian Domestic Law To International Human Rights

It remains unclear whether the ratification by Australia of various human rights instruments could be deemed to incorporate into

Australian law the universal human rights standards and norms, even though such provisions have not been adopted into the municipal laws.[28]

There are decisions of Australian courts where principles of customary international law have been incorporated into the domestic law so far as these were not inconsistent with any applicable statute law or with any binding precedent.[29] However, the consensus of judicial opinion seems to suggest that whilst it is open to have regard to such instruments as an aid to determining what the common law is in the event of doubt, e.g. the existence of a particular right, they are not by their terms incorporated into Australian domestic law. It is, nevertheless, permissible and useful to have regard to them in considering the exercise of discretion.[30]

Enforceability

To what extent are the provisions such as those in the *International Covenant on Civil and Political Rights* enforceable? Obviously, those provisions in the *Convention on the Elimination of All Forms of Racial Discrimination* are rendered enforceable by the *Racial Discrimination Act 1975* (Cth). It has been strongly argued in some cases that the *Human Rights and Equal Opportunity Act 1986* impliedly incorporates the provisions of the various international covenants into Australian law, particularly since five of those covenants have been appended to the Act in Schedules 1-5 and also because the Commission has been given an intervener function under the Act. However, an authoritative ruling on this point is still awaited.

There is however the mandatory reporting procedure under Article 40(1) of the *International Covenant on Civil and Political Rights 1966* whereby every five years each signatory State is obliged to submit to the Human Rights Committee a report on its own human rights situation. Mention may also be made of Article 41 which provides for an inter-State complaint procedure although this is rarely used for reasons of diplomacy. Finally, as already stated, there is also the procedure for individual complaints to the Human Rights Committee under the *First Optional Protocol* of the *International Covenant on Civil and Political Rights 1966*. It should be noted that this mechanism has not been invoked as yet in the Australian context. However, in a reference from Canada, called the *Lovelace case*, the Human Rights Committee observed that Article 27 of the Covenant does impose some positive duties on State parties to acknowledge the cultural rights of its citizens as individuals.[31]

Conclusion

The United Nations Universal Declaration of Human Rights affirms the principle of the inadmissibility of discrimination and proclaims that all human beings are born free and equal in dignity and rights and that everyone is entitled to all the rights and freedoms set forth therein, without distinction of any kind, and that this applies to indigenous peoples of the world. Every State which is a party to the international covenants on human rights has the obligation to ensure the equal rights of men and women to enjoy all economic, social, cultural, civil and political rights.[32] Undoubtedly, these covenants have a strong moral force.

Australia's accession to the *First Optional Protocol* combined with the Law Reform Commission's report into *The Recognition of Aboriginal Customary Laws*,[33] the report of the Royal Commission into *Aboriginal Deaths in Custody*[34] and the *Mabo* findings in 1992 clearly reveal a desire for reconciliation and to remedy the past wrongs.

Undoubtedly, the protection and promotion of Aboriginal human rights, including a grant of the right of self-determination,[35] will contribute to Australia's international prestige, and provide a basis for national pride. Enormous social and economic benefits will also emerge out of this, but most importantly, this will make the original inhabitants of this vast island continent feel at home in their own home. History is a witness to shameful miseries inflicted on this culturally profound and peace-loving peoples in the past two centuries. It will be sad if non-Aboriginal Australians are not able to recognise the universal human rights of the indigenous peoples, if for no other reason, then at least as a gesture of repentance for the wrongs of the past.

Finally, although the wrongs of the past can perhaps never be compensated in monetary terms, the developments of the present do manifest a commitment which, if maintained, is likely to lead to a brighter future. In such a future there would be no need to question whether the indigenous peoples of this country are being afforded their basic human rights because there would be no graphic discrepancies in the statistics of law and justice, health, housing, education and employment, to suggest otherwise.

Endnotes

1. This is an abbreviated version of the address delivered by the author to the International Commission of Jurists (Swedish Division) in Stockholm on 20 August 1993. The author acknowledges with gratitude the help given to him by his Research Assistant, Ms Ceri Mcdonald, in collecting the relevant material.
2. Australian Law Reform Commission's Report, *The Recognition of Aboriginal Customary Laws* (AGPS 1986) para 193. See also, P. Ford.

'Australia's Human Rights Record and the United Nations Human Rights Committee' [1989] Australian International Law News 38.

3. There is some controversy as to whether "Aborigine" or "Aboriginal" is preferable. However, there appears to be some preference for the expression "Aboriginal" people to the word "Aboriginal": see H. McRae, G. Nettherm and L. Beacroft, *Aboriginal Legal Issues: Commentary and Materials* (Law Book Co, 1991) at p vii. Note that Torres Strait Islanders, who are also indigenous inhabitants of parts of Australia, like Aborigines, have been greatly affected by European settlement. See further, Australian Law Reform Commission's Field Report no. 6, *The Torres Strait Islands* (1979).

4. See *Commonwealth v Tasmania* (1983) 46 A.L.R. 625 at 792-793. See also *Mabo v The State of Queensland* (1992) 66 A.L.J.R. 408, where Brennan J stated (at 435): "Membership of the indigenous people depends on biological descent from the indigenous people and on mutual recognition of a particular person's membership by that person and by the elders or other persons enjoying traditional authority among those people." A "Maori" is defined under section 2 of the *Maori Affairs Act* 1953 as "a person of the Maori race of New Zealand; and includes any descendant of such a person."

5. For a useful discussion, see *Report on Aboriginal Customary Laws*, above, note 2 at 68 et seq.

6. Reproduced from Fact Sheet on Australia, *Aboriginal Culture* (Department of Foreign Affairs and Trade March 1990).

7. See *Mabo*, above, note 4 at 450.

8. The *Human Rights and Equal Opportunity Commission Act 1986* (Cth) defines "human rights" in a broad manner, stating that "human rights" mean the rights and freedoms recognized in the International Covenant on Civil and Political Rights 1966 and other international instruments (section 3). These include the right to self-determination, right to life, right to liberty and security of the person, right to liberty of movement, right to equality, right to privacy, right to freedom of thought, conscience and religion, right to freedom of association, right to equal opportunity and right to enjoy one's culture.

9. J. P. Evans, "The critical issues posed for domestic legal systems is the concept of self-determination relating to indigenous minority group and the most appropriate course for resolving them" (1990) 3 *Ngulaig* at 1 alleges; "Dispossessed Aborigines, as one of the most visible 'deviant' groups in white colonial society, had been socially and environmentally

recast from a sovereign into an alien status and capacity by the destructive processes of Western colonisation."

10. See P. Dudgeon and D. Oxenham, "The Complexity of Aboriginal Diversity: Identity and Kindredness" (1990) 1 *Ngulaig* at 3: 'To Anglo-Europeans, Aborigines have been and still are perceived as savage, dirty, worthless, pitiful and animalistic, "sons of ham" and therefore not party to "divine creation." This is a damning criticism, but, regrettably, true account of some Anglo-Europeans.

11. *Commonwealth Electoral Act 1962.*

12. For a good discussion on this issue, see *Report on the Recognition of Aboriginal Customary Laws*, above, note 2 at 49 et seq.

13. *R v Murrell* (1836) Legge 72; *R v Wedge* [1976] I N.S.W.L.R. 581.

14. (1971) 17 F.L.R. 141 (the *Gove Land Rights* case).

15. But c.f *Delgamuukw v British Columbia* [1991] 3 W.W.R 97; (1991) 79 D.L.R. (4th) 185, and *Calder v Attorney-General of British Columbia* [1973] S.C.R. 313; (1973) 34 D.L.R. (3d) 145, In *Calder* in 1978 the Supreme Court of Canada held that Aboriginal title can survive British acquisition of sovereignty. In *Cooper v Stuart* (1889) 14 A.C. 286, the Judicial Committee of the Privy Council said that the introduction of the common law to the new colony was not on a wholesale basis: only so much of it as was relevant was introduced. It follows that as per the doctrine of continuity, rights which existed prior to colonisation continued through the act of colonisation. See also, *Johnson v McIntosh* (1823) 8 Weaton 543; 5 Law Ed (2d) 681, where Marshall J recognised that prior to the creation of any treaties, the aboriginal title did exist in the original occupiers.

16. *Mabo*, above, note 4 at 448. The Full Court of the High Court handed down this very lengthy decision on 3 June 1992. It consists of four different judgments. The Court comprised of Mason CJ, Brennan, Deane, Dawson, Toohey, Gaudron and McHugh JJ. This part of the paper containing a comment on *Mabo* formed part of a paper, entitled "The Demise of Terra Nullius in Australia" which the author delivered at the International Association for the Advancement of Teaching and Research in Intellectual Property (ATRIP) Congress at WIPO Headquarters in Geneva, June 29 - July 1, 1992.

17. The inadequacy of the present intellectual property regime, specially copyright law, for the protection of Aboriginal folklore is well-established. See *Report of the Working Party on the Protection of Aboriginal Folklore*, Department of Home Affairs and the Environment (Canberra 1981). For an analysis of this and related issues, see K Puri,

Australian Aboriginal People and Their Folklore NGULAIG Monograph 9, Aboriginal and Torres Strait Islander Studies Unit, The University of Queensland (Brisbane 1992).

18. *Mabo*, above, note 4 at 451 per Deane and Gaudron JJ.
19. The application of the doctrine of terra nullius to Australia has also been strongly criticised in H Reynolds, *The Law of the Land* (1987).
20. *Mabo*, above, note 4 at 451 per Deane and Gaudron JJ.
21. See generally, G Triggs, "Australia's Ratification of the International Covenant on Civil and Political Rights: Endorsement or Repudiation?" (1982) 31 International & Comparative Law Quarterly 278.
22. For a good historical account, see A. A. Trindade, 'Exhaustion of Local Remedies Under the UN Covenant on Civil and Political Rights and its Optional Protocol' (1979) 28 International and Comparative Law Quarterly 734. See further, J. Davidson, "The Procedure and Practice of the Human Rights Committee under the First Optional Protocol to the International Covenant on Civil and Political Rights" (1991) 4 Canterbury Law Review 337.
23. A copy of the text of this Convention is set out in the Schedule to the *Racial Discrimination Act 1975* (Cth)
24. See *Aboriginal Deaths in Custody - Response by Governments to the Royal Commission* ·(AGPS 1992) Volume 3 at page 1269. The Royal Commission was set up jointly by the Commonwealth, the States and the Northern Territory on 16 October 1987 in response to concern that deaths in custody of Aboriginal and Torres Strait Islander people were too common and public explanation too evasive. The Royal Commission published two reports - an interim report (December 1988) and the final report (April 1991). In eleven volumes and around 5000 pages, the reports looked into the circumstances of the (99) deaths, action taken by authorities following the deaths, and underlying causes, including social, cultural and legal factors. The Royal Commission made 339 recommendations covering reform of law and justice systems and measures to address endemic Aboriginal and Torres Strait Islander disadvantage. The Commonwealth, State and Territory Governments have responded to each of the 339 recommendations of the Royal Commission in the above-mentioned document in Volumes 1- 4.
25. These are (i) the International Covenant on Civil and Political Rights; (ii)

the Discrimination (Employment and Occupation) Convention 1958 (International Labour Organisation Convention 111); (iii) the Declaration of the Rights of the Child 1959; (iv) the' Declaration on the Rights of Mentally Retarded Persons 1971; and (v) the Declaration on the Rights of Disabled Persons 1975. The text of each of the above Covenant, Convention and Declarations is set out in Schedules 1-5 to the Human Rights and Equal Opportunity Commission Act 1986 (Cth).

26. *Mabo v. The State of Queensland*, above, note 4 at 422 (with Mason CJ and McHugh J concurring).

27. See *R v Stephen Lorne Astill* (25 August 1992) Unreported Supreme Court of NSW Criminal Division, No CA 060477 of 1991; *R v. George Stephen Greer* (14 August 1992) Unreported Supreme Court of NSW Court of Criminal Appeal, No 60495 of 1989; *Chow v. Director of Public Prosecutions* (4 September 1992) Unreported Supreme Court of NSW Court of Appeal, No. CA 40318 of 1992; and *Director of Public Prosecutions v. Saxon* (27 August 1992) Unreported NSW Court of Appeal. It should be noted that the Hon Justice Kirby, President of the NSW Court of Appeal is now the Chairman of the Executive Committee of the International Court of Justice, Geneva.

28. See G Triggs, above, note 21, at 209.

29. See, e.g. *Chow Hung Ching v. R* (1949) 77 C.L.R. 449 at 477- 479; *Polites v. Commonwealth* (1945) 70 C.L.R. 60, 80 - 81; Dietrich v. R (1992) 109 A.L.R. 385

30. See *Kioa v. West* (1958) 159 CLR 550 at 570, 630.

31. *Report of the Human Rights Committee*, GAOR 36th Sess, Supp No 40 (A/36/40), Annex XVIII, 166. For discussion, see *The Recognition of Aboriginal Customary Laws*, above, note 2 at para 176 et seq. Article 27 of the *International Covenant on Civil and Political Rights 1966* provides: "In those States in which ethnic, religious or linguistic minorities exist, persons belonging to such minorities shall not be denied the right, in community with the other members of their group, to enjoy their own culture, to profess and practise their own religion, or to use their own language."

32. These principles have been reiterated recently by the World Conference on Human Rights in Vienna, 14 - 25 June 1993.

33. *The Recognition of Aboriginal Customary Laws*, above, note 2.

34. Above, note 24.

35. It is significant to note that both international covenants, viz *International Covenant on Economic, Social and Cultural Rights and International*

Covenant on Civil and Political Rights, contain the same wording in Article 1: "All peoples have the right of self-determination. By virtue of that right they freely determine their political status and freely pursue their economic, social and cultural development." See generally, R. L. Barsh, "Indigenous Peoples and the Right to Self-determination in International Law" in B. Hocking (ed.) *International Law and Aboriginal Human Rights* (Law Book Co. 1988) 68-82; P. Ditton, '"Self Determination" or "Self Management"?' [1990] Australian International Law News 3.

Chapter Nine
RACE DISCRIMINATION AND SELF DETERMINATION: RECOGNISING, RESPECTING AND WORKING WITH DIFFERENCE.

by

Commissioner Irene Moss

Racism and racial discrimination in the economic and social spheres have been extensively documented in recent major reports such as the Royal Commission into Aboriginal Deaths in Custody. In current Government policy there are various initiatives aimed at reducing inequality, and improving conditions in these areas. However, an area which is perhaps less well understood concerns self determination, and the question of indigenous peoples' rights to manage the policies and programs which concern them. A more complex understanding of racial discrimination recognises that it is not only about levels and standards, but also about control and the values which underpin and determine the directions and objectives of programs. This paper examines some of the issues which are raised by the self determination debate concerning indigenous Australians with particular reference to the values and practices of Aboriginal and Torres Strait Islander peoples which may differ to those of non-Aboriginal people. It explores the difficulty raised for non-Aboriginal people attempting to devise and implement programs which will overcome the perceived problems while maximising self determination. The paper makes particular reference to current research being undertaken by the Race Discrimination Commissioner which looks at the need for appropriate technologies and services which take into account the particular cultural, geographic and other circumstances of the communities which are to benefit from them.

In recent years there has been a lot of discussion about the social and economic conditions of indigenous Australians, the appalling levels of health, the disproportionate rates of incarceration, the racial discrimination and the racist violence. These issues are crucially important, however, they are not addressed in this paper. They have been extensively documented in various reports, in particular in the Royal Commission into Aboriginal Deaths in Custody and the national inquiry into racist violence.

Rather than examining social, economic and civil rights in themselves, this study examines   political rights, which are in fact inseparable from the other categories of rights. This issue seems particularly pertinent in the current "post-Mabo" climate where the newspapers are suddenly full of references to "self-determination", "sovereignty" and "secession". But worse still the myths, hysteria, the hype which bears little on the real issues upon which we should be focusing and even worse than that the low level heroism, the hate mail and even violence of most people who are perceived to be supporters of the *Mabo* decision.

In Australia today, the debate is no longer just about the conditions in which Aboriginal people live, but about who "owns" the country, and who has the right to govern and make decisions about its future. These are questions which undoubtedly affect all Australians. However, they involve such complex concepts and arguments that it is difficult for many of us to take part in the debate in an informed and balanced way.

Any discussion of self determination must be set against the background of the history of control and paternalism which indigenous peoples have experienced. From virtually first settlement to the 1960s (and possibly even later) the dominant policy frameworks adopted by governments throughout Australia in relation to Aboriginal people were protection, and then assimilation. Both of these approaches saw Aboriginal people taken from their traditional lands, lifestyles and laws and placed on artificial settlements where they were controlled and directed by non-Aboriginal people. The aim was either to protect and civilise them, or to get them to live like all other (non-Aboriginal) Australians as members of a single community. This involved the grossest loss of control over every aspect of their lives.

Against this background, it is not hard to see why we are now hearing such vigorous and urgent calls from Aboriginal people for the power to make the decisions about issues which affect their lives. Calls for that elusive state of "self determination". But what exactly does self-determination mean? It is not possible to provide a definitive answer, to do so would in itself be contrary to the spirit of self determination, which demands that peoples have the right to speak for themselves, and to define concepts within their own framework. what is possible to do is to look at what self determination means in the context of racial discrimination, and discover some of the meanings it has been given in Australia and the world today.

Both the international covenant on civil and political rights and the international covenant on economic, social and cultural rights proclaim:

> All peoples have the right of self determination. By virtue of that right they freely determine their political status and freely pursue their economic, social and cultural development.[1]

Now this is certainly a fine sentiment, but unfortunately the term has all too often been invoked as a catch all phrase to cover a multitude of policies, practices, sins and virtues. Self determination has been the official policy of the Australian government in relation to Aboriginal and Torres strait islander people since the 1970s. Today it is used to cover a spectrum of meanings from self management at a local level, community control over policy, funding and decision making, partial self government, to a totally separate economic base, legal system and political system in an independent sovereign state.

The purpose of this essay is not to analyse these options, nor to pre-empt which option will best meet the aspirations of Aboriginal people within the context of the broader Australian community. It is rather to perhaps comment on what is at the heart of the matter, that is, a group's ability to have adequate decision making powers and control over their circumstances. This means being able to do so in a way which includes their cultural context and value system.

In an ideal democratic system, we would aim for all peoples and individuals within that nation to have the right to participate fully in the political process by which they are governed. In fact, if a democratic system really worked in representing the needs and interests of all groups, then they would be self determining. But, as we have come to see in many countries, even in countries which are formally fully democratic, significant barriers exist which inhibit the full democratic participation of particular groups. This means that the full range of human rights are not theirs to enjoy.[2]

One could respond to this observation by saying that no individual or group can be fully self determining in a large democratic system, and that all of us are spoken for and have decisions imposed on us constantly. But clearly, if we look around the world, we see that some groups are particularly disadvantaged and less adequately represented. In fact there is a consistent pattern of indigenous peoples in countries which have been colonised and taken over by a new culture finding themselves in just this position.

There are several compelling reasons for treating the demand for self determination for indigenous peoples as distinct, and not "just another minority". First of all, they were the original inhabitants of this country and their lands were taken without their consent. This involved the removal of their economic base and thus their bargaining power. Secondly, many Aboriginal people continue to assert that they never ceded their land or their sovereignty to the British colonisers, and as they were a distinct peoples before invasion, they remain so. Thirdly, as mentioned above, they have been subjected to disempowering and abusive treatment of a type which no other group has had to endure. And finally, the representative government and economically powerful interest groups would appear to be particularly unrepresentative of their interests.

There is a strong link between the demand for self determination and the position which indigenous peoples have occupied within the mainstream society. One of the main reasons that indigenous people are now talking about notions like a "separate state" and "full sovereignty" is that they have not received a fair go within the present systems.

Anti-discrimination law in Australia has, until now been designed to address the type of inequality where people suffer direct discrimination by being treated differently because of their race, e.g. being denied entry into a club, refused a job and so on, it has generally done so by applying the principle of "equal treatment before the law". This is a principle which is so deeply enshrined in our common law and in international law that it is rarely questioned.

However, as we become more sophisticated in our understanding of racial discrimination, we see that "fairness" cannot truly be achieved through the same treatment for all people. Look at justice. She stands holding the scales, but she is wearing a blindfold. Is she colour blind?

Is she blind to differences in race, culture and gender? Would the justice which she confers be even fairer if she could in fact discern those differences?

In Australia, when we have spoken about "one Australia", and indigenous people becoming part of the rest of society, has this meant that they would have to become just like everybody else? Is not the "everybody else" which we use as our measuring stick generally white (and male for that matter)? If a person belongs to a culture and a value system which radically differ to those of the "one system", will being treated just like everyone else in the system achieve their aspirations and needs? The point is that if we want to realise the rights of the individual, we need to recognise that individuals are not all the same. An important part of what an individual is derives from the racial, ethnic or cultural group to which they belong. For indigenous Australians in particular, their collective rights as distinct peoples, which occupy a unique position in Australia, are perhaps as important as what we term individual rights.

It seems that if our laws, policies and practices were able to truly reflect the needs and wishes of indigenous Australians, then it would be possible for them to freely pursue their economic, cultural, social and spiritual development in a spirit of coexistence with other citizens. It is when Aboriginal people feel that this is unachievable within the current system of one government structure and "one nation" that they call for more radical forms of self determination.

Today, when we hear calls for "culturally appropriate" treatment, and separate services or programs, they are frequently met with cries that this is different, and thus "discriminatory' treatment", and will result in the fragmentation of society. Fragmentation or dismemberment of a unified society is certainly not something that any state would desire, nor something which we should support. however, a "unified" society is only tolerable if it complies with certain principles, such as equal rights and self determination.

It is quite possible for equal rights and self determination to be achieved within a unified society where the government is representative of all people in its territory, without distinction. Where it is not, the right of self determination stands and must be realised. Having made these statements about rights and aspirations, the question is: How, in practical terms, do we achieve them? In Australia today we live in a multiracial, multicultural society which encompasses diverse groups, and diverse needs. So how do you support and balance diversity within an integrated community?

One illustration of the type of problem at issue is that of the sale and distribution of alcohol to Aboriginal communities in central Australia.[3] Alcohol abuse amongst Aboriginal people is not only having a devastating effect in terms of health and general well being, but is destroying the social and cultural fabric of communities. In the effort to control alcohol abuse amongst their people, various Aborigine communities have declared themselves dry. Unfortunately, in many cases this has not been all that effective. Either people buy and drink alcohol elsewhere and return to the community drunk, or they simply buy take-aways and, in defiance of the rules, bring them back to consume in the community. Some of these communities are now calling for governments to pass laws which will stop liquor being sold to their people all together.

One immediate response to this has been: "But you can not refuse to sell alcohol to a person because they belong to a certain Aboriginal community, that would be racial discrimination and is unlawful".

In response, many of the Aboriginal people say that they are trying to save their communities from total destruction; that the right of the community as a whole to safety and retaining its culture is higher than the right of the individual drinker to buy alcohol. So the communities say that they should have the right to regulate how their own people will consume liquor, and how their communities will be protected from the devastating effects of alcohol abuse. They feel that treating their people "in the same way as everyone else" in relation to liquor sales is having a detrimental impact on them, and that they should have the right to call for treatment which they believe will serve their needs and interests. In this case, that means being treated differently. So here we have a community which is seeking to increase its decision making powers, to have more say about how it will function, and it is facing barriers put up by the mainstream legal system. What is sought in our inquiry is a way to maximise the decision making powers of the community within the constraints of the law, and to allow them to determine how they will operate, without offending the broader community. This is a dilemma.

In conclusion, self-determination is an aspirational concept which provides a firm base for increasing the decision-making powers of indigenous peoples, and returning to them the control and dignity which have been so abused. A compassionate, just society must realise that difference must be tolerated and supported, and that in certain contexts only different treatment can achieve genuine justice for all its citizens.

One of the central principles of the Bahá'í Faith is the oneness of humankind. Bahá'í people have been trying to live peacefully within broader societies, and according to their Faith, they have suffered horrific persecution.

Our challenge is to find ways to recognise the oneness with both compassion and complexity so that we can see, without the blindfold of the old justice, that the oneness has many colours. When we insist that they are all the same, not only to we lose sight of true justice, we sacrifice and impoverish our humanity.

Endnotes

1. *International Covenant on Civil and Political Rights*, Article 1(1).
2. See <u>Working Group on Indigenous Populations</u>, Statement on Self Determination by Mr. Colin Milner on behalf of the Australian Delegation, 24 July 1992 (Geneva) at 3.
3. The author is currently conducting an inquiry on the subject.

Chapter Ten

AUSTRALIA'S INDIGENOUS PEOPLE: THE NATION'S SHAME

by

The Hon. Justice Marcus Einfeld

Australia has always regarded itself as a very lucky country indeed. The ideal of a "fair go for everyone" represents the commitment to equality on which Australians pride themselves. Yet these concepts contrast with the extent of inequality that exists in Australian society today. Our treatment of the Aboriginal and Torres Strait Islander populations is the most damnable example of this inequality. Our refusal to provide them with good land, equal or true opportunity, and a respectable and respected place in the community, is a reprehensible and continuing impediment to Australia's boastful claims of honourable behaviour and decent standards.

Australians of today speak of a great society, yet 265,000 of our citizens, or a sizeable proportion of them, are denied a basic quality of life! The gross inequality in the treatment of Australia's indigenous people as against other Australians in a number of areas including the law, employment, education, health and housing makes a mockery of our criticisms of other countries for their human rights violations. That is not to say such criticisms should be withheld. It is merely to require an acknowledgment of our own abuses. Whilst our general human rights record is undoubtedly better than many other countries, the standards by which we must be judged, and must judge ourselves, are those we set or claim for ourselves, not alien credos which we loudly and rightly condemn.

A constant problem for anyone attempting to research and monitor Aboriginal issues is a lack of data. Indeed the scarcity of statistical information is itself a manifestation of the low regard that Australia as a nation has for Aborigines' rights and state. The things Australians really care about, like sport and entertainment, are usually documented and tabulated to the point of absurdity. But there is almost nothing, except on an ad hoc or regional basis, about the descendants of our country's original inhabitants.

A 1988 report on Australia's Health by the Australian Institute of Health stated, for example, that in 1986 birth and infant mortality statistics were available only for 83,000 or only 37% of Australia's then recorded 227,648 Aborigines. Comprehensive data on Aboriginal deaths, except those in custody, are not routinely available for Aborigines in all States and Territories except Tasmania, are not routinely published, and their accuracy has not been established.

Nevertheless, what information there is indicates a shocking situation. Australia's indigenous people are grossly over represented in places of incarceration, and in chronic unemployment, while their health and housing are in some cases, of "third world" quality. In simple terms we have established a social system that has failed to recognise the special needs of Aborigines and Torres Strait Islanders while giving mobile phones and promising pay television to almost any one else who wants them.

A number of specific areas evidence the present, not past, inequality between indigenous and non-indigenous people. All these areas support the conclusion that the situation in Australia for many Aborigines and Islanders is horrendous and required urgent dramatic attention.

The Legal System

Before 1967, the Australian Government had no direct legislative power over indigenous people except those residing in the federal territories. In 1967, as a result of a referendum, the Australian Constitution was altered to permit the parliament to make laws with respect to the "people of any race for whom it is deemed necessary to make special laws".

Since that time, and particularly during the three years from 1972 to 1975 when the Whitlam Labor Government was particularly active, the Parliament has passed a substantial volume of legislation designed to improve the welfare of Aborigines and Torres Strait Islanders. Examples of such legislation include the Northern Territory's *Aboriginal Land Rights Act 1976* and the *Racial Discrimination Act 1976*. The Whitlam Government also greatly increased financial allocations to and for Aborigines and Islanders which have been continued and expanded since.

However, despite the increased volume of federal legislation and financial assistance designed to benefit the country's indigenous inhabitants from then to now, they still face a variety of disadvantages that are deeply rooted in history and the attitudes of the white community. Moreover, a dichotomy exists between the positive legal discrimination achieved by such legislation and expenditure, and the negative discrimination that still exists in certain areas of Australia's legal system, particularly the criminal sphere. Indigenous people have been confronted for many years with types of law which has created, and continue to perpetuate, a special inferior class of legal persons, law which ascribes to that legal class for generations immutable negative traits, law which bans as criminal, for that class alone, behaviour which is acceptable at large, law which controls Aborigines physically, mentally and geographically.

Law made Aborigines a lower class. Right up to the mid-sixties, in Queensland they could not enter into contracts, establish businesses, withdraw from savings accounts, own property or make wills without official permission. Any money they had was kept at the local police station and could only be released if authorised by a government official. In some States approval was required before an Aboriginal marriage took place and it was a serious offence, punishable by imprisonment, for any person other than an Aborigine to live or have sexual relations with an Aboriginal female. Aborigines could not be employed without government authority and any person who caused or induced them to leave any lawful employment without consent was prosecuted. In Western Australia, those living above a certain line of latitude were not entitled to certain civil and citizenship rights. Law created offences which only black people could commit: drinking, leaving a reserve, entering one when barred, refusing to work, even being cheeky.

As with all other areas affecting indigenous people, there are no clear statistics on the experience of Aborigines and Torres Strait Islanders with the legal system. What information there is suggests very clearly that they are in a severely disadvantaged position in contrast with white Australians. One of the starkest examples of the inadequacies towards Aborigines in the legal sphere has been the appalling incidence of deaths of Aborigines and Islanders in custody in recent times. In May 1991, the Final Report of the Royal Commission into Aboriginal Deaths in Custody was released after a three year investigation into the deaths of 99 Australian Aboriginal people and Torres Strait Islanders between 1980 and 1989 in police lockups, prisons and juvenile detention centres.

Aborigines and Torres Strait Islanders make up less than 1.6% of the total Australian population, and only 1.1% of the adult population. Yet the Royal Commission concluded that Australia's indigenous people are arrested and detained in police custody at a national rate 29 times greater than that of the general population. In Western Australia, the rate is 43 times higher. This severe over-representation also extended to incarceration in our prison system. According to the Australian Institute of Criminology, the rate of imprisonment of Aboriginal people has actually increased since the Commission began its work. The 1991 National Prison Census reported that Aborigine and Torres Strait Islanders were incarcerated in prisons at 9 times the rate of non-indigenous people in the Northern Territory, 10.5 times in Queensland, 14 times in NSW and South Australia, and a whopping 25 times in Western Australia. These appalling figures are even more alarming with respect to Aboriginal youths in custody, with roughly 35% of Australia's prison population of 24 years and under being Aborigines or Islanders.

Since 1980, almost 600 men and women have died behind bars in Australia: 18% were black, 82% white. If the proportions were right, the number of white people to have died would be about 6000. This would not have led merely to a Royal Commission, which itself would have had to be prised out of largely unwilling federal and state governments by large numbers of activist groups and on the eve of a Human Rights Commission investigation if they had not acted. It would have caused a revolution!

It is by now well known that the vast majority of people whose deaths were investigated by the Royal Commission were young Aboriginal men generally incarcerated in police lockups on relatively minor charges, mostly relating to intoxication. The given wisdom, then, is that the victim is drunk. He is thrown into a solitary cell on a concrete floor, with a blanket or a sheet or a towel, or some combination of those things, and the clothes he is wearing. Everyone knows the difficulty of trying to tie a sheet or a towel or a pair of jeans into a knot around anything, let alone a human neck. If it can be done, there is little left to tie in a knot around a cell bar. If socks are used and two are tied together, there is certainly nothing left to tie around anything else.

This means that a drunken man, in fact scores of different drunken men, with quite different heritages in quite different parts of Australia, thousands of miles apart, who have never met each other, find themselves sitting in dozens of different cells over a period of twelve years calmly splitting or slicing up blankets, sheets, towels or clothing, calmly tying the pieces together, calmly choosing the length so as to effect hanging, calmly knotting them around their own necks, calmly knotting the other end around different cell bars or other protrusions, and calmly hanging themselves to death.

How did they cut or slice the blankets or sheets or towels or clothing? With their hands or their teeth or their feet? If they did it with scissors or knives, where did the implements come from? How long did all this take? Why did official inspection not discover what was going on before it was all too late?

If they were all so drunk, how did they marshal their senses and presence of mind to hang themselves? If suicide was a cultural practice or personal inclination of Aborigines, why have not thousands of them, when drunk or sober, hanged themselves by throwing ropes over tree branches or in houses all over the country?

Yet if they were all suicides, what does this say about the sense of desolation, loneliness, neglect, and non-belonging of all these people, and so many others in precisely the same position? What does it say of us who have steadfastly failed to recognise the signs, refused to address the problems, and simply have not cared? And they are still dying. Since the Royal Commission stopped investigating four years ago, there have been 30 more deaths. While efforts in these regards may be improving, as long as any of the nation's citizens are forced to endure this type of suffering, Australia has a long way to go before it will deserve to call itself a civilised society.

A number of explanations have been advanced in the public debate concerning these events. They include the discrimination against Aborigines by the criminal justice system - that is, that they are arrested, persecuted and punished for offences which would not elicit the same response if committed by non-Aborigines; or they commit offences different from non-Aborigines to which the police react and which the courts punish relatively severely. There appears to be some substance in each of these hypotheses. Moreover, the isolation and despair of Aborigines deprived of their normal support mechanisms are crucial. Yet despite the enthusiastic acceptance by federal and state governments of the present author's proposal of five years ago to have Aboriginal Chaplains appointed to prisons and lockups in appropriate places in the country, most of Australia is still without them.

It is clear that Aboriginal people are much more likely than others to be arrested or detained by the police for minor alcohol-related public order offences. This is partly because many provisions in legislation or in by-laws concerning drunkenness or drinking in a public area, when socio-economic conditions and social prejudice are taken into account, are racially discriminatory. One recent example will suffice to illustrate this problem. Since 1990 there have been provisions in the *Local Government Act* of New South Wales permitting local Councils to designate certain areas as alcohol-free zones in which police may confiscate any alcohol or impose on the spot fines. The law was unashamedly aimed at Aborigines and is bound to cause more confrontation. Sober white people will suffer nothing but drink paid for by perfectly sober Aborigines may be taken from them with no right of recourse by the victim. If the police choose to do so, they can fine them as well. Because Aborigines will be unable to pay, it will cause additional incarceration. These are persons whose only offence is to possess liquor in an alcohol-free zone. It is a pity local councils are not all compelled to use the money involved in all this to offer jobs or job training to Aborigines.

Numerous studies have indicated that the relatively greater incidence of serious crime within the Aboriginal and Islander community is linked to the marginal status and alienated character of indigenous people within Australian society, of which lack of employment and of adequate housing, health care, education and training are the grosser examples. This phenomenon is in turn reinforced by the repeated criminalisation of large numbers of Aboriginal people for relatively minor offences, resulting in a self perpetuating spiral of criminalisation, victimisation and lack of self esteem.

An important part of any strategy to reduce the over-representation of indigenous people in prison must involve recognising their special vulnerability as prisoners, and the removing of factors which tend to be discriminatory in nature or practice. Clearly reviewing laws pertaining to alcohol offences, to public order offences and to the treatment of juveniles to take into account Aboriginal traditions regarding socialising in a public place, dress codes, language, and the economic reasons why so many people are vulnerable to alcohol, is necessary.

Another aspect of the differing treatment of indigenous people in the criminal law system is the over-policing of Aborigines and Torres Strait Islanders. There is a very high level of police presence and intervention in certain communities. Some observers have argued that one reason for the glaring disproportion in the number of arrests of indigenous people is the enormity of this presence.

The prevalence of such harassment and provocation also leads to a situation in which people accept an unusually high level of violence at the hands of the authorities as normal. It is clear that the degree and kind of control exercised by the police over Aboriginal life extends far beyond the level of police control over whites. The tensions inherent in the historical relationships between the police and indigenous people appear to contribute in a variety of ways to the discrimination against Aborigines found in our criminal justice system.

The point can be simplified. If an Aboriginal male swears at a policeman in almost any Australian town or suburb, he is arrested and charged. If he is fined and cannot pay, he goes to gaol where he may suffer far more than the appropriate penalty. He normally cannot pay because he has no work. He has no work because the opportunities for education and training supplied for virtually every other Australian have not been made available to him.

If on the other hand, a police officer calls an Aborigine a similar name, nothing happens except more hurt to the Aborigine to add to the other indignities heaped on his forebears for generations, and more likelihood of further disaffection with and revolt against white society. When the sense of affront bubbles over, they are accused of being drunk or unruly or antisocial or uncontrollable or dole bludgers. As if white people would not react the same way or worse in the same circumstances.

Not a thing of significance has been done concerning the police involved in the two disgusting videos that showed on television a couple of years ago where police poked fun and shouted obscenities at Aborigines wrongly killed by police. Why are Australian police allowed to get away with indecent racism against Australian citizens?

As a result of the *Report of the Royal Commission into Black Deaths in Custody*, steps are under way to address and redress this situation in part, but there is an urgent need for greater education of the police force and other law enforcers in relation to the treatment of Aboriginal and Torres Strait Islander people, and greater demand by other Australians for the accountability of all associated with the law in these respects.

Employment

There is no doubt that unemployment among Aborigines and Islanders is a chronic human problem. Even the most conservative estimate indicates that the present unemployment rate for indigenous people exceeds 30%. Among the young it is as high as 50% and more in some places. This represents something like three to four times the unemployment rate of the rest of the community, even in today's horrific levels of unemployment. This is not merely a problem of today. It is the result of two centuries of gross discrimination and neglect.

The position of indigenous people in the labour markets is even worse than these statistics suggest. In addition to high unemployment rates, there is considerable evidence that Aborigines and Islanders participate in the labour force to a much lesser degree than the rest of the Australian community. For example among 35-39 year old males, the participation rate for non-Aborigines is 95%, whereas the participation for indigenous people is around 20% lower, at about 75%. Among females of the same age group, the rate differential is even greater, at around 25%. At a national level in 1991, 26% of indigenous Australians were employed, compare with 62% of the rest of the population. Evidence also suggests that many Aborigines, although not considered to be in the labour force, are nevertheless interested in gaining meaningful employment but are not actively looking for employment due to the dispersed state of their local labour market. Only 57% considered themselves to be actively in the labour force compared with 71% of the rest of the population.

Of employed Aborigines and Islanders, one third have part-time work only, compared with one quarter of the non-indigenous population. Almost all of those with full-time employment are in low paid jobs, with a mean individual income of $11,500 compared to just over $17,500 for the rest of the population, and a mean family income of only $28,000, many thousands of dollars less than their white counterparts.

Over the years the federal government has attempted to redress the high levels of unemployment in the Aboriginal community, albeit unsuccessfully. There have been many special programs and indigenous Australians also have access to mainstream market programs, such as Jobstart, Skillshare and Jobskills.

However, despite the intentions of these admirable governmental policies, it is an inescapable fact that unemployment is still a major problem, and will remain so until such time as Aborigines and Torres Strait Islanders are given proper and adequate access to education and training programs so as to equip them with the skills needed to take advantage of a wider range of job opportunities whether in paid employment, self-employment or community ventures.

Education

Education is therefore of fundamental importance. Although school attendance is compulsory throughout Australia between the ages of 6 and 15 years, at least 10% of Aboriginal children of school age, more in rural areas, do not attend school at all. Moreover, the concentration of the black population in the younger age group disguises a much lower actual attendance level, with only about half of those between the ages of 15 and 24 still attending some form of education as compared with other Australians in the same age group.

As expected, this data confirms the pattern of Aboriginal disadvantage in attained level of schooling relative to the general population. A comparison of the qualifications of indigenous and other Australians reveals that whites are around three times more likely to have some form of qualification. A shocking 31% of Aboriginal people over the age of 55 have never attended school. These figures are comparable with educational levels attained by rural communities in many so-called Third World countries.

Low as the participation rates of Aborigines in primary and secondary education are, they are almost non-existent at the tertiary level, with only 9% of Aboriginal people obtaining tertiary education, compared with 26% of the rest of the population.

Studies of involvement in education present a similar picture. Teacher assessment studies indicate that at primary school level, Aboriginal children's achievement is substantially below the level considered average for white children in all but non-academic curriculum areas. This pattern is marked in the areas of basic intellectual skills in reading, oral and written use of language, and in mathematics. The picture at the secondary level is similar, with Aboriginal students being assessed by teachers as having lower performance in the vital skill areas associated with reading and communication.

To address the old racial superiority theories, still apparently espoused by some in the community, this should be put into perspective. By far the greatest participation and success rate of Aborigines in the education system occurs in all or mainly Aboriginal schools, whereas Aboriginal children's performance and attendance at mainly white rural schools is the lowest. This is not racism or racial segregation, still less superiority, practised by Aborigines. It is a reflection of the alienation felt by and prejudice practised against Aborigines by white students and teachers at mixed schools.

An example demonstrates the reality of this prejudice. In one rural district served by a mainly white school, the school bus which collects the children from Aboriginal towns and areas was known by everyone as the Coon Express. Some called it the Vegemite Special. Everyone knows about it but no one did a thing about it, not the teachers, the white parents, the bus driver, the clergy, the local council, the local member of parliament, no one.

The school experienced a substantial dropout of the Aboriginal children. It turned out that Aboriginal children were being singled out in front of the other children, some brought to the front of the class or the school assembly, for not having school uniforms or for being smelly or having head lice or unclean teeth. What was not told to the assemblage at the school was that there was no water in their home township for washing clothes or people because the river had run dry and the bore was not working. No one at the school explained that the river had run dry because it had been dammed by the government, and whereas the white cotton farmers up river had been told that if they needed water for their crops they only had to pay $10 for a 10 year licence and make a phone call to the dam supervisor, the Aborigines down river had been told nothing. And government is supposed to be for all the people. No one at the school said that the bore had stopped functioning because the bore pump had broken down and had not been fixed because local, state and federal governments were arguing about who should pay for the repair. Of course no one would train or authorise a local Aborigine to fix it.

Moreover, our education system needs to recognise the different skills and characteristics of Aboriginal students. First and foremost, Aborigines generally tend to be shy or overawed by white people in authority, a reflection and result of their historical experience. Second, Aboriginal children are taught at a very early age the art of being independent and self sufficient, and of respecting their elders. The constant questioning of parents found in many non-Aboriginal families does not occur with children learning from their own observations, and if necessary questioning their peers. Our traditional schooling system, particularly at the primary school level, does not suit these characteristics. Children are expected to obey the requests of the teacher immediately and without question and no time is given to "observe" or learn what is being done by other children. Thus, Aboriginal children who are slow to follow teacher's commands are often labelled as lazy or unco-operative.

The unavailability of education to the parents of the children has an especially adverse effect on this situation. Apart from the denial of their opportunity to be educational role models or helpers, their own lack of training and experience makes many Aboriginal parents ambivalent about the value of white schooling for their children. Schooling has often provided no economic benefits to families, especially in remote areas. In addition, formal education has sometimes served to divorce or alienate children from their traditional family and group affiliations without being able to achieve white acceptance in its place. Schools are often seen as white institutions ordered and administered by white people, and as vehicles for the continued subordination of blacks. These viewpoints are not wrong.

The result of this educational inequality at all levels it to leave the indigenous people at a marked disadvantage, not only in obtaining employment, but also in acquiring a due share of political power to facilitate negotiations for improved rights for Aboriginal people.

Although the Australian Government has made some small inroads in increasing their access to education, with schemes such as the Commonwealth Secondary Grants scheme and Abstudy, it must be recognised that a different approach is necessary to the education of Aboriginal children, at least in the early stages. There is still a long way to go before Aboriginal Australians have the same access to and derive the same benefits from education as do their white compatriots.

Health

Rates of Aboriginal health are, in every particular, worse that those for the wider community, and in some cases, many times worse. The 1979 Report on Aboriginal Health by the House of Representatives Standing Committee on Aboriginal Affairs stated:

> The standard of health of Aboriginals is far lower than that of the majority of Australians and would not be tolerated if it existed in the Australian Community as a whole. (p. iii)

The report also noted that there had been a number of reports on the subject, none of which seemed to have had any impact on governments or bureaucracies. Almost 15 years later, whilst there have been improvements in some areas, the situation in far too many areas is no better, and in some is actually worse. The 1988 Health Institute Report stated:

> Although the health problems differ, the overall [Aboriginal] standard of health is low throughout the country. For almost all disease categories, rates for Aborigines and Torres Strait Islanders are worse than for other Australians: death rates are up to four times higher, and life expectancy is up to 22 years less. (p. 105)

Only 4% of Aborigines are 60 or over, compared with almost 20% of the white population.

These mortality statistics, confirmed by a 1991 study, are comparable at the best end with those documented for Colombia, Mongolia, the Philippines and Thailand. The worst levels are comparable with the situations recorded in India, Haiti, Ghana and Papua New Guinea. There are also indications that morality rates are even higher than they were 20 years ago, an absolutely appalling indictment of a society which boasts of having done so much for Aborigines over that period in particular.

The Aboriginal infant mortality rate is three times higher than for the general population, and in remote areas there are about 34 per 1000 live births. The indications are that the high maternal mortality rates measured in the early 1970s have declined somewhat, but in 1982-84 the Aboriginal maternal death rate was still three to five times higher than for the general population. Indeed even more recent reports have indicated that this rate may be closer to eight times that of the general Australian population.

Rates of hospitalisation and lengths of stay are also indicative of the more serious and chronic nature of Aboriginal ill-health, the rate being two or three times higher than for the general population, and length of stay about twice as long.

Rates of infant development as compared with the general community confirm that young Aborigines still suffer significant disadvantage. Aboriginal babies characteristically weigh less than non-Aboriginal babies. The evidence suggests that they develop normally for the first four to six months, after which development is below normal up to about three years of age. A study in 1987 found that 14% of infants and 22% of children were underweight, suggesting mild to moderate under-nutrition.

The major cause of death for Aborigines is diseases of the circulatory system, including heart disease. This, of course, results from similar causes as the general community, viz. incorrect diet, lack of exercise, and stress. But the much higher rate at which these diseases afflict Aborigines is symptomatic of the environmental factors which affect, almost exclusively, Aboriginal communities.

Aborigines also suffer from some diseases which are regarded as non-existent in non-Aboriginal Australia. Almost all these diseases are also related to environmental factors quite outside the control of the people. They result also, of course, from the lack of adequate preventative or curative health care. Some examples illustrate the point.

One example is intestinal infections, particularly gastro-enteritis, caused by contaminated water, inadequate hygiene and overcrowding. These are serious, painful and debilitating infections, but for white people, even those who are seriously deprived, cases of true gastro-enteritis are quite rare.

For most Australians leprosy has nothing more than biblical significance. But its existence amongst Aborigines was discovered late last century. On the Northern Territory Register of Lepers in 1976, there were 710 Aborigines and 40 non-Aborigines. The situation has dramatically improved, but between 1982 and 1986 there were 19 newly reported Aboriginal cases in the Northern Territory and 31 in Western Australia. These figures are significant in the light of the fact that the disease is now completely unknown in the non-Aboriginal community.

Despite a TB inoculation program during the mid-1970s, there remains an alarmingly high incidence of this disease amongst Aborigines. Between 1983 and 1985, 169 new cases were reported. When a comparison is made with the non-Aboriginal community, discounting the occurrence of TB amongst newly arrived migrants, the Aboriginal rate is 20 times greater.

Recent research indicates a serious level of hepatitis B in the Aboriginal population. It is believed that somewhere around one third of Aborigines have been infected, and in some areas it is as many as 90%. A substantial number have been confirmed as chronic carriers, placing them at risk of the long term sequelae, chronic active hepatitis and cirrhosis and primary cancer of the liver, particularly hepacellular carcinoma (Health Institute Report, p. 117). In order to combat this problem, the Federal Government instituted an immunisation program for all new-born babies in communities with a carrier rate of 50% or more, but the condition is widely prevalent amongst Aboriginal communities.

Up to date research on the levels of sexually transmitted diseases in the Aboriginal community is not available, however, the 1979 Parliament report stated that in 1977 in the Northern Territory there were 703 Aboriginal notifications of syphilis. This constituted a rate of 27 per 1000 people, compared with a non-Aboriginal rate of 2. This situation has reportedly since improved but there is still a very high level of disease which has long been regarded as virtually eradicated from the non-Aboriginal community. The immense dangers which the HIV virus is now posing to Aborigines can not be overstated.

Recent research has indicated that Aborigines are also beginning to suffer from hypertension and diabetes, diseases associated with emotional, often financial and domestic, stress and poor diet. The 1988 Health Institute Report suggested that the incidence of non insulin-dependent diabetes in the Aboriginal community is as high as 16%, compared with a non-Aboriginal rate of 3.4%. This has also been connected with a high incidence of obesity, which of course also results from the inadequate nutrition of many Aborigines.

Alcohol

Alcohol is unfortunately another major health problem confronting many Aborigines. The 1977 Report of the House of Representative Aboriginal Affairs Committee on Alcohol Problems of Aborigines stated:

> Alcohol is the greatest present threat to the Aborigines of the Northern Territory and unless strong immediate action is taken they could destroy themselves.

Regrettably, that statement remains all too accurate today in many Aboriginal communities across Australia. Alcohol abuse is not one of the finer characteristics of western civilisation. Alcohol has always played a prominent part in Australian society, and the evil it can bring has been recognised since European settlement. The early colonialists and their convicted charges introduced alcohol to the Aborigines and Islanders. It was used as a currency in early New South Wales, and when Governor Bligh tried to break the monopoly of the Rum Corps in 1808, he had a mutiny on his hands.

The effects of alcohol in Aboriginal communities are particularly debilitating. This is no better understood than by many such communities themselves, which have initiated self-imposed alcohol restrictions or bans. Such initiatives cannot be praised too highly. However, there remain severe problems in many areas.

The 1990 Report on Aboriginal Alcohol Use commissioned by the *Royal Commission into Aboriginal Deaths in Custody* found that one half of all Aboriginal men drank at harmful levels, with estimates for women varying from 3% to 50%, depending on their age and living conditions. There seems to be a trend amongst older people away from alcohol, but 90% of 15 to 30 year olds surveyed were found by researchers to be current drinkers of significance.

The frequency of alcohol consumption among Aboriginal people appears to be related to where they live. Aboriginal people living in towns and fringe camps drink most frequently, while those living in remote areas are more likely to drink intermittently. An alarming correlation between drinking on the one hand, and mortality, incarceration, domestic violence and community well-being on the other hand, was found.

The report found that, contrary to widespread opinion, a substantial proportion of Aboriginal people, particularly women, do not drink alcohol. Estimates of the proportion of Aboriginal non-drinkers range from 10% to 35% of men, and 39% to 80% of women depending on the community. The proportion of Aboriginal non-drinkers is higher than in the wider Australian population, where the numbers are 12% of men, and 19% to 25% of women. In this regard a special tribute should be paid to women in Aboriginal communities who have played a significant role in the war on the use of alcohol, and whose particular commitment has been one of the principal factors, if not the single major cause, of the successes thus far achieved.

What, then, are the factors which lead to such high rates of ill health amongst Aborigines and Torres Strait Islanders? Reference here will be made to the well documented situation of the Aboriginal Communities of Toomelah and Boggabilla on the New South Wales/Queensland border.[1] It is not necessary to repeat the physical conditions which have been given wide publicity, but among the things learned was that Aboriginal ill-health can be attributed to three main factors: the living environment, lack of health services and lack of personal esteem. All these factors have to be addressed in order to solve the health problem. Even if we had the best health service in the world, nothing can be achieved if the people are living in unsealed broken down shacks without clean water, proper sanitation and fresh food, and without work, money or hope. The people at Toomelah suffered all these needs and more.

The nearest hospital to Toomelah is just a few kilometres away in Goondiwindi in Queensland. At the time of my Inquiry then in 1987, the interstate border represented a virtual "iron curtain" of denial of medical services to Aborigines just over the border in New South Wales. "Their" hospital was 120 kilometres away in Moree, no matter what or how urgent the condition. "Their" doctors lived even further away in Inverell. There was not even hot water available at the health station in the village, let alone trained personnel and a supply of drugs or equipment. Much of that gross mistreatment is now gone, and at Toomelah in particular there now exists excellent health services and facilities, but the human problem is still real in many other parts of Australia.

One of the complaints received by the Human Rights Commission was the hospital staff were uncaring and insensitive about Aboriginal patients, especially females who were pregnant or otherwise in need of obstetric or gynaecological care. It appeared that one of the major problems was a lack of understanding on the part of many Aborigines as to medical procedures. Some procedures which non-Aborigines accept and understand as being normal and necessary are not seen as such be Aborigines. This underlines the need for health professionals to be sensitive to such feelings and state of knowledge and to be forthcoming with explanations. There is a need to explain to Aboriginal patients the purpose and reason for the examinations and other procedures and to put them at their ease. If Aborigines are frightened or insulted by the white man's medicine, then the responsibility rests with the white carers to bridge that gulf with information, understanding and responsiveness to needs.

An Aboriginal Health Service and an Aboriginal Medical Co-operative[2] exist in New South Wales and do an extraordinarily good job. But they are hopelessly under-funded and under-resourced. A comprehensive and ongoing health information and education program in the schools and with the adult community is an urgent need. This should embrace everything from avoidance and treatment of heart and other serious diseases to baby and youth care and simple issues of daily personal hygiene, even down to the use of such things as hair shampoo and toothpaste.

Few Aborigines have had any professional dental treatment in their lives. Even in the bad old days of supposed state paternalism towards Aborigines, a dentist was rarely provided. Nor was training given in mouth and teeth care. Even now, progress is slow. Like in other health areas, the dental condition of Aborigines is affected by poor nutrition, environmental neglect and denial of basic services. In turn poor dental health affects wider good health, and of course job prospects and the accompanying capacity for self-esteem, advancement and determination.

It seems that what is most needed in Aboriginal health is for governments, bureaucrats and the medical community to open their minds and realise that the problems and solutions in this area are often quite different to those which commonly arise in health care provision generally. A lot more money and time is needed. Bureaucrats must be flexible and innovative in their response to Aboriginal health problems. They must be prepared to compromise, and to co-operate with other service providers, in order to combat differences of culture, the tyranny of distance and subject disorientation. They must also be prompt, recognise that the needs were urgent months and years ago, and acknowledge that action not words is now the only permissible choice.

Housing

The housing situation of many Aboriginal people is appalling. About 70% of Aboriginal families live in urban areas, in separate houses or medium density housing. Of that 70%, about 10% live in impoverished dwellings. In rural areas about 30% of all Aboriginal households occupy impoverished dwellings.

Most of the remainder of the Aboriginal population live in public dwellings. Almost 1 in 5 are inmates in prisons, correctional institutions or detention centres. Hostels for the homeless, night shelters and refuges account for about 6% of Aborigines and Islanders living in non-private dwellings. This is six times the figure for the rest of the Australian population.

The poor level of housing afforded to many Aborigines was brought into stark reality when my Inquiry first visited Toomelah. The housing situation which confronted the Inquiry was appalling. Forty houses accommodated an average of more than 12 people each, four times the State average of three persons per household. Twenty-two people or more lived in several two and three bedroom dwellings, and in one three bedroom house there were 30 people. The overcrowding problems were exacerbated by the generally poor standard of the houses. The houses built by the Aboriginal Welfare Board before 1969 were substandard and fundamentally uninhabitable, and some of the more recently built accommodation right up to 1987 had major defects, such as for example roofs with no gutters and downpipes so that when it rained, water ran inside the walls rather than outside into tanks that could have helped with the water shortage.

There were few flushing toilets, and showers or baths were only available with water collected in bottles. This situation existed at Toomelah until 3 years ago and still exists in many other places. There is still overcrowding at Toomelah brought about by an influx of people from extended families coming to escape the appalling housing they have had elsewhere. The tragedy continues.

In Boggabilla, houses erected for Aborigines were passed for habitation despite the fact that kitchen sinks did not properly drain and toilets did not empty on flushing. In one house the pipes were so negligently installed that the toilet overflow actually came back through the kitchen sink. Such houses stand beside dwellings occupied by white people which no local council would dare to approve for occupation if the same faults existed, and which all local councils do approve because the faults do not exist.

To call these houses 'jerry-built' would be a most charitable description. The local Moree Plains Shire Council has no jurisdiction over federally funded housing for Aborigines, so that new houses do not have to meet the standards, inter alia, of Ordinance 70 of the *Local Government Act*. It seems incredible that the government authorities which funded these houses did not have similar standards, but apparently they did not. Indeed the Inquiry was told that new dwellings were not checked at all before their new owners were allowed to take possession. These housing problems need to be addressed by government, for not only do they create many health problems, they prevent the happiness of Aborigines inside their own community let alone their successful integration into the general community, and tend ultimately to produce ghetto situations with all their associated problems.

Bureaucratic Indifference

Since the Inquiry first visited Toomelah, much has changed for the better, but much has not. One of the most horrifying images was that of raw sewage on the ground where children were playing. The sewerage pump broke down again last year and the stuff covered the ground. No government would give the people a spare pump, and no one would authorise the Aboriginal residents to fix it themselves.

Instead, a hepatitis epidemic broke out, children became ill, and parents could not cope, all this while the various levels of government argued about what to do. The bureaucrats' salaries, the paper, the stamps, the telephone calls, the medical treatment would have paid for twenty pumps!

And whichever government authority installed the pump chose a German model, not any of the quite suitable and available Australian varieties, so that the spare parts had to be obtained from Germany after three months delay, no doubt assisted by a visit to Germany by the appropriate bureaucrat so as to save an overseas telephone call and the cost of a spot in the cargo hold of a Lufthansa jet, and of course to avoid anything going astray in the post. Having a few spare parts on hand just for such emergencies was completely out of the question for these publicly paid "planners".

As in many Aboriginal townships, the water system set up involves bore water. At Toomelah the water is pumped from the bore into a tank 100 or more feet in the air, gravity feeding the houses. The tank sprang a leak last June, it needed a special crane to be reached and then a special jack to lift it off its base so as to get access to the leak. Or a new tank.

The local council would not lend the crane and the jack and it would not make them available for a fee until the State Government agreed to pay the cost. The State Government would not pay until the Federal Government supplied the funds. No one would supply a new tank without months of procrastination.

The rest of the story you can guess. As the months went by the unrepaired hole got bigger and bigger until a veritable torrent was pouring out so that if you were within 100 feet of the base, you were in a storm. As the tank emptied more and more, the pump in the bore overworked until it too broke down. Again no spare pump, no plumber to fix it without a guarantee of payment, no one to agree on who was to pay, and no one to train a local resident to fix it. The problem was eventually fixed, more than six months after the original small leak first appeared. Meanwhile the people did not have a safe and secure water supply for their children. This would never be tolerated for or by white people.

Although no council services are provided, no library, no swimming pool, no park or garden, no children's playground or other facilities, no street cleaning or garbage removal, nothing, the local council has the effrontery to charge them rates. Three years ago it sued the people for three years of unpaid rates despite the fact that no judgement could be enforced because by law the Aborigines do not own the freehold of their houses. The New South Wales Government had the power to waive the rates but refused to do so despite the reports from the Human Rights Commission and the Ombudsman urging it to be done.

Two years on, the federal government paid the five year old debt out of funds earmarked for Aboriginals, the final result of this mind-blowing standard of administration being that the local white population receives municipal services denied to Aborigines but paid for with Aboriginal money. And there are hundreds of Toomelahs, and worse, all over the country.

Conclusion

This is not a particularly uplifting catalogue of facts. But it is Australia in 1993. It illustrates clearly that the plight of our indigenous people in their International Year is indeed our nation's shame. The existence of such a discriminatory and unbalanced level of unemployment, ill-health, poor housing, and lack of education amongst one group in this country warrants nothing less than a judgement of appalling neglect, or worse, on the part of the rest of us. Australia prides itself on being a civilised country and, even worse, boasts of the highest standard of human rights. That must sound like a very poor joke to our indigenous brothers and sisters, and to nations and people overseas among whom we arrogantly strut telling all and sundry what they should do about the situation in their countries.

The bottom line in this unbalanced equation is not money. Around $1 billion in public funds is now spent annually on Aboriginal services and advancement for significantly less than a quarter of a million people. It has been gradually increasing in the 20 years since about $200 million was allocated in 1973. Of course funds are needed, but what is required more is the application of concern and ingenuity, and commitment to the traditional Australian concept of a "fair go", by the leadership, administration and people of our country.

Everyone in the country has by now heard of the case brought by the late Mr. Eddie Koiki Mabo. His eventually successful claim for recognition of his people's claim to be the legal titleholders of the Torres Strait Island of Mer, occupied by them for thousands of years, took 10 years to get through the court system thanks to the obstruction of the Queensland Government in the 1980s. Mr. Mabo died before he could savour the victory. Yet today some in our community are trying to make his name blacker than his skin. It is no use saying they should know better. Their insensitivity, arrogance and selfishness indicate they know nothing better, that is, nothing better than themselves and their own comforts, or perhaps their political agendas or financial interests.

Few, apparently, know what the decision in the case says, even those who have no excuse for no knowing. Many, apparently, especially those who do know, are deliberately stirring latent xenophobia by outrageously misrepresenting what the decision says and means. And they are doing so in the pretended cause of trying to help the country avoid economic and social ruin, while actually contributing immeasurably to division, confusion and fear, here and overseas. Hypocritically, they are causing what they say they want to overcome. This can only be mischievous and self seeking.

Why can white people not understand that Aboriginal attachment to land is basically spiritual, not commercial? That what they wish to do is to preserve and teach their children their heritage by reference to their history and to sacred and other sites on the land, quite similarly to the way the Jewish-Christian tradition explains the divine revelations in which they believe? Why does the white population react to any Aboriginal request for recognition of rights held by everyone else in the country defensively and ungenerously? Why would we wish to deny Aborigines and Islanders the opportunity to control and better the awful lot generations of white Australians have brought down upon them, by enabling them to access and use land as the white community has been doing for 205 years?

I have never met an Aborigine, and I suspect no one else has either, who has wanted someone else's backyard or the ground floor of David Jones. What they want is respect and security, training and education, employment and health care, and above all a future for their children. These are aspirations held, and expected of society, by everyone else in Australia and in virtually every other country in the world. Aborigines and Islanders, like everyone else, want Australia to prosper, if only so that they can do so themselves. Yet as they strive to rid themselves of the welfare mentality which everyone including the Aboriginal community itself strongly criticises, we unkindly refuse them opportunities to do so and in the process force them back into helpless dependency and still further deprivation. And some Australians including elected leaders have the temerity to try to justify this treatment on a racial basis.

The shameful public 'verballing' of the High Court for what it manifestly did not say in the *Mabo* decision is bad enough. As the Chief Justice Sir Anthony Mason has reminded everyone, Courts do not have national agendas or political goals. They decide cases and issues the parties ask them to decide. That is all that happened in this case. If the federal or state government, or the mining or any other lobby, had something to say or to warn the High Court about, all they had to do, as they well knew, was to go to the Court and ask to speak. But they chose not to do so. Their attempts to blame, even ridicule, the referee now that 'their' side has lost do not deserve a hearing.

Moreover, the failure of critics to acknowledge that Australia has long lagged behind many other countries in recognising the native title of indigenous peoples and that the High Court judgement was actually quite conservative and limited in world terms is simply irresponsible. Sensible reasoned debate has thus far escaped us.

Unquestionably the *Mabo* decision raises significant issues which should be debated and discussed. Every one of them can be solved. Yet the level of the debate must be raised beyond the sphere of self interest and short term gain. The people who hold differing views to the High Court on *Mabo* issues are of course entitled to their opinions and to express them. But it is discourteous and irrelevant to express or justify the difference in terms of personal vitriol. The personal abuse of the Justices of the High Court which has followed the Mabo decision is not only arrogant and unwarranted, it is also cowardly as the Court has absolutely no way of answering back. It will not help society or help solve Mabo issues to undermine the integrity and assault the reputation of our Judges.

Some of the responses to the Mabo decision suggest a desire by some in our country to perpetuate the wrongs of the past and stop at nothing to deprive some Australians of decency, honour and a reasonable life in order to protect the existing order of things. A thesis that whenever some of us cannot get our own way, we should pull everyone else down with us, including distinguished institutions like the High Court which has served the nation with such honour and distinction, is taking our "tall poppy" mania right over the top.

The recent particular attack on the High Court's Justice Brennan for being influenced in the writing of his judgement by his son Father Frank Brennan, over a few paternal beers it was apparently said, is difficult to distinguish from pure Goebbelsian fascism. Both Justice

Brennan and Father Frank Brennan are two of Australia's most outstanding sons. They have in quite separate but distinctive ways made greater contributions to Australia's progress, quality of life and standards of humanity and learning than any mining executive could ever hope to emulate. In any case, the supposed distortion of justice and right caused by Justice Brennan's alleged drinking practices and partners must have been contagious to his fellow Judges as, despite difference of emphasis and approach in the various judgements, five others upheld native title as well.

How can anyone affecting to be a serious participant in national discussion on a difficult subject matter indulge in such perversion of judgement, decency and taste? We should never allow ourselves to forget, as the moneyed classes and the financial and political bullies of society sometimes conveniently do, that nations ultimately prosper and progress not because of money, but by the commitment, sacrifice and achievements of their people. Totalitarian and repressive societies have long and frequently proved that people only function to the best advantage of their country if they perceive it to be fair, equitable and humane. To this cause, the Brennans have made a contribution of massive proportions. Their pointless defamation by one or two corporate nobodies and a small number of narrow-minded fellow travellers is the best example of the utter void of these people's arguments. The larrikinism of Australians was once regarded as one of our more attractive features, distinguishing us from the stuffy and conservative British. Most of us have or have had aspects of it. But larrikinism is no intellectual thuggery. If our country's interests are to be safeguarded by and vouchsafed to anyone, the Brennans of society are much the better bet.

If the idea of human existence and family life is to leave a better world and greater security to our children than we received, our generation has a big job to do in overcoming the consequences of its profligacy and self indulgence. The task is difficult enough as it is, but unless along the way we unequivocally disavow self-centredness, racism and intolerance, and the consequent disunity and division they create, we have no hope at all. It is imperative not to make things worse, and things certainly will worsen if we fail to act on the state of Aborigines and Islanders in our country today.

There are endless tiresome complaints about what the whingers call the guilt syndrome of the so-called guilt industry. We need not accept responsibility for a past in which we took no part and had no influence, though heaven knows, it is an appalling indictment of those who did - indiscriminate mass murder, even genocide, rape, exploitation, slavery, forced removal of children from their parents, gross racism and inequality, destruction of self-respect, language and culture. Far from truly being, as opposed to claiming to be, the country above all others of national decency and egalitarianism, far from truly being, as opposed to claiming to be, the people of the "fair go to everyone", Australians of the past certainly treated the indigenous people of the country abominably.

We may not be complicit in the behaviour of our forebears but our own generation is guilty of a major crime against humanity in its treatment of Aborigines and Islanders. For the fact is that at this moment Aborigines and Torres Strait Islanders have at best extremely limited access to the valued resources, facilities and services of the Australian economy. Of all existing groups within our society, they are without doubt the most conspicuously disadvantaged. By apathy and indifference at best, and positive policies of spiritual annihilation and at times intentional discrimination and exploitation at worst, we have allowed these appalling circumstances to persist right up to this very moment. We and no one else are to blame for that persistence. Some Australians are actually suggesting that it should continue endlessly into the future or prescribing approaches that will ensure it does. Whatever has been done in the past, history will hold us accountable for what we do or fail to do now. It is time things changed.

Endnotes
1. In June 1988 the Human Rights and Equal Opportunities Commission, when Justice Einfeld was president, reported to the community on an inquiry into the social and material needs of the Aboriginal communities in these areas.
2. Justice Einfeld is patron of the Aboriginal Medical Co-operative.

Chapter Eleven
THE IMPLICATIONS OF THE MABO CASE FOR INDIGENOUS PEOPLE

by

M.A. Stephenson

In *Mabo v. Queensland*[1] the High Court of Australia ruled that native title is recognised by the common law, and that indigenous inhabitants do have rights to their traditional lands. This was the first time the High Court had the opportunity to consider the question of recognition of native title rights and for the first time since white settlement judicial recognition was given to the rights of indigenous people with regard to land. This decision has revolutionised the notion of land ownership in Australia.

In examining the implications of the *Mabo* case for indigenous people it will be useful to consider first, the history of the action, secondly, the facts and the actual decision in the case and, thirdly the main elements in the decision and how a claim for native title can be made.

History of the Mabo Action

The *Mabo* case has had a long history. In May 1982, Eddie Mabo and four other Murray Islanders, who were members of the Meriam People, instituted legal proceedings in the original jurisdiction of the High Court, claiming rights to their traditional lands. Their traditional lands were the Murray Islands, in the Torres Strait, which consisted of three islands, Mer, Dauar and Waier, having a total area of 9 square kilometres. The claim was originally made on the plaintiffs' own behalf and on behalf of their family groups according to their traditional native title, their actual possession, use and enjoyment of their lands and according to their customs. The statement of claim was amended during the trial to seek declarations relating to the communal title of the Meriam people.

It was claimed that those rights survived the acquisition of sovereignty by the Crown at the time of annexation to the Queensland colony in 1879. In the statement of claim it was accepted that the Crown had sovereignty over the Islands. Thus, no issue of sovereignty arose in this case.

The *Mabo* case was remitted by the High Court to the Supreme Court of Queensland in 1986 for a determination of the issues of fact. This hearing was suspended while the High Court heard a demurrer on the question of the validity of the *Queensland Coast Islands Declaratory Act 1985*. This legislation was enacted with the objective not only of removing any doubt about the annexation of the Murray Islands to Queensland but also to retrospectively extinguish all rights and interest that the Murray Islanders might have owned and enjoyed, without the payment of compensation. The High Court in a 4:3 decision in *Mabo v. Queensland*[2] declared that the Queensland Act was invalid. The High Court found that the Act was inconsistent with section 10(1) of the *Racial Discrimination Act* 1975 (Cth). Because the Act was inconsistent with a Commonwealth law it followed that the Act was invalid by reason of section 109 of the *Australian Constitution*.

The majority noted that the right that is referred to in section 10(1) of the *Racial Discrimination Act* was a human right, not necessarily a legal right, to own and inherit property and this right was referred to in the *International Convention on Elimination of All Forms of Racial*

Discrimination (Article 5). The Court also noted that the *Universal Declaration of Human Rights 1948* (Article 17) recognised the right not to be arbitrarily deprived of that property. The Court thus found that the inconsistency with the *Racial Discrimination Act* arose because the Queensland Act of 1985, by arbitrarily depriving the Murray Islanders of their rights, limited the Meriam people's enjoyment of the human right to own and inherit property. The Court found that the Queensland legislation extinguished the traditional legal rights as claimed by the plaintiffs, while it confirmed the existence of other owners' legal rights granted under Crown Lands legislation.

The Facts in Mabo (No. 2)

The Meriam people, who were originally Melanesian, had been in continuous occupation of the islands from the time before European contact. They lived in groups of huts and houses that were organised into villages. Life was communal and based on group membership. They were primarily gardeners. The garden land was located in the central portion of the Islands. Garden land was identifiable by reference to a named locality and also by reference to the name of the relevant individual or family. Land was never held under a communal title, but was owned by individuals or family groups. The boundaries of the land were in reference to known land marks such as specific trees or mounds of rocks. The land was passed down from father to son for generations and a recognised system of inheritance was shown. There was no permanent immigration population on the Islands and therefore there was no question of other groups challenging the Murray Islanders' sole occupancy. The Meriam people were not nomads living by hunting and gathering of naturally occurring food. In this respect their society differed from that of mainland Australian indigenous inhabitants. Thus it was possible to show a very close and continuous connection between the Islanders and their lands.

The Decision

The High Court, ruled in a 6:1 decision that the common law of Australia recognised a form of native title, being the rights of the indigenous inhabitants in accordance with their laws and customs to their traditional land. Meriam people were entitled to the occupation, use and enjoyment of the lands of the Murray Islands (except for the operation of Crown leases and some land set aside for administrative purposes).

The title of the Meriam people was stated to be subject to the Queensland Government's rights to validly extinguish that title. Any such action would to be subject to the *Racial Discrimination Act 1975* (Cth).

The High Court indicated that the general principles in *Mabo* are applicable to mainland Australia. However, the circumstances of the Murray Islanders will differ from many mainland Aboriginals and native title may not be as easy to prove in the mainland.

The Court found that Australia was not *terra nullius* or unoccupied in 1788, native title survived the acquisition of sovereignty by the British in Australia. Furthermore, native title was recognised by the common law and that the Crown was not the owner of all land as previously thought. On the acquisition of sovereignty the Crown acquired a radical title which is a bare title and not complete ownership of land.

Potentially Claimable Land

What Land Can Be Claimed?

Land that is owned by the Crown may be subject to claims for native title. Thus vacant Crown land is potentially claimable and Crown land, where the Crown has granted an interest in the land that is consistent with native title, may also be claimed. Native title will exist concurrently with the interest granted.

National parks were specifically mentioned by the High Court in *Mabo* as being consistent with native title and claimable. However, the lighting of fires, the hunting of native animals and fishing are usually prohibited in national parks. These rights are often the basis of native title. This is a matter that will require resolution. It is also not entirely clear here whether claims may be made to forestry land or defence land.

What Land Cannot Be Claimed?

Land already granted in freehold, ie. a fee simple, cannot be claimed. Thus no claims could be made to settled rural or urban areas. Land leased from the Crown, for example, pastoral leases, cannot be claimed in Queensland under *Mabo*. This is, however, subject to the *Racial Discrimination Act (Cth) 1975* as discussed below.

Pastoral leases have been the subject of speculation in the area of claimable property. The High Court did not have to address the issue of pastoral leases in the judgement. However, both Brennan, Deane and Gaudron JJ. did comment regarding leases generally. Deane and Gaudron JJ. found that a lease conferring exclusive possession would extinguish native title. Brennan J found that the tenant acquires exclusive possession and the Crown acquires the reversion on termination of the lease. The effect of this is at the end of the lease period the Crown's title becomes absolute ownership, as opposed to a radical title.

Thus, if a pastoral lease was granted, native title would be extinguished. However, rights of native title may continue if, for example, the lease reserved to Aboriginal inhabitants their traditional rights in relation to the land, such as rights of access to enable Aboriginal people to procure birds, fish and other foods. It is also arguable that the lease itself, being a grant of exclusive possession, would extinguish native title. Therefore the rights reserved would owe their existence to either the lease document or the relevant legislation which protected such rights. The issue is where do those protective rights derive? Do the rights derive from the lease or legislation, or are they sourced in native title itself?

Brennan J found that the grant of a sardine factory lease over two of the Murray Islands would have extinguished native title, even though the lease contained a special condition that provided that the tenant was not to obstruct or interfere with the use by the Murray Island natives of their tribal gardens and plantations on the leased land. There appears to be no protective or reservation clauses dealing with native title and pastoral leases in Queensland, nor are such clauses contained in the *Land Act 1962* (Qld). Therefore, in Queensland, pastoral leases would extinguish native title. The position may be different in other states such as Western Australia, South Australia and the Northern Territory, where reservations clauses still exist.

Effect of the Racial Discrimination Act

Grants of fee simple or leasehold made before 1975 when the Commonwealth *Racial Discrimination Act* was enacted are immune from claim under *Mabo*. However, the situation may be different for title to privately owned land and for Crown leases granted after the *Racial Discrimination Act 1975 (Cth)*. This has yet to be tested.

The principle behind the *Racial Discrimination Act* is that

Aboriginal people should not be treated less favourably than other people. Sections 9 and 10 of that Act provide in effect, that if Aboriginal people are deprived of certain rights, by discriminatory laws, then those rights are not lost. The question here is what right is being denied to Aboriginal title holders because of discriminatory laws. The right being denied is the right not to be arbitrarily deprived of property. This could mean that a right to the land itself will continue to exist, in which case title granted, including freehold title, since 1975 could be invalid. It could also mean that the right that is denied is a right to compensation, in which case titles granted would be valid but subject to a payment of compensation by the Crown. Under State legislation such as the *Acquisition of Land Act 1975 (Qld)* the holder of an interest in land acquired by the Government is entitled to compensation for loss of that interest in land. Therefore, if native title can be proved, titles granted since 1975 will be subject to either a claim for native title or a claim for compensation from State Governments.

Extinguishment of Native Title

Land cannot be claimed by Aboriginal people if native title has been extinguished. Once native title is extinguished it cannot be revived for contemporary recognition.[3]

Native title can be extinguished by Government action. All judges in the *Mabo* case agreed that native title could be extinguished by legislation that showed a clear and plain intention to extinguish native title.[4] Brennan J., with whom Mason C.J. and McHugh J. agreed, found that native title could also be extinguished by executive action, and in Queensland that could be action by the Governor-in-Council under the *Land Act 1962*.[5] An example of executive action in Queensland would include action by the Governor-in-Council under the *Land Act 1962 (Qld)* (Crown leasehold provisions) for reservations of land and alienations.

Therefore native title will be extinguished as follows:

1. By grants of freehold title, that is, privately owned land;

2. By grants of leases, as leases are a grant of exclusive possession; and

3. By grants of interests in land that are inconsistent with native title.

The majority of the Court in *Mabo* agreed that if the Crown grants an interest pursuant to a statutory authority which is inconsistent with native title then native title will be extinguished to the extent of the inconsistency.[6] Native title may not continue where the Crown has appropriated land to itself and where land is dedicated or reserved or set aside for roads, railways, post offices or other permanent works.

It must be remembered that in the third case (above), native title is a bundle of rights. It may be that not all rights of native title are lost, only some. Here the facts of each case will need to be examined.

Action by the native title holders may also extinguish native title. Native title can be surrendered to the Crown voluntarily.[7] Native title will be lost if the native title holders cease to acknowledge their laws and customs, or have lost their connection with the land.[8] Native title would also be extinguished on the death of the last member of the group or clan.[9]

Can Native Title be Extinguished Without Compensation?

The High Court was divided on this issue. Although notional majority in the *Mabo* case found that no compensation was payable, it is arguable that the extinguishment of native title would be subject to payments after 1975. The reason for this is that the legislation which extinguished native title could infringe the *Racial Discrimination Act 1975 (Cth)*. No compensation will be payable in relation to native title extinguished before 1975, but extinguishment of native title after 1975 will be subject to the *Racial Discrimination Act*.

Also noteworthy in the context of whether compensation must be paid when native title is extinguished is the judgement of Toohey J.[10] who considered that Governments were in the position of a trustee in relation to native title holders. His honour considered that compensation might be payable for breach of this duty of trust, if, for example the Government sold the land without the native title holders' consent. However, Toohey J. was in the minority on this point and such arguments for compensation may not be successful.

The question of compensation raises the important issue of how native title is to be valued. If native title is not the equivalent of a fee simple, if it is more akin to a right to use the land,[11] then the value must be assessed accordingly.

Proof of Native Title

There are four elements necessary to prove native title, firstly, a traditional connection with or occupation of the land must be shown.[12] It is not entirely clear from the decision, exactly what connection with the land is required. Certainly physical occupation will be sufficient. But what connection less than physical occupation will be enough? A spiritual relationship alone would probably not suffice. Likewise it appears that it would not be sufficient to show that the group had an historical connection with the land. In the *Mabo* case, there were no difficulties in showing that the Murray Islanders had a *close connection* with the *land on a continuing basis*. The Meriam people lived on the land, and cultivated gardens on their land. It is arguable that "visits" to traditional land over a number of years, may be sufficient maintenance of the traditional connection. This is yet to be tested

Secondly, there must be a substantial maintenance of that connection. The High Court has not specified a time period during which the connection needs to be maintained. One would expect that the native title holder's connection with the land would have had to have been in existence in 1788. After all it is unlikely that a burden on the Crown's radical title could develop where no title existed in 1788. Certainly the implication is that recent occupation or modern user will not qualify. Therefore clans could not occupy the land now for the first time and claim a "connection with the land".

Thirdly, the traditional connection must be maintained under the laws and customs of the community. The High Court has accepted that laws and customs can be those as currently observed. If all real acknowledgment of traditional law and any real observance of traditional customs have ceased then native title would also cease because the traditional connection with the land would be lost.

Finally, there must be in existence an identifiable group or community. Native title can be held only by indigenous inhabitants and their biological descendants.

The Concept of Native Title

Rights

The content of native title is to be found in the traditional customs and practices of the native community.[13] These customs and practices will determine the extent of the rights relating to the use of the land and its resources.

The main issue with regard to the content of native title is whether native title is restricted to traditional laws and customs as at the time of the Crown's acquisition of sovereignty or whether native title includes not only past uses but also present and future uses of the land. The answer is not entirely clear from *Mabo*. The High Court has accepted that traditional laws and customs can be those as currently acknowledged and observed. It is implicit in the judgement that the laws and customs may have undergone changes over the years, yet may still be accepted as traditional ways. Thus the content of native title will not be frozen in time, as at the moment of settlement. However the issue is how much change is permissible before the laws are no longer classified as traditional laws and customs. It is accepted that customs are not immutable. It is in the nature of customs that they change to adapt to new circumstances. The thrust of the High Court decision in *Mabo* suggests that the content of native title should adapt to change. Therefore it is arguable that commercial development of traditional lands, held under native title should be permissible in Australia.

The actual content of native title is not clear and will depend upon the customs and practices of the claimants in each case. Native title will in most cases, include basic rights to use the land for traditional forms of sustenance, for example, hunting and fishing and food gathering. But what further rights will it comprise? Does native title include the minerals and petroleum in the soil, the timber on the land, the rights to the air space and rights to the fish in the seas? It is unclear from *Mabo* whether native title includes such rights. It is arguable that indigenous rights to traditional land would include rights to the areas of land that are not utilised, for example, the subsurface and minerals, and that rights to land should include all rights to land. It is also arguable that if the traditional rights to land did not include minerals and the utilisation of subsurface areas, then the rights of native title holders today would not necessarily include minerals. The question would be similar for other aspects of ownership.

Communal Title

Aboriginal native title is communal and the rights under it are communal rights enjoyed by the whole clan.[14] Individual rights to land will exist provided they are consistent with, and recognised by, the traditional laws and customs.

Transferability of Title

Native title is usually not transferable; it cannot be sold or leased. The question of its transferability depends on the laws from which it is derived, and those laws have traditionally forbidden transfer of title.[15] Thus, native title cannot be transferred to people outside the traditional group unless the pre-existing laws and customs of the tribe permit this. Could it be argued that alienation outside the clan could become part of the culture and customs? The problem of assignment to a third unrelated party is that it would be difficult to show that a group's traditional connection with the land has been maintained. If the traditional connection is lost then native title would be lost.

Status of Native Title

Type of Interest Created

The High Court indicated that the rights conferred by native title did not constitute an interest in the land and the rights of native title are personal or rights of user of the land only.[16] These are called *usufructuary* rights. However, the Court did recognise that these rights constitute legal rights. Apart from Toohey J., none of the judges in the High Court was prepared to recognise native title as a "fee simple".[17]

Brennan J noted that a community, which asserts and asserts

effectively that none but its members have a right to occupy or use land, has an interest in land that must be of a proprietary nature as there is no other proprietor.[18] This requires exclusive possession and not all Aboriginal communities would satisfy this test. Brennan J indicated that the fact that individual members of the community enjoy only usufructuary rights that are non-proprietary, would not prevent the recognition of a traditional proprietary title.[19] These views are difficult to reconcile. If the community title is proprietary then it would be expected that an interest in land is conferred.

Native title cannot be easily categorised. The best approach is to note that it is outside our known system of land law. It is *sui generis* (i.e., the only one of its kind or peculiar to itself.) It appears to be a usufructuary right with some of the characteristics of the proprietary title.

The Enforcement and Protection of Native Title

Native title is recognised by the common law as a legal right and can be protected by legal or equitable remedies that are appropriate to the particular rights and interest held.[20] Protection of native title would be available for the infringement of rights, for example, to prevent trespass to land provided that the native title holders had exclusive possession of the land. However, the protection of native title by such remedies would not be available to prevent the valid extinguishment of the interest by the Crown.

Conclusion

The High Court has provided basic guidelines to deal with native title. These are:

- that native title could not be claimed against freehold land;
- the elements necessary to prove native title; and

- the methods by which native title can be extinguished.

The following issues remain open:

1   The effect of the *Racial Discrimination Act (Cth)* and whether native title survives grants of interest in land made after 1975 or whether rights are commuted to rights of compensation and if so how these compensation rights are to be assessed.

2   Whether mineral resources legislation effectively appropriates minerals to the Crown and whether mining leases and licences extinguish native title.

3   Whether leases with reservation of rights in favour of Aboriginal communities extinguish native title.

4   Whether the Aboriginal community's customary rules would allow transferability of title or whether the commercial development of traditional lands would be permitted.

5   The precise content and nature of Aboriginal title.

6   The nature of the traditional connection which needs to be proved.

In conclusion, Brennan J. found that the recognition of native title can be incorporated into our system of land holding without fracturing the skeleton of legal principle.

The High Court in *Mabo* has provided a new dimension to our legal system for land holding: a scheme which responds to current notions of justice and equality in Australia. It is appropriate then that the issues raised by the *Mabo* case should be resolved in accordance with these notions of justice and equality.

Endnotes

1.   (1992) 66 A.L.J.R. 408.

2.   Ibid., at 33.

3. Ibid., at 430
4. Ibid., at 431 - 432.
5. Ibid., at 452.
6. Ibid., at 434 - 436.
7. Ibid., at 435
8. Ibid., at 435
9. Ibid.
10. Ibid., 491 - 495.
11. For example, a right to take game from the land.
12. *Mabo*, op. cit at 430.
13. Ibid., at 429.
14. *Mabo*, at 452.
15. Ibid., at 430.
16. Ibid., at 452.
17. Under the Torrens System a fee simple is tantamount to absolute ownership.
18. *Mabo*, at 426.
19. Ibid., at 426.
20. Ibid., at 433, 452.

PART 3:
INDIGENOUS
CULTURE
AND
SOCIETY

Chapter Twelve

UNITY IN DIVERSITY, A VISION IN FILM

By

June Perkins

This paper discusses how the indigenous people of Australia, especially women, have been represented in film. It will cover early representations of Aborigines in film and reveal highlights of the history of Aboriginal women in film and look at how principles of the Bahá'í Faith might apply to forging new representations. It seeks to achieve these aims in four ways, firstly, by outlining those films, secondly by looking at what they were trying to say when they came out. Thirdly by looking at what they, with hindsight, say now. And fourthly, by looking at the significance of those films in the history of representation of Aboriginal women and men.[1] Current scholarly debates indicate that there is a discourse of Aboriginalism:

> Europeans have forged a collective identity through a discourse that sets them apart from non-Europeans, especially the "Aborigines." In particular, many European Australians have constructed Aborigines as the primordial or primitive other, a paradigm of originality and antiquity. In this representational discourse, Aborigines figure as "savages" or as "an ancient people living in an ancient land" or as "stone age people.
>
> Aborigines and Aboriginality' in this discourse come to represent a place, which Europeans have left behind in order to assume "civilisation" or enter into modernity, whereby Aborigines stand for the past, for our origins or beginnings, the childhood of humankind.[2]

Current discussions of the discourse of "Aboriginalism" centre on the appropriation of Aboriginal Australia, an example of such an appropriation being boomerangs becoming national icons. Current theorists of Aboriginalism believe that if we look closely at the historical background of how this discourse was produced and reflected in screen (cinema, video and television) representations of Aborigines, we will find that "these representations of the other (the other in this case being the Aborigine) were inseparable from the colonists' exercise of power."[3] It is interesting to see that past prejudices which have shaped the present in representation are now being acknowledged openly, a recent example of this was the production of a whole journal dedicated to deconstructing the discourse consisting of prejudices and stereotypes about the indigenous people of Australia.

A film's most powerful element is its visuals. It has sometimes been said that a good film cannot be understood without its pictures. We all have eyes with which to see images but what our eyes see is shaped by our life's history, our cultural upbringing, and perhaps our religious experience; thus many spectators will see a film differently. We all have different tastes, prejudices and biases that unbeknown to us are sometimes shaping these tastes. Often we cannot control images put before us. These images are being shaped by the views and life history of filmmakers (director, producers, writers, camera person) and co-workers (actors) which in turn are shaped by the people who fund these films. The best way for us to question our eyes and how they have perceived indigenous people of Australia is to think critically about the images put before us and how we see them. Shoghi Effendi, (the Guardian of the Bahá'í Faith, Grandson of 'Abdu'l-Bahá who was the son of Bahá'u'lláh), said:

> If we allow prejudice of any kind to manifest itself in us, we shall be guilty before God of causing a setback to the progress and real

growth of the Faith of Bahá'u'lláh. It is incumbent upon every believer to endeavour with a fierce determination to eliminate this defect from his thoughts and acts... The fundamental purpose of the Faith of Bahá'u'lláh is the realisation of the organic unity of the entire human race."[4]

It would seem that what we see on the screen, applying these words, needs to be shaped by a belief in the "organic unity" of the human race. This means actively and critically reflecting on why we see the world the way we do.

Early Representations

The first film made in Australia was the 1896 Melbourne Cup. Other early Australian films were those made by the Salvation Army, one was titled, Soldiers of the Cross.[5] Perhaps the earliest film with an Aboriginal actor in it playing the part of an Aborigine was *The Birth of White Australia* (1911). It was a film that portrayed Australian history as that of white Australia. The Aboriginal character in the film is portrayed as comical, whereas the Asian characters are made to appear threatening. Such ideas as the following were being written in history books at that time:

> When people talk about 'the history of Australia' they mean the history of the white people who have lived in Australia. There is a good reason why we should not stretch the term to make it include the history of the dark-skinned wandering tribes who hurled boomerangs and ate snakes in their native land for long ages before the arrival of the first intruders from Europe... for they have nothing that can be called history.[6]

The indigenous people of Australia were often portrayed as the faithful companion bushrangers, in a series of films now known as the Bushranging Genre (spanning 1900-1912). Examples of these films in which Aboriginal characters appeared were *Robbery Under Arms* (1907), *Dan Morgan* (1911), *The Assigned Servant* (1911) and *Assigned to His Wife* (1911). The aboriginal parts in these movies were played by non-Aboriginal actors in blackface.

Another way in which the indigenous people of Australia were represented in early Australian films was in corroborees. This was to authenticate the film as Australian. However this was often done disrespectfully and in such as way that the sacred appeared as a novelty. This disrespect manifested itself in some corroborees being performed by actors in black face or being made to resemble ballet. In the bicentennial year 1988, Maureen Watson, an Aboriginal story teller, commenting on the sacred said:

> I think if you ask yourself what is human, what is the meaning of human being or perhaps humane being, and how do white people treat the sacred places and places of worship and the things that are important to white people from other countries, if any human beings have any sort of sensitivity... then not only they themselves are going to respect our arts and crafts their... children.... grandchildren... will too.[7]

The Bahá'í Faith possesses a view that some things are too sacred to be portrayed on the screen; they are not in the domain of the camera to possess. In the Bahá'í Faith the three central figures (The Báb - forerunner of Bahá'u'lláh -, Bahá'u'lláh, and 'Abdu'l-Bahá) cannot be portrayed, their words can be used but no figure can be used to represent them.[8] The spiritual is not to be possessed and displayed for material gain. This is similar to Aboriginal attitudes toward the display of their sacred ceremonies, dances and sacred sites.

Other indigenous people who feature in Early Australian film history were New Zealand Maoris in *A Moari Maid's Love* (made in Australia) and in *Mutiny on the Bounty*, but strangely New Zealand Maoris played Tahitians in Mutiny on the Bounty, and a European woman played the major role of a part-Maori woman in *A Moari Maid's Love*, which could have been played by a New Zealand Maori.

A European woman was represented as a Jungle Woman in *A Jungle Woman* (Frank Hurley, 1926), an adventure "documentary" which was really more the fantasies of its filmmaker. Many of these documentaries were adventures of pure fantasy that revealed their tone in their titles, for example, *Uncivilised* and *Pearls and Savages* (Frank Hurley). These films seemed to serve no social comment or purpose other than "fantasy".

Early ethnographic films and documentary films are dominated by representations of Aboriginal male ceremonies because European men were the dominant filmmakers. In early photographs of male filmmakers with their "subjects" one photograph sums up the attitude of the filmmaker's superiority to their subject: "Picture Charles Chauvel standing on a rock to look taller than his "subjects" as he (Chauvel) was a short man. Perhaps we should ask ourselves why he would want to look taller than his subjects?

Looking back at these early Australian films we see:

a. Aborigines are background figures and even when in major supporting roles these roles are rarely played by Aborigines;

b. there is a marked absence of Aboriginal women and their ceremonies; and

c. many of the early films used Aboriginality within their films to further overseas sales.

In conclusion, Aborigines were "subjects" or "objects" in early Australian film. As they had no access to making these films themselves, they were unable to enter the realm of film-makers. It was to take many years for this situation to be rectified.

Jedda (Charles Chauvel 1955)

Jedda was the first Australian film with starring roles for an

Aboriginal woman and man. It is also significant in Australian film history as it was the first colour feature film made in Australia, the first film to have an Aboriginal cast central to the story and one of the first Australian films to make it to the Cannes Film Festival. It had female involvement in its making care of Elsa Chauvel, Charles Chauvel's wife. Her involvement made it possible for the Aboriginal actress to take part, as she could chaperone this actress.

When the film was released it was the mid 1950s, the time of Happy Days Music and clothes. Aborigines were still not considered to be Australian citizens. Many continued to live on missions and reserves. The 1950s was a period in which "assimilation" was becoming the catchcry of policies concerning Aborigines. The Aboriginal child with partly "European blood" was in particular considered redeemable. Many children were taken from their parents during this period, in a sorry continuation of what had been done in the past.

Jedda was a significant step forward in the representation of the indigenous people of Australia as it dealt with the theme of romance and acknowledged the common humanity of Aborigines with their fellow Australians. But despite this appearance of a full feature film with Aboriginal actors in it, the audience were mostly white and those Aborigines brave enough to come into the cinema were subjected to "apartheid" and had to sit downstairs. Robert Tudawali, one of the stars of *Jedda*, was given the special privilege of being allowed to sit with the non-Aboriginal filmmakers, but chose to sit with his wife downstairs when he went to see it.

Jedda was described as follows in a review:

> Jedda the Uncivilised. An unusual documentary-type drama about the aboriginal territory of Northern Australia, this is offbeat fare best suited to art houses. Music is in the weird native tradition.[9]

In Jedda a white woman adopts a part aboriginal girl (Jedda) as her own, the girl is then attracted to a tribal aboriginal (Marbuk) who kidnaps her, they are chased by both the white people and the tribal elders. She has a part Aboriginal boyfriend who loses her to Marbuk.

In visuals of the film we see Jedda up against the rock, after she has left "civilisation". She is semi clad. In other scenes in the film the white mother is weeping, and Marbuk is doing aboriginal things such as making spears and listening to the didgeridoo. There is a dramatic final scene in which Jedda and Marbuk end up at the bottom of a cliff. Perhaps implying that by going back to her Aboriginality Jedda has chosen to end up there, although this is balanced by the fact that Marbuk has ended up there because he defied the elders.

In an exotic pose from the film, featured on a poster advertising the film, Marbuk carries Jedda. The picture reminds one of a caveman with his wench. Other film posters described the film as an adventure which shows the wilds of Australia (by implication its wild people also). Others have suggestive descriptive titles like Jedda, Eve in Ebony.

Jedda was an exotic love story with tragic proportions. It was like an Aboriginal version of *Romeo and Juliet*. However, the film's message (one possible reading) that "assimilation" is necessary for Aboriginal people to survive is out of date and gives the film a patronising tone. It did nothing to change the trend of marketing the "wilds" of Australia for an overseas audience. This was a trend that earlier filmmakers had set, and it stressed in its advertising that it was a story about the "uncivilised". It did little to review and change the accepted role of women for Jedda the "Eve in Ebony" is seen to cause the fall of Marbuk (Adam).

The film's assimilative attitude is now seen as prejudiced in an insidiously patronising way. It is now seen by many as a film that reflects poorly a history in which people of part-Aboriginal parentage have suffered greatly: this is a story that gives no foreground in its plot. Shoghi Effendi, although writing specifically on blacks and whites in America, is applicable here as he deals with the attitude of patronisation:

> Let the white make a supreme effort to contribute their share to the solution of this problem, to abandon once and for all their usually inherent and at time subconscious sense of superiority, to correct their tendency towards revealing a patronising attitude towards the members of the other race, to persuade them through their intimate, spontaneous and informal association with them of the genuiness of their friendship and the sincerity of their intentions, and to master their impatience of any lack of responsiveness on the part of a people who have received, for so long a period, such grievous and slow healing wounds.[10]

Eliminating patronisation in the tone of films about Aborigines might be one way to heal the wounds of the past.

The Film Revival and Aborigines

At the close of the 1950s there was a general demise in the local film industry. Some Australian television shows had regular Aboriginal characters and television was on its way to becoming a popular medium. In the 1970s a film revival began, this was helped by Government investment and subsidy. In the beginning of this revival the commercial feature film industry avoided Aborigines being placed in major roles as they were seen to be, as Pike would put it, "politically delicate" subjects.[11] Producers of independent 16mm films were more willing to give Aborigines major roles and deal with their social and political issues.

The 1970s was the time of Skyhooks, platform shoes, and Gough Whitlam. Cinema audiences were less likely to be just Anglo-Celtic so perhaps this is why Aborigines appeared in many films such as

Walkabout, a story about a young aboriginal boy's unrequited love for a white girl; *The Last Wave*, in which aboriginal myth and legend are incorporated into a suburban mystery of the supernatural; *Storm Boy*, a story of a young boy who loves pelicans and a film in which Aborigines are associated with ecology and *The Chant of Jimmy Blacksmith*, which is based on Thomas Kenneally's novel of the same name.

In the 1970s the parts for Aboriginal males widened, as an Aboriginal you could be an actor, but still in many cases Aborigines were presented as a part of nature or a victim. There were also only a few major stars, such as David Gulpilil, who got most of the major roles. Aborigines were more and more in the cinema audience. They could now vote, having had citizenship as of 1967 via a referendum.

In the 1970s, and early 1980s documentaries featuring Aboriginal woman began to appear. Women, according to Jennings, in traditional Aboriginal society had been rendered "invisible" by male historians and anthropologists located within a male "dominated profession constituted" by a "patriarchal society".[12] The importance of Aboriginal women in their traditional societies, their ceremonies and function and the way in which they perceive their relation with their men is more fully understood through the work of various (mostly female) anthropologists, such as Dianne Bell.[13] Black female activism has been paralleled by the emergence of the feminist movement, and with the development of sustained and prolific feminist film making activity.[14] In the late 1970s, there was the adopting of a broader perspective by white feminist film makers. Examples of documentaries that were made:

Bread and Dripping (1981) on the lives of four women during the depression includes the reminiscences of an Aboriginal woman.

Sister if Only You Knew (1975)

My Survival as an Aboriginal (1979)

Two Laws (1981)

During the 1980s Aboriginal involvement in filmmaking was beginning to extend into the areas of writing and production, but this was mostly in non-fictional film forms.

Fictional Film in the Feminist Genre

Another film representing an Aboriginal woman during this era was *Journey Among Women* (Tom Cowan, 1977), a fictional film in the feminist genre.

Journey Among Women was one of the few feature films of the 1970s to have a part for an Aboriginal woman. It possessed an Aboriginal character, the symbolic Kameragul who is the guiding spirit to help the women survive in the bush. The film presupposed racial equality and that the original inhabitants of the land are teachers of the new comers.

It is an eighteenth century story of a group of women convicts who escape with the daughter of a judge of the colony and experience freedom (as well as male oppression, especially violence and rape from the soldiers).

At the time it came was released it was seen as contributing to a cinema information about the role and status of women. Many of the people involved in the filming were outspoken feminists or involved in the women's movement. When the film came out it reflected a feminist agenda by telling the history of Australia from a woman's point of view. It had an amazonic attitude, that women can create a just society and survive without men. The film reflected a radical feminism, yet ironically the director of this ground breaking film was a man.

Looking back on this era and the Australian films that were made with Aboriginal characters we see:

a.   A growing political and social awareness of the Aboriginal people from Europeans and other non-indigenous peoples;

b.   The documentary form being used as self expression by Aboriginal people;

c.   The effect of the Women's rights movement and its role in bringing Aboriginal women into film (non fiction and fiction);

d.   Aboriginal men still dominating as subjects in fictional forms that are being presented; and

e.   Aborigines are still not very involved in writing and directing Aboriginal Drama.

In the 1980s Australia recognised the need for more equality. Land rights for Aboriginal people was beginning to become an issue, the environmental movement was developing, and multiculturalism[15] was becoming the catchcry of government policies.

Other significant events during the 1980s were the creation of SBS television and video going into remote areas in the outback and video casette recorders becoming more affordable.

Manganinnie (1980, John Honey)

In the 1980s many films began to portray Aboriginal woman in more foregrounded roles, one example of this was *Manganinnie*.

Manganinnie gave to the cinema perhaps the first major starring role for an Aboriginal actress, since 1955. It was a positive contribution to combating prejudice in that Manganinnie was shown to be a worthy mother and guide to the white child, Joanna. Peter Malone outlines the story of *Manganinnie* as one of:

...a lone Aboriginal woman separated from her tribe during the Black drive in Tasmania in the 1830s. In her search for her people Manganinnie finds Joanna, a settler's child whom she adopts to her tribe. Joanna learns to survive in the hostile bush and is initiated into the mysteries of the Dreamtime...

As Manganinnie and six year old Joanna are lost in the bush and journey together, bonds, kinship between women and girl are strongly formed...

Joanna sheds her clothes and dresses like Manganinnie, she communicates with Manganinnie as she is sensitive to her feelings of joy and sorrow. They share myths of the moon and when Manganinnie loses the fire Joanna makes fire from flint. She frees Manganinnie from the convicts but it is too late. Out of respect for Aboriginal rites Manganinnie's body is cremated.[16]

Manganinnie is narrated through the eyes of the grown up Joanna. It is loosely based on a novel written by non-aboriginal Beth Roberts. It is a very visual film. Its use of imagery is reinforced by the almost complete lack of dialogue (other than the voice of Joanna and the sequences in which Joanna is back with her family). It uses the music of Peter Sculthorpe extensively. For Virginia Duigan, a reviewer of the film, *Manganinnie* has "the quality of a fairy tale". It is lyrical and emotive. Duigan writes, "it is the kind of gentle film that influences attitudes and combats prejudice. It would be encouraging to see it made required viewing in schools throughout Australia"[17].

Manganinnie (the character) was seen by some critics of the film to represent Truganinie, the defeated Aborigine. Joanna, a child with a family, represented the future and a continuation of the dreamtime. Some Tasmanian Aborigines felt that the film, rather than deconstructing misunderstanding between indigenous peoples and others, increased it by keeping alive the myth that Tasmanian Aborigines were wiped out. Although this argument has validity, it does not completely eliminate the film's lyrical beauty and or its effect of encouraging children to be free from prejudice.

Women of the Sun (writers Hyllus Maris and Sonia Borg, 1982)

The television series *Women of the Sun* is included in this discussion of film because it had Aborigines moving into roles other than acting, for example, Hyllus Maris, one of the co-writers of *Women of the Sun*, was Aboriginal. One of *Women of the Sun's* most important contributions to the history of representation of Aboriginal women is that it was co-written by an Aboriginal woman and a European woman. Thus, "Unity in Diversity" was demonstrated in the writing of a script, in that two women of different cultural backgrounds combined their talents to produce a script about the effects of racism on women.

Women of the Sun is significant in the history of the representation of Aborigines in films, because it was the first major television series to have Aborigines in starring roles. It was one of the first fictional representations of Aborigines to use native language with subtitles and one of the first representations in which the emergence of the Aborigine, who survives and triumphs, was apparent. It was ground breaking because not all its characters end up at the bottom of cliffs or in the funeral pyre. Indeed, it presents heroes and heroines for Aboriginal and non-aboriginal people to admire. *Women of the Sun* won AWGIE awards for original television writing, and the United Nations Association of Australia Media Peace Prize. This is testimony to the fact that this series combined art and social purpose.

Women of the Sun consists of four episodes *Alinta, Maydina, Nerida, Lo-arna* (1982).

Alinta, set in 1824 to 1834, is the story of an Aboriginal girl, Alinta, growing from puberty to adulthood. Her tribe accepts and takes in two escaped convicts, much to the chagrin of the female elder who foresees doom. One of the convicts commits rape and is put to death for his crime. The other becomes part of the tribe and good friends with Alinta's husband to be, but this convict then betrays them to the Europeans when he is offered land and a pardon. Alinta's tribe is massacred and she is left alone with her child.

Maydina set in 1890s, in South East Australia, is the story of Maydina and her daughter, Birri. They begin the film as virtual slaves to a group of sealers and then escape and meet an old Prospector, who after Maydina's refusal to be his defacto wife, takes Maydina to a mission run by Mrs. McPhee and her son. Maydina and Birri are given Christian names. Maydina serves as a domestic while her daughter is "educated" by Mrs. McPhee, a widower who has never had a daughter. Mrs. McPhee becomes attached to Birri. Maydina befriends a man Joala/Charlie. They escape with their children to live in the bush and escape Mrs. McPhee and Reverend Bligh's Christianising and destruction of their culture. They are pursued and chased and Joala/Charlie is shot, and the rest are returned to the mission. The children are taken away by the Government.

Nerida is set in 1939 on a Government Reserve in Victoria. Nerida returns from the city to the rest of her family who live on a reserve. The manager runs the place very badly and corruptly. He gets sexual favours from one Aboriginal girl in exchange for giving her more rations. He expects this from Nerida but she will not do this. He tries to rape her, and Nerida gets blamed by the local Reverend and the manager's wife for leading the manager on. The manager also makes it difficult for Nerida and her family to get her sick father to hospital. The Aborigines on the reserve have a big meeting to try and work out a way to instigate change. This results in Nerida, her brother and a friend being taken to court by Felton for "treason". They win their case but are not given an opportunity to speak the whole truth in court. They then stage a walkout from the Reserve because of the horrific conditions there. Nerida's brothers join the army to escape constant harassment from the police. Aborigines can fight in the world war, but ironically still do not have their citizenship rights. Nerida's father dies from war wounds.

Lo-arna is set in a Victorian country town in 1981. It is the story of Alice Wilson and her daughter Lo-arna who were separated when her white father "stole" her. Her father passes her off as his adopted child from the Pacific islands. Alice Wilson is involved in the political rights movements for Aborigines, and educating children about Aboriginal culture, at the time when she locates her daughter. Lo-arna, when she learns the truth about her origins, is at first very scared of her aboriginality because of Australian society's attitude towards Aborigines. This is exacerbated by her parents' fear, her adoptive mother is particularly fearful. Lo-arna's European boyfriend tells her it does not matter to him what she is, she is still the same person. Lo-arna develops a need to know her mother and bravely makes the step to go and see her at the end of the film. She arrives at her mother's home but her mother is out. Lo-arna drives away and her mother chases her down the road. The car stops and the episode ends which leaves the viewers to draw their own conclusions as to how the story ends.

Continuous themes throughout the episodes are separation of mothers and daughters by administration and colonialism; the impact of government policies and colonialism on women and children; the representation of women as strong survivors; Aboriginal women having their own rites and ceremonies separate from men; the issues of land rights; relations of men and women (Aboriginal and European) including the impact of missionaries on Aboriginal culture.

Each episode of *Women of the Sun* represents stories of what happened to real Aboriginal women. Although "Lo-arna", "Maydina", "Atlinta" and "Nerida" never really existed, women like them did.

The series seeks to render their stories because the authors and directors perceived an absence of these stories in representations of Aborigines in the media. Sonia Borg began the project of co-writing this series with the following aims in mind:

"Why not show phases of Australian history through the eyes of Aboriginal women? Let them set the record straight! Let them say what they must have wanted to say for two hundred years."[18] Speaking specifically about what she and Hyllus Maris wanted to show she writes; "We wanted to show the clash of two cultures, the tragedy of racism."

The writers of *Women of the Sun* claim to be able to represent the reality of Aboriginal women as one of them is Aboriginal and her perspective should be more realistic than that of a European male. The writers were then concerned with showing the truth about what had happened to Aboriginal women. The directors and producer used predominantly 'realist' methods in relation to time and costume, to realise this goal. Realism as a mode, according to Lesley Stern, is meant to:

> ...articulate images as though the process is a transparent representation of reality... the marks of cinematic production are effaced or contained so that the meaning appears to unfold naturally.[19]

Spectators tend to regard film images as "realistic" as they reproduce "real" life in "real time" (time as it is from second to second, hour to hour) on the screen.

Episodes of *Women of the Sun*, due to its epic proportions (the covering of different historical periods), are now used in courses at

TAFE and teacher training courses, to teach educators about Aboriginal history. The realist mode of the series lends it to this environment, but its semifictional form perhaps makes it more "palatable" than a straight documentary.

Fringe Dwellers (Bruce Beresford 1985)

Another film during the 1980s that represented Aboriginal men and women was *Fringe Dwellers*. The significance of *Fringe Dwellers* was that it was the second film with predominantly Aboriginal cast to go to the Cannes Festival (1986). It was the official Australian entry. *Fringe Dwellers* deals with "modern day" Aborigines, and is based on a novel by a non-aboriginal. It made it on to video release in mainstream video stores and screened on television, thus reaching a wider audience than the original release of the film. It was nominated for 7 AFI Awards and two of its Aboriginal actresses were nominated for best actress awards.

This film is the portrait of an Aboriginal family. It follows the story of the Comeaway's, focusing especially a young woman named Trilby. It looks at what it is like for an Aboriginal family living on the fringe of a town and reveals what happens when they move into a house in the town. Trilby's brother is a good artist and her sister, Noonah, is studying to be a nurse. Her father does odd jobs here and there, at one stage in the story he goes away looking for work and later turns up home. Trilby gets pregnant to her boyfriend and "accidentally" drops her new born baby, then she leaves the town on a bus.

At the time it was released the makers and actors of the film said that it was more concerned with the story of the Aboriginal family rather than with being overtly political. Some Aboriginal activists were upset by the film because they felt they were portrayed as pathetic victims. They felt that the "typical white man's view" of Aborigines in a country town was endorsed. The director and producer of the film said that he had found the Aboriginal audience not offended by it. He felt it was truthful, and that all the characters were affectionately played. Kath Walker (Oodgeroo Noonuccal) felt the film did not bring hope but showed life as it was, that is, many Aboriginal people still live on the fringes. Bob Merritt (Aboriginal playwright) and others were upset with the film's lack of analysis, historical, political, social etc., but others have felt the whole point is that the fringe dwellers have lost much of their culture. It represented the non-tribal Aborigines. It was a bleak look at possibilities for a future which seemed to lack heroes and role models. Peter Malone, in his analysis of the film, felt that it could help build bridges between all Australians, by bringing about greater understanding of the plight of the fringe dwellers.

Fringe Dwellers and *Manganinnie* are both based on novels that were not written by Aborigines, thus it seems the next step forward in reshaping representation patterns of Aborigines in the feature film industry would be for Aboriginal writers to come to the fore, as they have already begun to do in television.

Tracey Moffat

In the period spanning the late 1980s to the 1990s, Aborigines, such as Tracey Moffat and Archie Wheeler, were among the first to have their stories made into films. Archie Wheeler had a novel, *Day of the Dog* (1992 James Ricketson), made into a film and Tracey Moffat, coming mostly from a still photographic background, writes, directs and acts in her own films.

Tracey Moffat's major films are *Nice Coloured Girls* (1987), *Night Cries: A Rural Tragedy* (1990) and recently the short story trilogy, *Be Devil* (1992/3). She is an interesting filmmaker who uses avant-garde techniques and has a universal outlook. Her comment on *Be Devil* demonstrates this:

> I like to have an array of very interesting faces, Chinese Italian, Greek and so on... I reflect what I see in Australian society. For me Australian society is now a very mixed society, very multicultural, a hybrid society.[20]

Nice Coloured Girls (1982) won the prize for the most Innovative Film at the 1988 Festival of Australian Film and Video Frames. One of its aims was to show strong black women survivors but without didacticism and with an avoidance of cliches.

Bob Hodge and Vijay Mishray[21] saw a distinct absence of erotic encounters between Aborigines and their colonisers in film and other texts, even though historically it was a reality. They consider Moffat's Nice Coloured Girls to be a reinscription of this forgotten 'fact' into history.

Hodge and Mishray see an ambivalence in the Australian attitude to Aborigines and their culture. They see a double-movement of fascination with it and suppression of it. They read Moffat's film as portraying white men who beget without responsibility both in the present and at the time of the founding of the nation (1788). Moffat's film is then, for them, a "deconstruction of the foundation myth of white men", who believe the pioneers built this nation by suffering and who sought to resolve the "Aboriginal problem", and who met with little or no resistance from the people.

In *Nice Coloured Girls* three young Aboriginal women go out to Kings Cross, Sydney, and pick up a captain (sugar Daddy), have a good night and roll him (dump him). The urban Aboriginal woman's experience is compared to that of the Aboriginal woman at the time of colonisation through voice overs and images of the past being combined with this narrative.

Night Cries, A Rural Tragedy (1990s) is perhaps one of the finest short films made in Australia. The plot outline does not reflect the process of the film, for it is non-linear and uses experimental techniques. It needs to be seen on video from a University Library and viewed shot by shot. *Night Cries*, a more recent example of Moffat's work, is more surreal, more concerned with the interior of one Aboriginal woman's memories. It explores the subconscious and the psychology of being physically depended upon and middle aged. It departs even more radically than *Nice Coloured Girls* from what an 'Aboriginal' film might be expected to do.

Night Cries is about a white European mother and her Aboriginal foster daughter. It alternates between the childhood memories of the daughter being looked after by her mother and the present reality where she looks after her mother, now old and frail, in the outback. The film traces the day to day tedium of the daughter taking her mother to the toilet and feeding her. This is interspersed with memories of the mother washing the daughter as a girl and dressing her. The European mother takes her daughter to the beach (here the daughter gets tangled in seaweed by some boys while mother is not there). The film ends with the death of the mother and her daughter lying in a foetal position with the soundtrack of a baby crying. A singer called Jimmy opens, appears throughout and closes the film by crooning the song of "Jesus on the Golden telephone."

Night Cries has been described as a sensitive film about menopause[22]. Others have sought to categorise it as a film about the "assimilationist era" of the fifties. Although bringing up some issues of race it seeks to balance this against considerations of the film's universal concerns and concerns with woman. The issue of "race" can enter into readings of the relationship between mother and daughter because the daughter is black and the mother is white.

Conclusions.

This survey has shown a range of films about Aborigines and some by Aborigines. It has traced how Australian films progressed from a patronising representation dominated by "black face" actors to a cinema where most parts are reserved for Aboriginal males who are predominantly victims. It has depicted a cinema that portrayed Aboriginal women as the downfall of Aboriginal man's progress, change to a cinema where strong Aboriginal women are portrayed as the backbone of their society and the ones who help keep their culture alive. It has shown that the absence of Aborigines from the realms of writing, producing and acting, well and truly ended and the disrespect of the sacred by non-indigenous peoples has become a major issue in the treatment of Aborigines in film and in relation to their sacred sites.

The art of the indigenous people of Australia is changing and adapting to those forms and mediums it comes into contact with. Film is one of those mediums. Indigenous films, films made by Aborigines and with Aborigines, need to be recognised as a legitimate contribution to their culture. Consider the following quotations from Aborigines and another indigenous person.

> Aboriginal arts and crafts people today who are not doing bark painting, who are not doing traditional dance, but who are doing other things which fit in with their way of life, these people must be recognised. Their art must be given its rightful place. And it must have recognition as legitimate Aboriginal arts and crafts.[23]

> People have a history that is reflected in the art they produce today as much as it is in the art that was produced on bark, or carving or whatever years ago.[24]

> It is illusory to think that which we comfortably label 'traditional' art was in an earlier time immune to changes in style and form, it is thus unproductive to lament change that reflects current realities.

Continuity with earlier forms will always be found; the present day community values ensures the arts will survive.[25]

The arts and the spiritual may have their reconnection hurried by the work of indigenous artists due to the strong respect many have for the sacred and for their communities. Johnny Harding, an Aboriginal playwright who has written about film, commented recently:

> Everything is interconnected and affects everything else. The arts in general in white Australia seem to be a very separate entity to the mainstream community. Elements of accountability and responsibility do not bind the two together. Thus a community sees no link between the arts body its taxes pay for, spending the majority of its funding supporting activities that a minuscule percentage of the population participate in and in fact they should be irate about it.[26]

Harding stresses here the way the social and the spiritual are interconnected. He feels that the arts should benefit the whole community.

Bahá'u'lláh has written:

> The purpose of learning should be the promotion of the welfare of the people, and this can be achieved through crafts. It hath been revealed and is now repeated that the true worth of artists and craftsmen should be appreciated, for they advance the affairs of mankind. Just as the foundations of religion are made firm through the Law of God, the means of livelihood depend upon those who are engaged in arts and crafts. True learning is that which is conducive to the well-being of the world, not to pride and self conceit or to tyranny, violence and pillage.[27]

Bahá'u'lláh stresses the social responsibility of the artist to the community, something integral to many indigenous artists.

Unity in diversity, and the elimination of prejudice will be reflected in the arts allowing all, including indigenous peoples, to reflect their culture in mediums. 'Abdu'l-Bahá stated:

> The Diversity of the human family should be the cause of love and harmony, as it is in music where many different notes blend together in the making of a perfect chord.[28]

Unity in diversity is a concept proposed by Bahá'u'lláh, in which people of different nationalities and cultural backgrounds are unified through a common belief in the oneness of humanity, religion and God. Unity in diversity recognises that many cultures have many elements that need not be changed, but rather celebrated as they make the world like a wonderful rose-garden of different cultures and colours. How uninteresting the world would be without some of these differences. However, Bahá'u'lláh teaches that there is one planet and one humanity which need to learn not to be divided by their different cultures. People need to live together free to develop to their full potential. Whatever their cultures, people need to realise that there is one people on this earth, the human race, and the existence of different cultures does not negate this experience.

The discourse of Aboriginalism is at odds with the concept of "unity in diversity" but the critique of Aboriginalism shares some points with the concept as it seeks to break down discourses that are founded upon prejudice.

There is hope in the future as we see the beginnings of future artists with spiritual values emerging from:

a.   Co-productions between indigenous artists and their European and non-indigenous friends.

b.   Imagery beyond negative images of destruction and victim obsession.

c.   The emergence of indigenous filmmakers and support for them by film financing bodies; and

d.   Cheaper access to film through video.

Some of the steps of deconstructing Aboriginalism as a discourse are in harmony with the broader aim of eradicating prejudice. These are outlined by Atwood:

1.   Speaking of Aborigines not for them!
2.   Acknowledging that ones own background effects what one says and observes.
3.   An exchange of knowledge is possible through dialogue.
4.   Creating a professional code of ethics and values in discussing another's culture.
5.   Consultation between Aboriginal communities and non-Aboriginal Communities.
6.   Changing theoretical terms; a shift from collection of objects to engagement with the subject, and
7.   A "provision of new ways for mutual becoming". As Bernard Smith suggested, creating grounds for 'an effective cultural interchange, neither patronising or exploitative' between Aboriginal Australians and other Australians.

In the USA, North American Indians have film co-operatives passing stories on through video. An Australian example is the video, Tidalk the Frog, which is an Aboriginal legend told by puppets and Bob Maza.

Overall there is a sense of responsibility emerging amongst indigenous people and their friends when making creative work. Carriers of prejudices need to be overcome in practical terms. This will help develop the vibrancy and integrity of indigenous and Australian culture. It is this responsibility that is seeing aborigines increasingly reflected on the screen free from stereotypes and patronisation.

Films Depicting and Representing the Indigenous Peoples of Australia.

The Birth of White Australia (1911)

Robbery Under Arms (1907)

Dan Morgan (1911)

The Assigned Servant (1911)

Assigned to His Wife (1911)

A Moari Maid's Love

Mutiny on the Bounty

Jungle Woman (Frank Hurley, 1926)

Uncivilised (Charles Chauvel)

Pearls and Savages (Frank Hurley)

Jedda (Charles Chauvel, 1955)

Walkabout

The Last Wave

The Chant of Jimmy Blacksmith

Storm Boy

Sister if Only You Knew (1975)

My Life as An Aboriginal (1979)

Journey Among Women (Tom Cowan)

Bread and Dripping (1981)

Two Laws (1981)

Manganinnie (John Honey 1980)

Women of the Sun (Hyllus Maris and Sonia Borg, 1982) [television drama]

Fringe Dwellers (Bruce Beresford)

Nice Coloured Girls, (Tracey Moffat, 1987)

Night Cries: A Rural Tragedy (Tracey Moffat, 1990)

Day of the Dog (James Ricketson, 1992)

Bedevil (Tracey Moffat, 1992/3)

Heartland (1994) [television drama]

Endnotes

1. The author uses both the word Aborigine and the term "indigenous people of Australia".
2. Bain, Atwood, "Introduction", Vol. 35, Nov 1992 *Journal of Australian Studies*. Latrobe University Press in association with National Centre in Australian Studies, Monash University.
3. ibid.
4. Shoghi Effendi., *The Advent of Divine Justice* at 33, cited in *Lights of Guidance* at 405.
5. The Salvation Army were the backbone of the film industry's early link with religion and the sacred.
6. W. Murdoch., *The Making of Australia, An Introductory History*, (Melbourne 1917), cited in Atwood, above, note 2.
7. Maureen Watson, "Aboriginal Art, The Politics of Consumption and Display.", *Art Link*, (June-July 1984), No's 2 and 3 at 28 - 33.
8. See letter written on behalf of the Guardian to individual believer, 19 August 1951, at 167, in *Lights of Guidance*.
9. From a newspaper review cited in Carlson Chauvel's, *Charles and Elsa Chauvel, Movie Pioneers* (University of Queensland Press, 1989).
10. Shoghi Effendi, *The Advent of Divine Justice* at 33.
11. Pike, *Aboriginals in Australian Feature Films* at 598.
12. Karen Jennings, "Ways of Seeing and Speaking About Aboriginal Women: Black Women and Documentary Film", *Hectate* 8.2 (1987-1988) at 113.
13. Dianne Bell, *Daughters of the Dreaming*, (George Allen and Unwin, Sydney 1983).
14. Jennings, above, note 12 at 114.
15. Multiculturalism is: The recognition and promotion of diverse cultures

within society. Ideally, in such a society, there are rights and opportunities for all, regardless of ethnic origin. Australia, though having inherited predominantly British political and social forms, and with English as the one official and commonly spoken language is now labelled a multicultural nation.... governments have structured their ethnic affair and immigration policies on the basis of multiculturalism. See *Penguin Macquarie Dictionary of Australian Politics*, Macquarie University, Sydney 1988, at 227-228.

16. Peter Malone, *In Black and White and Colour; a Survey of Australian Feature Films*, (Nilon Yubu Missological, 1987). This has excellent information in listing lots of films which represent Aboriginals. It is also a good source for people making a viewing list.

17. above n. 16.

18. Sonia Borg, 'A Glimpse of Wisdom', Hyllus Maris and Sonia Borg, *Women of the Sun*, (Currency Press, Sydney, 1983).

19. Lesley Stern, 'Independent Feminist Filmmaking in Australia,' *An Australian Film Reader: Part Four: Alternative Cinema* ec. Albert Moran and Tom O'Regan (Paddington: Currency Press,1985).

20. See this in Kathy Bail, 'Fringe Benefits' *Cinema Papers*, (1986) at 58

21. Bob Hodge and Vijay Mishray, *Dark Side of the Dream: Australian Literature and the Post-Colonial Mind* (Sydney: Allen and Unwin, 1991) at 68-9.

22. Caryn James 'Woman on the Subject of Menopause,' *New York Times* (September 26th, 1990).

23. Maureen Watson, 'Aboriginal Art, The Politics of Consumption and Display.', *Art Link*, 4. No. 2 & 3 June-July 1984, 28-33.

24. John Mundine, 'Aboriginal Art, The Politics of Consumption and Display.', *Art Link*, 4 No. 2 & 3, June-July 1984, 28-33.

25. Chike C. Aniakor, an Igbo schola cited in James Clifford, 'On Ethnographic Authority.' *Predicament of Culture*, Harvard University Press, Cambridge, 1988, at 21-54.

26. Johnny Harding, 'Canons in the Camera', *Cinema Papers*, 87, March-April, 1992 at 42-43.

27. From a Tablet translated from Persian in *Compilations of Compilations*, *Vol. 1*, Bahá'í Publications Australia, Sydney, 1991, at 3.

28. Quoted in *Advent of Divine Justice*, at 32.

Chapter Thirteen
ALCHERINGA
by
Fr. Rod Cameron

The Aboriginal word for "Dreamtime" is "Alcheringa". In this short paper Father Cameron explores its meaning and shares with us the things that he has learnt from his Aboriginal friends in many parts of Australia. The ancient spirituality is like a camp fire which burns in the night and can become a source of light, not only for Aborigines but for us all.

The word "Dreamtime"[1] came into our language when Spencer and Gillen wrote their account of their studies of Aboriginal tribal life amongst the Aranda people in Central Australia. Their work was published in 1899. The Aranda word they translated was "Alcheringa"

It is not easy to capture the deep meaning of Alcheringa, but Aborigines of the area say[2] that it refers to a sacred past which is ever present. It is eternity touching time. It is the Eternal Now. The human experience is that we live in time, but meaning and value are derived, ultimately, from the sacred (Eternal life) which is forever bearing down on us.

This Aboriginal mind-set is expressed in sacred story. When the teller says "In the Dreamtime" it is the present, now, that is involved in the theme.

Journey of the Crab

In the Dreamtime the creatures were all searching for their proper place in the world. The Crab found himself amongst the forest people. They treated him as one to fear because he was so different. They were aggressive and hostile. But the unhappy crab one day heard the music of the Land. It was the sound of the didgeridoo which, as the call of the Sacred, was calling him. He followed the call and came at last to the wide world of blue ocean and blue sky. His own people welcomed him and to the sound of the rolling waves and the drone of the didgeridoo, there was dancing on the beach.

Camp Fire Experience

Stories were told by the campfire. After the day's experience, they gathered in a circle about the fire to share their food. As a result, the fire became the symbol of the Sacred which is the centre of the land and the centre of human life.

The Kembla Story

The old man Burrendong was dying. Young Kembla stood beside him as the old man lamented the passing of his tribe. He asked Kembla to go to the sacred cave and ask the Spirit to speak: "Ask the Spirit to explain not why we die, but why we live."

Kembla went to the cave but the only sound he heard was the murmuring of the wind. As he stood before the sacred paintings on the wall of the cave he noticed that his own shadow was on the wall amidst the sacred spirit people painted there. To Kembla this was a sacred moment, for he saw himself as a carrier of the Dreamtime.

He returned to Burrendong, but found the old man dead. Sorrow filled his mind. Taking the old man in his arms, he carried him to the top of a hill. Holding the old man asleep in death, Kembla sang a tribal song that was heard on the far horizons of the earth.

The Rainbow Snake

This is a symbol of the sacred, uniting heaven and earth like the rainbow. An old Aborigine once described[3] the initiation ceremony in which he was as a boy involved. He and a few other boys were seated in the centre of the sacred ground. Along came a line of dancers, painted to represent the Snake. They coiled about the boys till the boys were out of sight. "I was swallowed by the Snake!" he said. "I was swallowed by God." Then the dancers withdrew and the boys stood up as men. It was the sacred that made the boy a man. All human identity is in the Sacred.

The Sleeping Snake

An Aborigine in Coen related[4] that when the Snake goes to sleep in the cave, the rains do not fall, the land begins to thirst and animals die.

But then the elders must go and call the Snake to awake. When the snake awakes the rains come again and all the world is renewed.

The old Aborigine said, "The Rainbow Snake is now asleep, but he is about to wake up."

Endnotes

1. Over thirty years ago, the author was commissioned to study the "Dreamtime" with a view to increasing the appreciation of the "Dreamtime" amongst white Australians.
2. From information derived from the author's travels and conversations with Aborigines.
3. *ibid.*
4. *ibid.*

Chapter Fourteen
LITERACY AT HOME AND IN SCHOOL AN ETHNOGRAPHIC CASE STUDY OF ABORIGINAL AND TORRES STRAIT ISLANDER CHILDREN

by

Farvardin Daliri

This paper is based on a major research project funded by the Australian Research Council which started in February 1990 and is still continuing. The chief investigators are Professor R. Smith, Head of the School of Education of James Cook University, Dr. Allan Luke, Reader and Associate Professor Michael Singh, Lecturer in the Department of Education. Mr. Daliri's PhD is based on this project. In addition he is co-ordinator and research assistant for the project.

Mr. Daliri sets out to find out how the cultural differences of indigenous children with main stream children is implicated in their school achievement. Culture is a core of a language, and every language is a complex activity which involves learning a culture as well. Knowing that Aboriginal and Torres Strait Islander children come from a home environment with a distinct and different culture which is very much alive, it would be of importance to find out how this process of learning a new language and a new culture takes place and how the cultural transition effects their learning and achievement at school.

There is one important question to be studied in this context: What is the Aboriginal and Islander children's level of literacy and numeracy achievement at the time of transition from home to school in relation to

grade one classroom expectations.
In the concluding part, the writer analyses the whole research project in
the light of the Bahá'í theoretical basis of emancipation of indigenous
people.

Many indigenous Australian children face educational problems in their early years. Various ethnic, cultural and racial groups have presented to educationists various levels of achievement in the early schooling years, thus this problem has been investigated and researched extensively in the past.

It is a well established finding that Aboriginal and Torres Strait Islander children are disadvantaged in formal schooling.[1] Most of the problems faced by indigenous students can be traced back to the early years of schooling.

As a key moment in educational development, transition from home to school has been the focus of educational research in the past two decades. In the case of Aboriginal and Torres Islander children the initial years of schooling have far reaching significance and implications. But there is no accurate description of the formation of knowledge, identity and achievement of Australian indigenous children in early primary school education. Further, there is no extensive published research on the progress of urban Aboriginal and Islander children in early literacy and numeracy. Most of the data and theories we have are drawn from either remote community studies or "mainstream" work. It was against this background that, in February 1991, an Australian Research Council Study Project commenced. This study focused on grade one classrooms which had a high percentage of indigenous children. The chief investigators were Associate Prof. Michael Singh, Head of Program, Initial Teacher Education, Faculty of

Education, University of Central Queensland and Dr Allan Luke, Reader at the School of Education, James Cook University of Northern Queensland.[2]

The Australian Research Council project involved two parallel studies. The first comprised of case studies of literacy and numeracy "events" of Aboriginal and Torres Strait Islander early primary age children in home and community settings. The intended outcome was a description of what counts as literacy and numeracy in the indigenous home and community sites.

The second comprised of case studies of grade one classroom programs in state primary schools which focused on the kinds of literacy and numeracy tasks children face at school. The background of this project was based on various reports which have recently shown that indigenous children are presented as underachievers in school reports. This has caused teachers to expect lower achievement from indigenous children, and in turn this causes lower self-expectation in indigenous children and families.

One of the possible outcomes of this expectation may be described as *normalisation of abnormal situation*. This means that some educationists over a long period of time, may form a stereotyped view of the situation and consider the failure and underachievement of indigenous children to be normal. As a result, instead of looking into the educational institutions for the cause of the problem, they may blame the victim. There are two interrelated hypotheses or questions one can ask in this context, Firstly, whose needs and requirements are catered for in our schools? Secondly, how do schools relate to the experiences and knowledge systems of indigenous children? In 1986, Shirley Brice Heath published a paper in which she reported findings of her ethnographic research. She studied a problem which, in one form or another, has vexed most classroom teachers where there is a difference between the cultural background of the teacher and that of some or all of the children in the classroom. In this study, which took place in USA, a group of Afro-American children were compared with a group of mainstream children and a group of white working class children. The aim was to study the reasons for the underachieving of Afro-Americans as compared with white working class children. Some of the findings are relevant to the Australian context and problem of underachievement of indigenous children.

According to Heath, the means of making sense from books and relating their content to knowledge about the real world is but one "way of taking", and that this process is often interpreted as "natural" rather than learned. Teachers (and researchers alike) have not recognised that ways of "taking" from books are as much a part of learned behaviour as are ways of eating, sitting, playing games and building houses.[3]

As school-oriented parents and their children interact in the pre-school years, through modelling and specific instruction, adults give their children ways of taking from books that seem natural in school and institutional settings such as banks, post offices, businesses and government offices. These mainstream ways exist in societies around the world that rely on formal educational systems to prepare children for participation in settings involving literacy. In some communities these ways of schools and institutions are similar to the ways learned at home. In other communities the ways of school are merely an overlay on the home-taught ways and may be in conflict with them.

Let us elaborate on this issue with a few examples. Children growing up in mainstream communities are expected to develop habits and values that attest to their membership in a "literate society". For example, the bedtime story is a major literacy event that helps set patterns of behaviour that reoccur throughout the lives of mainstream children and in classroom interactions at school. The bedtime story is generally accepted as given and is considered to be a natural way for parents to interact with their child at bedtime. During this familiar ritual, mother or father in a series of reading cycles alternate turns in a dialogue. Children in mainstream homes start paying attention to books and written signs from six months of age. Their rooms contain bookcases and are decorated with murals, stuffed animals and posters. When children begin to verbalise the contents of books, adults extend their questions from simple requests for labels ("What's that?".. "Who is that?"), to ask the attributes of these items ("What does the doggie say?", "What colour is the ball?"). It is beyond the scope of this paper to detail the literacy events of mainstream homes. However, in short, Heath argues that children brought up in those homes achieve certain levels of literacy and numeracy skills before going to school. And when they do go to school, the very same type of literacy events and interactions take place at school. One example of these events is story reading, which is repetition of the bedtime stories at home. In other words, literacy and numeracy tasks children face at school are familiar to what mainstream children have already faced at home.

What happens to those children who come from homes which have no bedtime stories similar to the bedtime stories in mainstream homes? For example, Afro-American parents do have bedtime stories. Instead of reading from a book, the grandfather or grandmother tells a story orally in which children take part and contribute. This type of story telling has a different educational function than book reading and is equally educative and important. However, it is different from the practices of mainstream homes and schools.

In reading stories at bedtime, the following habits and values are reinforced:

- Books and book related activities have authority.
- Learning to love books.
- Learning to entertain yourself with books and to work independently.
- Interactive participative role in book reading is discouraged. Children listen and wait as an audience, store what they hear, and, on cue from the adult, answer a question.

This style of learning is termed *analytical or field independent.* The analytical or field independent style is generally presented as that which correlates positively with high achievement and general academic and social success in school.

In oral story telling in Afro-American homes, *field dependant or rational* style is used. Whatever merits this style may have, it is not used in schools. Therefore children coming from homes with a different cognitive style of learning are disadvantaged from the beginning. They face new situations which are foreign to them and they have to make an extra effort to adapt to the new situation, often by the time they catch up with the new style they are already left behind.

To return to indigenous Australian children, there are strong indications that our educational system is not geared to cater for the specific needs of indigenous children. These children when they start their school life, not only do they have to face many problems related to their cultural differences with the main community, they may also be facing a cognitive style in terms of educational practices which is new to them, whereas all mainstream children have already learned that style at home. It should be emphasised here that different cognitive styles are ways of taking meaning from books which are not natural or genetic, rather they are learned.

In our research project, we commenced two parallel studies: one is the case study of Aboriginal and Torres Strait Islander children in the home setting, and the other at school. By running these two parallel studies we studied the literacy and numeracy events at home, with their associated cognitive styles, and on the other hand we studied the kinds of literacy and numeracy tasks children face at school.

Comparison of these two studies show to some extent how far the school program matches or mismatches indigenous children's cognitive style, discursive competencies, and literacy and numeracy achievement at the time of transition from home environment to the school setting. Finally, the findings of this study may be used as a guideline for future intervention programs for indigenous children at school.

To report on the process and progress of these two parallel studies, consent was first obtained from three Aboriginal and Torres Strait Islander families with children in grade one.

The relevant community was approached through their meetings and through friends in various organisations. The purpose and benefits of the project were explained many times to many people. The study involved visiting a family for a few days and nights each week for a whole year. Their reactions to such approach were predictable. As soon as they were told about the research, they commented, "Oh research, too many of them, so many people come with papers and surveys and use our community, gather some data, cause some inconvenience and go away for good. What do we gain from them? We don't want to be used."

After some persuasion, a few questions were asked: "What do you think of the education of Aboriginal children?", "What do you think of

229

the schools?". Then they came up with all sorts of statements which may be summed up in the following terms: "Our children are not learning at school." "Schools are not about our education." "We know our children can learn as well as anybody else." "Who is responsible for their failures?"

During the course of this study, regular visits were made to the ten families who agreed to participate in the qualitative ethnographic fieldwork. The purpose was to gather accurate information on the process of early socialisation of children: What kinds of literacy and numeracy events were in homes? What, if any, was the style of bedtime stories? Which television programs did they watch? What outdoor literacy related activities, topics of table conversations and formation of cultural identity were conducted at home?

The findings of this research may be summarised as follows:

First, all the parents seemed concerned about the education of their children. They were co-operative in educational programs initiated at school. They asked questions about the educational system and had their opinions about educational issues.

Second, those families possessed a very strong sense of cultural and philosophical identity which is very different from mainstream Anglo-Saxon culture and philosophy.

Third, although they enjoyed various levels of friendship with individual members of the white community, they felt strong racial hatred and prejudice against themselves from most member of the mainstream community.

Fourth, they were concerned about their social integrity, self esteem and cultural pride.

Fifth, they felt powerless to talk to school authorities about their viewpoints in relation to the educational problems of their children.

The second project took place in schools. This study had a different technique altogether. Three state primary schools with large indigenous populations were targeted and four grade one classrooms were selected. The selection process involved a series of negotiations with the education department, school principals, teachers and in some cases parents.

The actual classroom setting was filmed for many days while teachers were engaged in their professional practice. The focus was on the kinds of literacy and numeracy tasks children face rather than the methodology of the teachers.

Two professional cameras were set up in the classroom. At first the children showed signs of disturbance and fascination, but by the second day, they forgot all about the cameras and things resumed as normal. About 100 hours of the classroom interactions in its actual setting were filmed. This huge body of collected data is the first of its kind. Hopefully by July '93 the first summary of the report will be published, and by mid '94 the results of the analysis of the findings and the final conclusion of the project will be made available to educationists.

At this point the following points should be noted:

Firstly, as mentioned before, the families studied had a strong sense of cultural identity which prevailed in their family interactions. Everything was seen, said or expressed from an Aboriginal perspective. Having this in mind, it was interesting to know that, after going through all those video tapes, not a single event of reference is to be found to the Aboriginal or Torres Strait Islander cultural and racial identity.

This finding gives more insight about what is happening in the classrooms, what constitutes useful knowledge in classrooms, what are acceptable ways of displaying knowledge, and how parts of some human knowledge and experience may be unconsciously ignored or dishonoured in an educational setting.

Secondly, during hours of filming and observing grade one classroom interactions, it was noticed that Aboriginal and Torres Strait Islander children were mostly listening to the teacher, paying attention, and trying their best to be involved in whatever topic or activity was going on. Of course their success in doing their tasks is a different question altogether.

It is hoped that the conclusion of this research will help develop school programs which cater for the special needs of indigenous children. These programs need to be responsive to different cultural identities and they need to be committed to the educational needs of children who have learned different ways of taking meaning from books and who have different cognitive styles.

Endnotes

1. See Bourke and Perkin (1977) and Seagrim and London, Furnishing the Mind, (Academic Press, Sydney 1980).
2. The present author is associated with this project as co-ordinator and research assistant and is writing his Ph.D. thesis on this topic
3. See Heath, S. B., Ways With Words (Cambridge University Press, Cambridge 1983.)

Chapter Fifteen

DESPAIR, ANGER AND BEAUTY - THE RISE OF ABORIGINAL WRITING IN THE MODERN WORLD

by

Camilla Chance

This paper first examines the importance of story and song in Aboriginal culture. Next it explores the emergence and nature of Aboriginal writing in the modern world. A number of Aboriginal works are reviewed including poetry, novels and television productions. Aboriginal perspectives, history and experience are examined through this review, as well as European attitudes to the Aboriginal experience. The emergence of this literature represents Aborigines telling their own story, which has only recently begun to displace a situation in which Aborigines were only seen by Australian society through European eyes.

A great many years ago, an Aboriginal young man reproached the author, a white woman, for violating an Aboriginal custom. I had spoken to him in front of and involving someone else of a matter he had told me about quietly. "You still don't understand!" he had exclaimed. Communications among Aborigines is almost always one-to-one. If an Aborigine says "I'm having a talk to so-and-so. Do you mind?", the other people present will mentally switch off. Maybe, a white person has to experience this to believe it, but the Aborigines present genuinely will not hear the speaker's words on any level, knowing that he or she would instantly be aware if they did. This is one of the many ways in which psychological privacy is maintained in often physically crowded surroundings.

The present author thought that it was no use offending a whole race. In order to speed up the progress of her understanding she borrowed an "Aboriginal Encyclopaedia" from the library, and sent for every single reference work the editors had consulted. In no time, a small study at her house was completely crammed with books, stacked from floor to ceiling. She read them all. Two outstanding facts emerged: first, none of the books overlapped in information. Aboriginal culture is a truly vast subject, which explains the despair expressed so strongly by Aborigines at the time of her reading. They were in real danger of losing this culture, while having nothing they saw as worthwhile to replace it. The second fact to emerge was the gigantic silence on the subject of Aborigines that lay between the forgotten writings of the early white settlers to that time.

The stories of the Creator Ancestors that were kept alive from generation to generation fostered in Australian Aborigines (as they would in any indigenous society) the love, trust and deep sense of security which made their tribes flourish for over 40,000 years in what white people saw as an inhospitable and hostile land. Stories told to Aborigines from childhood gave them great happiness from the powerful sense they conveyed, that the spiritual world and their ancestors were all around them. Aborigines truly pity members of the white race for having cut themselves off from such awareness - they see this cutting off as the main source of white people's fears, tension and sadness.

Not only the exploits of Creator Ancestors, but also those of ordinary human beings were exalted in song. A young woman might be kidnapped by a man from another tribe, and her tracks - broken branches, deep grooves made by her heels in the soil - would bear proud witness to her heroic protests. Stories and songs were so important that they expanded according to the age and worthiness of a tribal member. A baby or a young woman would be offered a simplified version of the ancestor's exploits. Once a male baby grew to manhood, he had to prove himself worthy to hear more by undergoing a complex and often excruciatingly painful initiation ceremony. Females had their own stories, but their initiations tended to be gentler. After all, women underwent the pain of childbirth, and so would soon become naturally worthy in many respects. A woman past menopause was greatly respected, and usually allowed to witness otherwise exclusively male ceremonies.

Years after his initiation, a young man would undergo further tests and teaching which would qualify him to hear the more secret parts of those same stories. But in no way would he be permitted to know the definitive versions until he became an Elder. That is how important the Aboriginal religious stories were.

European arrival in Australia meant the discovery by outsiders, to quote George Johnson, from his book *The Australians*[1], that

...the trees were different, the birds were different, the insects were different, colour was different, the light was different, the very scale of the landscape was different, sounds were different. . . Even the heavenly constellations were upside down or totally unfamiliar... When the battler did find rivers they sank into the sand and vanished quietly into deserts. His lakes were terrible, salt-rimmed, brine-bitter..

in this land that sought to murder ambition with its massive indifference.

There grew up a love-hate relationship with the land which is so strongly reflected in white artistic expression that, when a recent modest American-Australian collaboration appeared on our television screens, the film was mocked severely as being "corny" by all white Australians the author met who saw it. It contained a jolly song which appeared to be titled "Off we go to the Bush". To most white Australians, even a day trip to the bush meant contending with poisonous spiders and snakes, leeches, death-dealing ticks, bull-ants, infinite hordes of flies and memories of the long-term hardships which beset our earlier explorers. The small production on our television screens violated a cynical tradition which we are so used to in our art and literature that we can hardly recognise as a work of art anything which does not contain this traditional ambivalence towards our land of extreme heat, fire, flood and drought. Of course, Australians of European origin love the bush, but they also see it as a threat.

Off went our television sets, but Aboriginal acquaintances insisted: "That film had something which other films we've seen didn't have. It wasn't so bad." They meant that it expressed the quality of uncontaminated love and trust with which they themselves regarded the bush. Every movement of Aboriginal people is normally in harmony with what they feel the spiritual world wants of them at that time, therefore, if a white person asks them to do something different from this, they will react with anger. Aborigines take it for granted that they will be given premonitions of danger, and that, if harm is about to befall a loved one, the spiritual world will tell them. So, unless interfered with by white people's ways, the Aborigines move through their own tribal country and that of friends in perfect confidence.

White people in Australia have produced a vast body of writing - "tall" stories, folksongs, factual matter, novels, plays, poetry and short stories. Societies have been formed to give writers moral support, and certain prizes are funded. As far as one can categorise anything Australian fiction today falls into five main groups. First, "rural" writing, carefully crafted. Next, an introverted style where the setting is usually not important - and indeed a recent trend in Australian fiction generally has been the setting of novels overseas. Experimental work has also come to the fore. Thirdly, there seems always to be a place for humour in Australian fiction, but totally humorous books are almost always "ocker" aggressively masculine. Feminist literature, which is still very much alive and well in this country, forms the fourth category.

Inside Black Australia[2], edited by Kevin Gilbert, contains Aboriginal writer Maureen Watson's poem "Stepping Out". It begins:

> I'm stepping out, don't mess about,
> Don't tell me to be patient.
> I've been wedded, enslaved, white-washed and saved,
> But now, I'm liberated."

But note that the poem continues:

> "I've been patted, and moulded, and shaped, and scolded
> And I learned real fast how to please 'em,
> I "Yes sir'ed" and "No Ma'amed",
> I was cursed and damned,
> And all for no good reason.

Aboriginal women writers see themselves as Aboriginal first, and feminism as part of that struggle.

The fifth category is the recent rise of Aboriginal writing. From 1961, conventional thinking in Australia and the previous decade could best be described as stifling. People like Barry Humphries and Germaine Greer are still haunted by that decade's stultifying climate, and actually send it up. Patrick White then published *Riders in the Chariot*.[3] It was about people who suffered because they differed from the norm in their thinking - their outlook was characterised by its creativity, which others around them seemed to do their best to destroy. One of those individuals considered "worthy" to ride in Patrick White's "Chariot" was an Aboriginal artist. It could be considered objectionable that of all the main characters in the novel, only the

Aborigine was created in such a way that the reader could not "get inside" him. The objection has often been answered with the words, "I defy any white person to get inside the savage mind." And yet, critics of Aboriginal Sally Morgan's *My Place*[4] have insisted that Sally Morgan merely had a dreamy, artistic temperament, with no facets that differed from those of thousands of white people.

One cannot have it both ways. One cannot use both savagery and sameness as excuses to avoid paying attention to Aboriginal thought. The rise of Aboriginal writing has meant that we must all open our eyes.

The year 1964 marked the first publication of an Australian Aborigine's book of poetry. Its title, *We Are Going*[5], blatantly referred to the fact that Aborigines were seen (even by themselves) as a dying race. Although the volume became very popular, and although Kath Walker, later known as Oodgeroo Noonuccal, has written a great deal of good material since (and the very changing of her "white" name to her Aboriginal one makes a statement), it is fair to say that *We Are Going*, with its resigned title, did nothing to stir white complacency.

The Track to Bralgu[6] was published in Britain in 1978, and soon after became available here. This was a book of short stories, ostensibly by an Aborigine, "Banumbir Wongar". It expressed the kinship Aborigines feel with all animals, and their belief that a human being can turn into one so as to be effective in a crisis.

Although the works of Banumbir Wongar showed Aboriginal consciousness, one feels that they could not be by an Aborigine. It was then common for Aborigines not to have the slightest idea of how white people thought. When flashes of understanding did occur, they were deeply shocked. Wongar did have the clear-cut yardstick of knowing how white people thought, which enabled him to point out so succinctly the contrasting Aboriginal outlook. He turned out to hail from Yugoslavia, though he lived in Australia.

In 1981 and 1982, *The Australian* published a its first reviews of books by and about Aboriginal people7. The title of the opening review, chosen by the editors but inspired by the review's contents, was Aborigines *have gifts for the world*. The article began by referring to *The Day of the Dog*[8], a gripping novel by Aboriginal writer Archie Weller, which had been runner-up for a Literary Prize sponsored each year by *The Australian* and *Vogel's Bread*.

The reviews sought blatantly to bridge the gulf between Aboriginal and white views - to stimulate understanding. They came out alongside a series of reports about the condition of Aborigines on early missionary settlements in Queensland. Suddenly white readers, the vast majority against their wills, became well-informed about Aborigines.

The dialogue of *The Day of the Dog* has a poetic strength, and never falters. Published in 1981, the book is about urban Aborigines. Doug Dooligan, its hero, tries to break free of his society's outlook, but the pressures are too strong.

Women of the Sun[9] is a mini-series of four episodes jointly written by the Aboriginal poet and sociologist Hyllus Maris and respected scriptwriter Sonia Borg. This work was televised in 1982. It immediately won the 1982 United Nations' Media Peace Prize, and also many other awards. It was published in 1983 as a script, and in 1985 as a novel.

Some critics have claimed that *Alinta*, the first episode, recreates the 18th century writer Rousseau's "noble savage". This is not true. Hyllus Maris and Sonia Borg have forced the Australian consciousness to make a much bigger jump than that. People of European descent are proud of their languages, developed from ancient Greek, Latin and other roots. What makes them imagine that Aboriginal languages do not have just as interesting and illustrious a history? (Just as "burro" means "butter" in Italian and "donkey" in Spanish, so the same Aboriginal word can have two different meanings in the north and the south.)

For no rational reason, everything to do with Aborigines was devalued in the Australian mind, languages included. But white Australians did have enormous respect for films in foreign languages by master filmmakers, such as Ingmar Bergman. These films were never dubbed, but subtitled. The actors in *Alinta* spoke in their own language. Viewers had to be content with subtitles. The actors played members of the extinct Nyari tribe of South-eastern Australia - an imaginary name which represented the spirit of many tribes. As a result of the subtitles and other devices, our respect for the film's characters and everything to do with them grew to be enormous.

In the episode *Alinta*, which begins in 1824, we are excessively aware of nature's abundance. Aborigines generally moved among the fertile areas of Australia, leaving them for arid parts only when white people took over. In *Alinta* two escaped convicts, Finlay and McNab, are found by children, and saved by the Aboriginal tribe from a certain death. One of them, Finlay, is later speared for trying to rape a tribal girl (his crime is seen as not only attempted rape but also incest, the girl having become his tribal sister). The other convict, McNab, becomes a fully initiated Nyari man. Alinta's promised husband, Murra, visits the tribe with presents, and some years later arrives to take her away. Prospective white settlers invade. McNab finally leaves with them, and returns to claim the land from the Nyari people. We see his action, through Alinta's eyes, as treachery. We see his ambition and acquisitiveness through tribal eyes: as character flaws.

Enormous trouble has been taken in *Women of the Sun* to create Aboriginal characters with whom we feel empathy. We are moved by Alinta's excitement and anxiety about her forthcoming marriage, when she will have to leave everyone she knows. We are moved by Murra's beautiful promise to make Alinta happy: "See how the wind plays with the flames? That's me, Murra - the West Wind. He knows I'm here - see how he makes the flames dance? That's you, Alinta... You are the fire... Where does the fire go, Alinta?"

Because we have identified with the Aboriginal characters, we are ready to learn about the very particular concerns of Aboriginal people generally. We are ready to question the conventional values of white society, and acknowledge the strength and warmth of Aboriginal life both before and after white settlement. Suddenly, a white audience has become involved with Aborigines as human beings.

Punishment among the Nyari never involves humiliation - as seen when Finlay screams out in fear when two young Aboriginal warriors miss him with their spears, and Morrorra (a tribal Elder) decides to end his display of cowardice by spearing him accurately. At initiation ceremonies, too, the Elders would put the boys known to have a low threshold to pain through the Law first.

Episode Two of *Women of the Sun, Maydina*, is about the situation described in the song:

Between her sobs, I heard her say,
Police bin taken my baby away.
From white-man boss that baby I have -
Why he let 'em take baby away?

It was somewhat confusing to Aboriginal women that white men who fathered "brown-skinned babies" did not love them and did not normally want anything to do with them. In fact, they were often the ones who reported them, without acknowledging fatherhood, of course - to the police in order to have them removed and put into orphanages.

In every state of Australia, children were taken away from their mothers - babies up to teenagers. Two generations grew up institutionalised. Government files were kept on all these children; but, until recently, Aborigines were not allowed access to those files. The files gave details such as their subjects' relations' sexual lives, and whether they were "lazy". Recently, some libraries and record offices have taken to employing Aboriginal people whose job it is to go through the files, index them and make them available to their subjects' families.

In Maydina, set in south-eastern Australia in the 1890s, an Aboriginal woman is forced to work for white sealers, by whom she is used sexually. She has a daughter, Biri, by a white man. Running away from the sealers, she meets another white man, Gustav Muller, a German gold prospector. He appears to be an inherently good man. He wants Maydina to stay with him. Maydina is tired of drunken men who mistreat her and her child and wants to return to her own people. Muller tells her they are all gone. The audience has no way of knowing if this is true, but the audience must realise, "If it is not, it soon will be." The authors of the story did intend Maydina to be the last of her tribe - as Alinta became, at the end of the first episode. Muller goes out of his way to take Maydina and her daughter to Balambool Christian Mission, where he thinks she will be "safe", and he expects gratitude for this. But Maydina would have liked to have gone to her own country, and seen for herself whether her people were all gone.

Now comes the most unbearable part of the film - the spiritual destruction of a race. Muller, Maydina and Biri arrive at the mission while the burial of a child is in progress. The Aborigines look at the newcomers as prisoners would eye a new arrival. Maydina is frightened, and wants to leave: "No like this place... no like this place... All gonna die all same that one... " Indeed, most of the Aboriginal people there appeared to have given up hope.

There is no way of getting through to Mrs. McPhee and her assistant, the Reverend Bligh, who run Balambool Christian Mission, that goodness and godliness exist other than in the narrow interpretation of these qualities which they serve - that other people can have a sense of right and wrong, of justice and injustice. Maydina and Biri are renamed "May" and "Emily". "It's easier to train those who have white blood in them," says Mrs. McPhee, for whom self-denial and denial of what they believe in and are habits that must be imposed on children, and adults who remind you of children.

When the missions established by the Christian churches were gradually taken over by the government-run "Protection Board", the separating of children with white blood from their parents became official policy. Episode Two ends with Maydina, arms outstretched, running forever after the buggy taking her child away to an orphanage. The sight of mothers running after their children until they collapsed has been a familiar one to Aborigines.

Nerida Anderson, of episode Three, leads six hundred people off an Aboriginal reserve because of the appalling conditions. The exodus on which the episode was based was actually led by men, but in spirit the incident is Cummeragunja Mission in 1939, based on the experience of Hyllus Maris's family, who lived through it.

Episode Four of *Women of the Sun* is called *Lo-Arna*. The beautiful young girl of the title has been adopted as a baby into a comfortably-off white family and renamed Ann. The episode shows with great strength the reactions of Lo-Arna, now a teenager believing herself to be French Polynesian, when she finds out suddenly that her mother is Aboriginal. She experiences great shock, to Lo-Arna it is as if she has come from a rubbish dump. But the episode ends with a reversal of *Maydina* - with Lo-Arna physically accepting her Aboriginal mother.

The song by Archie Roach,

.. And then they took the children away.
Torn from their mother's breast,
Said it was for the best..."
ends with the triumphant:
"The children came back!

Back to their culture, their customs, the outlook on life which made them whole individuals and Aborigines rose again.

Suddenly, white people said, "Did that really happen? We have a lot to answer for, haven't we?", realising that the black mothers and brown children suffered as much as white Australians would have if *their* children had been taken away forever, through no fault of their own. The vast majority of white Australians simply had not known that it was happening. They also had not known that many more massacres occurred than were recorded in history books, that Aborigines had not been allowed to farm land for profit, or that the rape of Aboriginal women was commonplace. When these subjects were brought up, the White Australian always seemed to reply with the phrase, "I *know* terrible things happened." This stock answer meant that the listener didn't know and couldn't bear to know. Not until the Aboriginal children started coming back could white people face unwritten history. And, now, when history is being rewritten through Aboriginal plays, poetry, novels and songs, maybe white people will learn to live with their own consciences and cease to regard the land as hostile.

Some of Aboriginal activist-turned-playwright Jack Davis' work may be too painful for most audiences to bear, but he lets us know what really happened. *Kullark* was first performed in 1979, *The Dreamers* in 1983 and *No Sugar* at the 1985 Festival of Perth. His plays, like Sally Morgan's autobiography, My Place, and the biography of Jack McPhee, *Wanamurraganya*,[10] bear witness to a basic faith in white people's capacity to act morally when offered overwhelming evidence of past injustice.

We respond to this trust in Sally Morgan's *My Place*, which uses a novelist's techniques. We are made to identify with the author's search for the truth, and therefore enter a state of mind where we do not block out the differences between her family and ours, her outlook and ours. The book establishes a link of common humanity between Aborigines and outsiders, shunning accounts of extreme cruelty which might make the reader mentally "switch off". Such accounts do exist.

Apparently Sally Morgan's natural writing style is more literary than that of *My Place*, but the tape-recorded speech of her relations, which she transposed in it, was less so. A meeting-point had to be found. The result is a warm, clear, delightful style which caused one tourist to observe that during the summer of the books publication, every second person on the beaches he visited was reading *My Place*.

Sally Morgan, her brothers and her sisters grew up in Perth, in the 1950s and 1960s. Her grandmother had been taken away from her great-grandmother, and her mother had been taken away from her grandmother and brought up in an orphanage. Now the two women were together again, they made a vow that this generation of children must never know of their Aboriginal blood. "Don't tell anyone you're Aboriginal," Sally's grandmother used to say almost till her death. "If you do, bad things will happen to you." Sally did not suspect her Aboriginality but not until she was aged about fifteen. She was told the truth after six years of questioning when her mother admitted it. After that Sally wanted to know her past and to meet her relations. She visited the area where her grandmother had been born, and was helped to find her place in the kinship system. "You don't know what it means," commented one old full-blood lady. "No-one comes back. You don't know what it means that you, with light skin, want to own us." Sally's grandmother's brother, Arthur, and her mother and grandmother eventually told their life stories also.

At "Writers' Week," 1990, part of the biennial Adelaide Festival, Ms Morgan said: "We need to determine our own destiny and our future without other people telling us what we should be and how we should live." She has received a great many letters from Britain and North America, especially from black Americans. They reported that when they read her book, they realised why they had been unable to obtain information about Aborigines.

Published in 1987, *Wanamurraganya*, the story of Jack McPhee (Sally Morgan's tribal grandfather) is graphic, living proof of the song:

Prison's nothin' special

To any Nunga I know:

'Cause the white man makes it prison

'Most everywhere we go.

("Nunga" means "Aborigine".) Jack McPhee is not able to move anywhere without the permission of the "Protector of Aborigines", and he is only able to meet with family or friends by coincidence because they have been sent to work in the same place. Touchingly, thinking that the "Protector of Aborigines" must have his best interests at heart, he writes requesting permission to remain with a boss who wishes to will him his property. The "Protector", of course, immediately organises a large distance between boss and workman. Aborigines were not allowed to own land. At "Writers' Week", Ms Morgan said, "I have no doubt Jack would be a millionaire today, because he worked so hard, if he'd been given a normal chance

The Dreamtime is never far away. It was once the case that when, for example, an Aborigine of the kangaroo skin group saw a kangaroo, he would go into a dreaming state. He would feel forcefully the spiritual world surrounding him, confirming its love for him and reminding him of his ancestors. Today, sometimes an urban Aborigine will go into the bush, and the full force of its beauty will send him into such a state again. This is an aspect of his artistic temperament which the Aborigines with him understand and respect. They will not attempt to disturb him or destroy his experience.

The *Kadaitcha Sung*[11], an angry book by Sam Watson, was published in 1990. The book is extremely clear about certain Aboriginal ways and feelings. For example, we have Aboriginal awareness of agony in the origin of a certain desk - the desk "spirits" are screaming out because the desk was made from Aboriginal coffin-wood.

The Kadaitcha Sung's clarity embodies a step forward in Aboriginal-white relations. Its main theme of resentment, hatred and the outcome of revenge highlights an Aboriginal reaction to conquest that has been simmering for a long time.. .. At last *The Kadaitcha Sung* has expressed that Aboriginal reaction in quite extreme terms - and in a book that has become a best-seller among white people. A large number of white people have therefore now been told, and may have modified their thinking and behaviour as a result. Some Aborigines may have experienced an emotional release because of this. They may have been able to put their most self-destructive feelings behind them, and look clearly at what they want to do now and in the future. The revenge for white conquest is uncomfortably convincing: that one in every hundred white people will be tormented by a greed that can never be satisfied.

The style of *The Kadaitcha Sung* is marvellous, for example, "The smaller spirits of the mighty winds scudded across the outstretched fingers of the restless heavens...". The fact that in Aboriginal culture, nothing physical existed without its spirit, and nothing spiritual existed without its physical manifestation, has been tapped into by Sam Watson to great artistic effect, resulting in many passages of enormous beauty.

There are many fine Aboriginal writers whose works have not been discussed here, and Sam Watson's novel has been followed by work of art after work of art from a large variety of authors. Aborigines are speaking out at last.

Endnotes

1.   G. Johnson, *The Australians* (Rigby Pty Ltd, 1966).
2.   K. Gilbert (ed.), *Inside Black Australia* (Penguin Books, Vic, 1988).
3.   P. White, *Riders in the Chariot* (Eyre2 Spottiswoode, London 1961).
4.   S. Morgan, *My Place* (Fremantle Arts Press, 1987).
5.   K. Walker, We Are Going (Jacaranda Press, Brisbane 1964).
6.   B. Wongar, *The Track to Bralgu* (Pan Books, London 1980).
7.   The reviews were written by the present author.
8.   A. Weller, *The Day of the Dog* (Allen & Unwin, Sydney 1981).
9.   H. Maris and S. Borg, *Woman of the Sun* (Currency Press, Sydney, 1983).
10.   *Wanamurraganya*, Fremantle Arts Press, (1987).
11.   S. Watson, *The Kadaitcha Sung* (Penguin Books, Vic 1990).

Chapter Sixteen
INDIGENOUS WOMEN
AND LABOUR STANDARDS IN
PAPUA NEW GUINEA

by

Margaret L. Elias

The challenge for indigenous people here in Australia, in Papua New Guinea, in the Pacific Islands and across the globe is to address closely and give attention to the enormous problems of economic, social and politics threatening their existence and to participate in decision making in order to find amicable solutions to these problems. The focus of this paper is specifically "Indigenous Women and Labour Standards in Papua New Guinea"[1]. It draws upon the author's professional experience as Chairperson of the Industrial Conciliation and Arbitration Tribunals in Papua New Guinea.

This paper is dedicated to all the women workers in Papua New Guinea. Its purpose is to contribute to an improved understanding of the position of women workers not only in Papua New Guinea but also in Pacific Island nations and other third world countries.

Generally speaking, Papua New Guinea comprises the eastern half of the island of New Guinea and several hundred islands to the east and north. The land area is 464 thousand square kilometres with a population of 4 million, largely Melanesian in character. There are many resources including plentiful arable land, extensive forests, rich mineral deposits and hydroelectric potential.

However, much of the terrain is mountainous which makes travel and communications difficult. Some 700 local languages are spoken and allegiances are closely tied to clan or kinship groups. While social obligations differ among kinship groups, most land is commonly owned and members assist others in need. For many Papua New Guineans, contact with the modern world is recent and access to health, education and other social facilities remains limited.

The potential for future development in Papua New Guinea is extremely good. However its realisation will be a function of appropriate domestic policies, a supportive international community and future social and political evolution. Development in all its forms, in order to be enduring, will need to contain centrifugal tendencies emerging in our changing society.

In PNG today, there is need for dedicated women - knowledgeable and skilled in the specific areas of labour standards as they apply to women workers. This is of critical importance to the development of women and their increasing participation in the wage labour force.

The topic "Indigenous Women and Labour Standards" includes:

- Discriminatory practices relating to female workers;
- Inequality of educational and training opportunities including vocational and in-service training for women;
- Improved legislation and better implementation, monitoring and enforcement of existing legislation;
- Increased participation of women in trade unions;
- Changing inappropriate social attitudes towards women in the workplace;
- Provision of child care and maternity benefits;
- Accurate research and statistics on the conditions of working women;

- Appropriate training for women in leadership roles;
- Better counselling and placement services so that female workers demonstrating potential are fully informed of the available opportunities;
- Improved benefits including insurance provisions for female workers; and
- Better working conditions including environmental health, safety and recreational facilities.

It is necessary to facilitate the full participation of women in the socio-economic development of Papua New Guinea. There is a need for women leaders, in management, in the union movement and in other community organisations to be aware of the aspirations and needs of women working in the wage labour force whether in the public sector or the private sector. What follows is a review of the small segment of Papua New Guinean women in formal wage employment.

The Department of Labour and Employment estimates that in Papua New Guinea today there are some 233,000 persons currently engaged in the formal sector wage employment. Of these approximately 11.6% (27,000) are women. These working women are concentrated in lower level clerical and related work. A comparatively small number of women can be found in professional and technical occupations. The principle occupations for women are identified as clerks, typists, shop assistants and nurses. Papua New Guinean women are grossly underrepresented in other occupational categories in the formal wage sector especially managerial and administrative work, sales and service occupations, agriculture, forestry and fisheries, production, and transport and related work.

In attempting to explain this situation three main areas will be addressed. The first factor influencing the position of women in the wage labour force is the sheer male predominance in the work force. One could reliably say that for every 100 trainable men there are 11 trainable women. This statistical ratio is somewhat generous - less that 11 women per 100 men is more likely the case. At the executive level the employment ratio appears to approach 300 men to 1 woman.

A contributing factor affecting the employment of women is educational and professional qualifications. The education of women has long been adversely influenced by traditional, parental and community attitudes. In many societies in Papua New Guinea the primary role accorded to women remains that of subsistence food gardener, wife and mother   In many patrilineal and to a lesser extent in matrilineal societies, there remains a perception that women typically have a short wage earning life to fill the gap between the end of school and marriage. This enduring perception decreases both the career opportunities and the personal growth opportunities for women.

Furthermore for women who establish themselves in a career, there remains a tendency to be engaged in typically "women's" occupations such as nursing, clerk typist, shop assistant, secretary and so on.

However, with the increasing importance of the money economy in the lives of Papua New Guineans, women, particularly in urban areas, not only have to contribute to their family incomes but must earn more for a comfortable lifestyle. For this reason, increasing numbers of women desire long term wage employment. They have to compete with usually better qualified male counterparts (better qualified in terms of education and work experience) for jobs and further training. Furthermore, the Papua New Guinea economy has a very narrow industrial and manufacturing base and consequently competition for wage employment is fierce. This further disadvantages women desiring wage employment who are seen to have the alternative occupation of homemaker and mother.

When women succeed in acquiring a job in such a competitive labour market, other social factors have a bearing on their access to training and advancement through to supervisory, administrative and executive positions. These factors concern perceptions of economic return on investment in human capital and "fear". Fear that training of a woman is counterproductive to the organisation's goals because a woman's domestic obligations will adversely affect her work performance. Women are perceived as being unable to handle the combined pressures and responsibilities of family life with those of a working life. A woman's performance and commitment at work is assumed to fall upon marriage. The potential reliability of women employees in general is reduced because of the possibility of the husband's transfer to another location. Last, but not least, the potential threat to male supremacy can keep a capable Papua New Guinean woman out of training and career options. Conversely, some Papua New Guinean women fear the move into male dominated supervisory, middle management and executive positions, perhaps through a perceived inadequacy in themselves or because it has not been "the done thing" for a woman to occupy such a position within the organisation.

In Papua New Guinea, one can argue that the root cause of this difficulty for women does not lay in legislation or governing principles of the country as much as in the attitudes of Papua New Guinean society in general. It is never an easy or quick task to educate people away from their entrenched attitudes. However, it must be done in order to release the innate potential of women in the workplace and in the community in general. Parental attitudes and the guidance offered to their children needs to be realigned to this end.

As a Bahá'í, I take comfort and strength from the message of the Universal House of Justice to the Bahá'í's of the World, Ridván 1984 which said:

> The equality of men and women is not, at the present time, universally applied. In those areas where traditional inequality still hampers its progress we must take the lead in practising this Bahá'í principle. Bahá'í women and girls must be encouraged to take part in the social, spiritual and administrative activities of their communities.

Similarly, the formal education system should cater for a more equal participation rate for females relative to males at all levels of schooling. Greater access to post primary education is essential if Papua New Guinea is to fill an estimated manpower need of over 6,000 citizens for managerial posts by 1995.

In the workplace, access to career opportunities and promotion must be based on performance and not on gender stereotyping or assumptions about a Papua New Guineans personal life. Papua New Guinean women have a right to equal education opportunities, vocational training and employment opportunities, and to conditions of employment which empower them with real choices about their own lives.

Women's rights to equal employment opportunities have been long acknowledged in principles enshrined in the Constitution of Papua New Guinea and in appropriate legislation. Similarly in the Bahá'í teachings such principles are strongly supported and nurtured with direct guidance and support form the Universal House of Justice:

> The principle of the equality between women and men, like the other teachings of the Faith, can be effectively and universally established among the friends when it is pursued in conjunction with all the other aspects of Bahá'í life. Change is and evolutionary process

requiring patience with one's self and others, loving education and the passage of time as the believers deepen their knowledge of the principle of the Faith, gradually discard long-held traditional attitudes and progressively conform their lives to the unifying teachings of the cause.[2]

However, there still remains significant discriminatory practices in employment, promotion and conditions of pay and service which unfairly disadvantage women. Sex stereotyping of occupations in particular, limits choices and options of all women, and at the same time restricts the society's ability to fully utilise the human resource potential of its citizens.

Papua New Guinean women are capable of a lot more involvement and meaningful participation and area such as the industrial relations arena not only in the role of union organisers and delegates but also in mediation, conciliation and advocacy roles. Both private and public sectors will benefit substantially from the greater real involvement of Papua New Guinean women.

The challenge is for the Government, employers and their organisations, and workers and their organisations to positively reaffirm the prerogative of all women to participate to their full potential in the wage labour force. To some extent this will require enactment of legislation proscribing discrimination on the basis of gender and marital status. All industrial awards and determination should include clauses proscribing discrimination. Discrimination against women because of child bearing age should be eliminated and the universal right to job protection during pregnancy, child birth and maternity leave should be properly acknowledged. Equal pay for women should be made something more of a reality by including overtime, penalty rates, overtime payments and other benefits in equal pay legislation.

Co-operation between government employers and unions is necessary to develop training and re-training programmes, to remove the stereotyped perceptions of certain jobs as being "male" or "female" and to eliminate job classification, recruitment and retrenchment practices which discriminate on the basis of gender. The competent authorities need to support the objective of expanding the occupational choice for women by putting in place a combination of strategies including appropriate apprenticeship programmes, special counselling for supervisors, vocational guidance and appropriate skill development programmes for women in the work force.

Finally to the male counterparts, there is great responsibility on them to encourage women to eradicate male assumptions of superiority and to offer sincere, genuine and constructive encouragement to women in all areas of development and advancement.

To my fellow Papua New Guinean women and Indigenous women from around the globe, I respectfully urge you to strive, to press on in the face of adversity, to uplift the attainment of women so that our children will enjoy the fruits of our efforts and respect the God given equality of male and female. I would like to leave you with this quotation:

> In this wondrous Dispensation the favours of the Glorious Lord are vouchsafed unto the handmaidens of the Merciful. Therefore, they should, like unto man, seize the prize and excel in the field, so that it will be proven and made manifest that the penetrative influence of the Word of God in the new Dispensation hath caused women to be equal, and that in the arena of tests they will outdo others...[3]

Endnotes

1. The words "indigenous women" in this paper refer to Papua New

Guinean women.

2. From a letter on behalf of the Universal House of Justice, 25th July 1984.

3. From the Writings of 'Abdu'l-Bahá compilation *Women* prepared by the Research Department.

Chapter Seventeen
THE GARDEN RITUALS OF THE WAMPAR IN MELANESIA AND LUTHERANISM

by

William Ferea

Introduction

Three basic things may happen when two cultures meet:

1. The stronger culture eliminates the weaker completely;

2. The stronger culture prevails but the weaker survives and emerges at the appropriate times. Often aspects of the weaker culture are used to reinforce the dominant culture;

3. The fundamental ideas of the two cultures forge or integrate to form a new culture.

The Wampar Tribe

The Wampar tribe consists of eight villages: Tararam, Zifasing, Gabsongkeg, Ngasowapum, Munun, Gabanchiz, Wamped and Mare. The Wampar area covers the lower half of the Markham valley in Papua New Guinea's northern province of Morobe. The Markham (or Wanchef) river flows towards the east through the Wampar area and reaches the Huon Gulf where the city of Lae is situated on the river's north side. The Wampar total about 8,000 people and they speak "Zob-Wampar" or the Wampar language. "Zob-Wampar" is one of the three Austronesian languages that reaches the furthest inland on the Island of Papua New Guinea.

The Pre-Contact Wampar Cultures

The Wampar live in small hamlets based on clan lineage. Membership of the clan follows the father's line. Land is clan owned. The Wampar are hunters but they also domesticate pigs. Living of the fertile valley, the Wampar are great gardeners planting taros, yams and their staple food, banana. They grow over 20 species and varieties of eating and cooking bananas, some are: rao, oriyaz, mayamas, ngaropopok, wampong, mpi-a-ziap, kokwarak, gaen-a-mpas, banchem and anang, etc. Besides the brideprice, funeral and initiation ceremonies, the banana harvest ceremonies are one of the most elaborate among the Wampar. Huge pyramids are built with bunches of bananas which will be redistributed to guests. This is to thank people who helped with the gardening and to show-off their gardening prowess. The Wampar are also fierce warriors. They settled in the valley after chasing away the Ahi, Hengali, Waing, and Labu tribes towards the coast. These coastal people have taro and fish as their staple food.

The Garden Rituals

The rao banana is a ritual banana plant. It must be planted in the middle of every garden. After planting the garden with other bananas and food crops the garden is restricted for entry until the garden magician splashes bamboo water throughout the gardens. The women can then enter and weed the garden. The "buzug" or bamboo knifes which the women use for cutting dry banana leaves must be placed at the base of the rao banana - so is the magicians bamboo used for carrying the water. The rao has an unusual radiant color that seems to resemble the radiant sunlight. The first fruits are left to rot in the garden as a sign of fertility and abundance, but, the later fruits are harvested in the pyramid ceremony. Feasting and dancing of the med-

259

a-gom (garden songs) and the med-a-mpuang (miming dance) are associated with these ceremonies.

The Lutheranization

In 1886, Johaness Frierl set up the first station of the Nuendetelsau Lutheran Mission Society at Simbang near Finchafen. Conversion progressed along the coast but stopped abruptly along the Wampar borders. The Wampar warriors were still raiding the coastal tribes even in front of the German missionaries and planters. Attempts by missionaries and gold prospectors like Dammkohler and Oldorp always ended in tragedy. But in 1909 a curious German anthropologist, Dr. Richard Neuhauss, convinced the missionaries of peace prospects by establishing trade links with the Wampar. It worked and the Wampar accepted peace with the coastal tribes for a long time. Oertel and Panzer set up the first Wampar mission station in 1911 at Gabmazung.[1] Soon after Sturzenhofecker arrived replacing Dertel and helping Panzer to Christianize the Wampar.

The Conversion

The conversion took place in several stages:

1. The missionaries made sure that the people gave up magic and sorcery. All effigies and paraphernalia involved in magic were discarded into the Markham River.
2. Children were baptised while adults were all confirmed and then converted into Christians.
3. Church schools were built in which people were taught the bible and the related Lutheran liturgies using the church lingua Franca-Yabim.
4. Selected young men were further trained to become Lutheran Catechists or pastors among their own people.

The author's grandfather Ferea (Christianized as Benjamin) became the first Lutheran pastor from the Wampar tribe. Panzer became the most influential of all the missionaries. He spoke Wampar fluently and published three books in the language, thus disseminating God's word effectively.

The Integration

While many rituals were discouraged by the missionaries, some of the Wampar ceremonies were allowed to merge with the Christian church activities. The banana harvest ceremony is one major example of that integration. During the church congregational meeting which is held every three years, called the Sam Siga, the host village in the Wampar area will harvest the bananas and build huge pyramids with it. While the bananas are for feeding the church delegates to the Sam Siga, the various host villages also have the chance to show-off their gardening prowess as used to be done during the pre-Christian era. And during these church festivities the traditional garden songs and the med-a-mpuang (miming dances) are freely performed. Other instances of integration as with the initiation rituals of the adolescents and the Lutheran confirmation remain for another time.

Conclusion

The German missionaries may have sought to uproot the Wampar Melanesian cultures at the very beginning, but these people and their cultures have firm foundations that could not bend all the way for Christianity. Nor did the Wampar merge the Christian theology with their cosmogonies to create a new religion as with the cargo cult movements among some tribes in Melanesia. The Silas Eto religion of Malaita, the Solomon Islands and the Paliao church of Manus, Papua New Guinea are advanced forms of this integration of the old and the new. Often mixing is violent but the Wampar embraced Christianity as another alternative way of worshipping God or Garaveran. They adapt Christianity into their cultural life by integrating their tribal ceremonies like the initiation and banana harvest ceremonies. However, the ancestral spirits still remain an immediate concern for the Wampar Melanesians. In private people would appeal to the spirits for fishing, hunting, healing the sick or gardening, etc. There seems to be religious dualism in the Wampar area. Whether a Melanesian theology will emerge in the long run remains to be seen.

Endnotes

1.   P. Sack; 1976 at 69.

www.ingramcontent.com/pod-product-compliance
Lightning Source LLC
Chambersburg PA
CBHW072116270326
41931CB00010B/1573